An Immigrant's

Journey

into the

Cosmos

An Immigrant's Journey into the Cosmos

A Memoir

Dr. N Y Misconi

iUniverse®

AN IMMIGRANT'S JOURNEY INTO THE COSMOS
A MEMOIR

iUniverse books may be ordered through booksellers or by contacting:

iUniverse
1663 Liberty Drive
Bloomington, IN 47403
www.iuniverse.com
1-800-Authors (1-800-288-4677)

ISBN: 978-1-4917-5332-3 (sc)
ISBN: 978-1-4917-6165-6 (hc)
ISBN: 978-1-4917-5333-0 (e)

Library of Congress Control Number: 2015903753

Print information available on the last page.

iUniverse rev. date: 5/28/2015

To my father and mother for their love and encouragement

Contents

Abbreviations

AFOSR   Air Force Office of Scientific Research
ESA   European Space Agency
FIT   Florida Institute of Technology
IAU   International Astronomical Union
ISPM   International Solar Polar Mission
NASA   National Aeronautics and Space Administration
NATO   North Atlantic Treaty Organization
NEP   Nuclear Earth Penetrator
NOAA   National Oceanic and Atmospheric Administration
SAL   Space Astronomy Laboratory
SFA   Spaceport Florida Authority
SOHO   Solar Heliospheric Observatory
SUNY   State University of New York
TRDA   Technological Research and Development Authority
UCF   University of Central Florida
UF   University of Florida

Introduction

I wrote this book with two purposes in mind: to serve as an autobiography of my career over the years and to share my research experience with other researchers. My memoirs include many life experiences and history of my country of origin, Baghdad, Iraq, as well as descriptions of the political upheavals in that part of the world.

In middle school and high school I learned from American Jesuit Fathers who established Baghdad College near the Tigris River. I then went to college in Istanbul, Turkey, and earned a degree in astronomy. I learned much about Turkish culture during college.

After school I returned to Baghdad and taught at the University of Baghdad. While in Baghdad, I had the opportunity to make several appearances on the Baghdad Television *Science for All* program, talking about astronomy and space science.

I then pursued my lifetime dream of immigrating to the United States and pursuing my PhD degree. After that I was involved in major NASA missions, such as *Pioneer 10* and *11*, Skylab, space shuttle *Columbia*, the International Space Station's Gas-Grain Simulation Facility, and more.

I was also involved in the Strategic Defense Initiative (SDI), commonly called "Star Wars." I performed a total solar eclipse experiment and helped launch the first rocket in Mexico's history. I conducted a rocket experiment launch at NASA's Wallops Flight Facility and designed laser body armor for the US military.

I also spent three decades doing research in the field of astronomy and astrophysics. My research was primarily in the field of the solar system, with some other spin-off research. Part of this book is a series of chronicled topics on what I think is the best approach in doing research based on my long experience. I explore the unique way of pursuing research in the United States, with emphasis on how to conduct research in a successful manner. I also emphasize the importance of carrying out research on so-called soft-money, which on many occasions makes you more competitive and successful. I reveal the necessary factors that go into acquiring funding for your research ideas and explain the criteria of writing a successful proposal to land you a research grant. I also include some of my political views and my scientific outlook for the future.

Chapter 1

The Early Years

My full name is Nebil Yousif Misconi. I am the second son of Yousif Yacoub Misconi, a Christian Catholic. My mother was Columba Salim Dawood Kako. I was born in 1939, and I have five brothers and one sister. We jokingly called each other the Magnificent Seven after the famous American western movie.

My father was a well-known scholar in Iraq, specializing in the fields of Arabic history and literature, Mesopotamian history, and world history. My father published several books in these fields, and some of them have serial numbers at the Library of Congress in the United States. His accomplishments throughout his career earned him great respect and love from the Muslim community in Iraq and abroad. Since his passing in 1971 there have been many writers and scholars who still write articles in newspapers and magazines about him even until today.

My Near-Death Experience

When I was seven or eight, I developed an abscess in one of my teeth. This may not sound especially noteworthy, but this abscess is the closest I have ever come to death. At the time there was no cure that we knew of, and we had never heard of penicillin. My father and mother took me at eight o'clock at night in a rented horse-drawn carriage through the streets of Baghdad to the dentist's office. Unfortunately, he had just closed his clinic and gone home. Luckily my father saw a pharmacist he knew who was just closing his shop, and he told the pharmacist about my problem. The pharmacist told my father that I was very lucky because they had just gotten a new medication called penicillin a few days ago. We got a nurse to stay with me overnight and inject me every four hours with penicillin. It was so tough that I had black–and–blue marks on my bottom that made it difficult to sit for several days. The next day, the dentist said if it weren't for the penicillin, I would have died during the night. I'm not sure which year that was when penicillin came to Baghdad, but my guess would be either 1946 or 1947, shortly after the end of the Second World War.

Baghdad College, an American High School

After elementary school I enrolled in a new school called Baghdad College, which was run by American Jesuits. It was called a college but actually was a junior high and high school, covering grades 7 to 12. To my knowledge the Christian archbishop in Baghdad contacted the pope in Rome and told him that a lot of Christian students were not getting any Christian education, so the pope suggested sending American Jesuits to Baghdad. The American Jesuits built a fantastic high school that looked like a college in the United States. The school was put on acreage on the periphery of the city. Most of the American Jesuit fathers were from Boston, Massachusetts. The College was the only school in Baghdad that introduced green chalkboards in the classrooms, colored chalk, yellow pencils with erasers at the end, yellow legal pads, and other things that were kind of amazing. They had six yellow buses, similar to the ones in the United States, that were named after the vowels *A*, *E*, *I*, *O*, *U*, and *Y* because they said that Y was sometimes a vowel.

The American Jesuits also built a university in Baghdad, Al-Hikmah University. *Al-hikmah* in Arabic means wisdom. I guess you could call it the Wisdom University. The president of this university was the late Jesuit father Richard McCarthy, who in my opinion was the most brilliant Arabic scholar ever to come to Iraq, or to the Arab world for that matter. He was fluent in Arabic and even wrote several books in Arabic. His language skills were really remarkable. He gave a graduation address at Al-Hikmah University, which my father and I attended, in the presence of Abdul Karim Kassem, Iraq's prime minister at the time. He gave the speech fluently in classical Arabic. Classical Arabic is different from colloquial Arabic, which is what is spoken on the street. There are differences in the use of words and the way it is spoken.

At Baghdad College all the subjects were taught in English, so I learned science and math in English. Sadly, though, the Jesuit fathers were forced to leave Iraq in 1968, shortly after the Ba'ath Party came to power. The Iraqi government then took over Baghdad College and also Al-Hikmah University. The Jesuit fathers where disheartened because they really enjoyed living in Iraq and had good relationships with the students and their families. Father Richard McCarthy had to leave Baghdad and his legacy of brilliant work in Arabic literature and Islamic history. In 1971 when I was in the United States, I contacted Father McCarthy, who was in Boston, and visited him. He spoke endlessly of his memories of his time in Baghdad and kept saying how he missed those days. I saw him again in 1974 along with my mother when she came to see me. He passed away a couple of years later as I recall. I hope that one day Iraq will remember the contributions of Father Richard McCarthy to Arabic literature and Islamic history.

Hollywood Movies

Going back to my years in high school, I recall that Hollywood movies were very popular. They were shown in major movie theaters in Baghdad and other major cities with Arabic subtitles. So I saw many classic American movies, such as *Gone with Wind*. In those days many American actors, like Jimmy Stewart, Gregory Peck, Robert Mitchum, Clark Gable, and Marilyn Monroe, were icons in the minds of the educated class in Baghdad who followed these movies.

The USIS

In those days I also used to go regularly to the USIS, which was the US information service center in Baghdad, which was basically an American library. There were also USIS centers in Cairo, Beirut, Istanbul, and many other cities around the world. The USIS had a lot of books on every subject, including all major science fields. On one of these visits I picked up a book titled *Stars*. It was an introductory book on astronomy with beautiful photos of spectacular nebulae, galaxies, and stars. I must have read this book at least five times; I couldn't let it go. It inspired me so much and made me curious about astronomy. I told my family about this book and what I learned from it briefly, and they were impressed and interested in hearing what I had to say.

Reading this book was my first encounter with astronomy and my first window to the universe. Another book that captured my imagination also came from the USIS, a biography about the great rocketeer Dr. Wernher von Braun. So two books, one that dealt with the essential basics of the cosmos and one about the basics of rocket engineering, captivated my imagination. This took place in 1956 while I was in my final stage of my graduation from high school. The two fields, in my opinion, were interrelated since at that time I thought that rocketry could play a role in space exploration of the solar system and perhaps beyond. Added to this was the fact that there were no astronomers in Iraq at the time and no institute to teach astronomy or rocketry.

I was excited by the idea of perhaps being the first male astronomer (Iraq had one female astronomer who had moved to the United States) or the first rocket scientist in the country. That was just an added bonus to my real enthusiasm for astronomy and rocketry, though. I had to make a big decision about which field was more exciting, which one would be more rewarding, and which field would satisfy my curiosity better. I believe that these major conflicts are common for young people, and having to make this choice certainly played a major role in helping me achieve my goals better.

I learned early on that I could be an astronomer or an astrophysicist. The difference between the two titles is somewhat nebulous. An astronomer is a scientist who is trained in astronomy in both observations and theory fields. An astrophysicist could be a physicist who just decided to get into the field of astronomy. Actually both titles are often interchangeable. However, typically an astronomer could be dealing with observations only or observations and theory, while an astrophysicist deals mostly with theory and not necessarily observation methodologies. Some physicists claim that astronomy is a branch of physics. Classical astronomers disagree and consider astronomy as the father of sciences. The argument goes on and on, but in this book I will use the two titles interchangeably.

I was extremely impressed by Dr. von Braun's career and his accomplishments in the field of rocketry, so he became my role model. I always thought that maybe one day the United States could put a man on the moon and that certainly Dr. von Braun would play a major role in this fascinating endeavor. So I started concentrating on the field of rocketry with the idea of specializing in chemical engineering so that I could participate in building rockets that one day could carry men to the moon and beyond. I started visiting a relative of mine, George Misconi, who graduated from a university in Denver, Colorado, in chemical engineering. George was a brilliant chemical engineer and a brilliant student in school at all stages. The American company Kellogg, which was building the first petroleum refinery in Baghdad, hired him. He listened carefully to my dreams regarding rocketry, and he told me that chemical engineering was only a part of rocket engineering.

After finishing high school I heard of scholarships being offered by the Baghdad Pact, an alliance similar to NATO, that included the United States, Great Britain, Turkey, Iran, and Pakistan. The scholarships were for Iraqi students to enroll in the University of Istanbul, Turkey. This was an opportunity for me to enroll in either chemical engineering or astronomy, both of which were not offered in the University of Baghdad and in Iraq as a whole. I immediately applied for these scholarships and was granted one. I began preparations to travel and enrolled in the University of Istanbul.

The only drawback of this endeavor was that everything would be taught in Turkish, which meant that I had to learn Turkish. After considering this requirement I thought, *Well, why not learn another language?* Learning Turkish turned out to be an easier task then I originally thought simply because Turkish has about thirty thousand Arabic words in it.

The Trip to Istanbul

In early September 1957 I bought a ticket on the Orient Express to make the journey from Baghdad to Istanbul. The journey, which took four days and three nights on the train, was the most wonderful trip. I went through Syria and then southern Turkey and to Istanbul. The Orient Express had two cars dressed with magnificent mahogany wood that belonged to a British company called Thomas Cook. These two cars provided lodging, and I got to sleep through the nights in my own cabin. The journey was very special mainly because the scenery was breathtaking. For the first time I was introduced to mountainous terrain that I was not accustomed to, since Baghdad is a flat land. My best friend and later my roommate was Asim Mustafa Al-Tikriti, who was a relative of Tahir Yahya Al-Tikriti who was prime minister of Iraq in the late 1960s. Asim was impressed with my ideas about rocketry, and so he also decided to enroll in chemical engineering.

I spent a whole academic year learning Turkish, as I could not enter the university until I passed the language exam. As it turned out, I excelled so much at learning Turkish that the teacher asked me not to attend class anymore and to study on my own because I was so much more advanced than the other students. This arrangement gave me a lot of extra time to spend reading about astronomy and rocketry along with magazines, such as *Life, Time,* and *Newsweek* during my

The Iraqi Consulate Celebration Party

In another incident I was invited to the Iraqi consulate for their celebration of the coup d'état that removed the royalty and instated General Abdul Karim Kassem as the prime minister of Iraq. I interviewed the consul and photographed the display they made for the revolution, which included a statue of General Kassem made out of ice. I wrote an article in the newspaper describing the ceremony and my interview with the consul. I mentioned that as time passed by, I watched the statue of the prime minister melting. After the article was published in the newspaper, I became worried that I may be reprimanded or punished in some way for the comment about the statue melting. Luckily nothing happened, and slowly my fear disappeared.

Gala at Sultan Abdul-Hamid's Famous Palace

I received another interesting opportunity because of my journalism during my third year in Istanbul. I heard that there was a gala for local and international journalists to be held in Sultan Abdul-Hamid's palace, which had been built during the Ottoman Empire. The gala was held inside a huge room where Sultan Abdul-Hamid used to receive the ambassadors from Europe. The room had a huge crystal chandelier and beautiful rugs, along with magnificent decorated walls and ceiling. Among the attendees, I recall seeing Miss France and European actresses. For the first time in my life I had to rent a tuxedo to go to this gala, and I invited one of my student friends to go with me. We took a cab to the palace, and when we arrived, we told the driver to go passed the gate to the main building.

The driver said, "Are you kidding me? I can't go inside the palace; it is forbidden."

I told him, "Don't worry. I have passes, and they will let us in."

He said, "Oh my God, this is something special. I never dreamed of doing this ever."

The gala made us feel like we were in Europe, and the butler announced our names as we came in. The attendees were mixed, with ladies and men, and the ladies were wearing the latest fashionable gowns. The band played American and European songs, and everybody was dancing, including me. I asked Miss France for a dance, and she accepted. To say the least this night was one to be remembered. At the end of the gala they had a lottery for all kind of goods, such as refrigerators, cameras, and so on. My friend won a camera, and I was shocked as I won only a hair comb, the least expensive gift in the whole ensemble. However, that misfortune did not take away from the thrill I had that night.

Writing Poetry in Turkish

Since I had a year to study Turkish, I decided to indulge in Turkish poetry and started buying some poetry books. Turkish poetry was not necessarily written with rhyme, but I enjoyed reading the poetry that was written with rhyme the most. I tried sometimes to compose some lines, but I wasn't really good enough with the language yet to write good poetry. As it turned out, after four years in Turkey, I perfected the language so well that I wrote my own book of poetry, *Iki ve* üch *yanyana*, meaning *Two and Three Side by Side*. When I wrote the book of poetry, I was twenty-three years old. The first poem explained that when you say two and three side by side, it could mean thirty-two years or twenty-three years.

My best friend in the later years in Istanbul was Burhan Said. His father was Arab, and his mother was Turkish, so he had relatives from his mother's side living in Istanbul. Burhan read my poems and liked them very much. He said they should be published, and it so happened that one of his relatives was in the publishing business. He asked me if I wanted to ask his relative to help me publish the book, and I said yes. His relative, whose name I don't remember, asked me if he could show the book to a Turkish literature professor at the University of Istanbul, a standard procedure before publishing a book. I was a little nervous when I saw the professor reading my book of poems and didn't know what the outcome would be. The professor emerged after a couple of hours and said it was very good and should be published on good shiny paper.

I was delighted to hear the professor's recommendation and was very thankful. Burhan's relative put in motion the process of publishing. An art student friend of Burhan's relative made the cover, which was very nice. I paid Burhan's relative a small amount of money to get the project started. Unfortunately Burhan's relative had some financial crisis. I never heard from him again, and the book was never published. Burhan kept apologizing to me about this unfortunate outcome, but I told him not to worry. I said we could do it some other time and that I was very busy with my studies anyway. The book never saw the light of day and is still unpublished.

Harassment by Turkish Students

My first year in Istanbul I stayed in a Turkish dormitory with Turkish students and some Iraqi students who had the same scholarship as me. There was some slight harassment from the Turkish students in the dormitory once they knew that we were from Iraq. They often told us that we came from one of their colonies that they had in the Ottoman Empire. Others said that we had their oil and were selling it to the world and making money, which should rightfully belong to them. Whenever they engaged me in such political arguments, I tried to change the subject and not involve myself in the discussion. I was a Christian, so I was careful not to engage in anything dangerous for me, but my other colleagues had a lot of arguments with them and sometimes contentious ones. At times things came close to physical threats and action by the Turkish students, but none of it really happened, thank goodness!

What Dating...Girls?

On the romantic side, I was really miserable because I only dated three or four Christian girls during my entire stay in Istanbul. This was primarily due to the fact that I was Christian and was afraid to date any Muslim women. My other friends were Muslims, so they were in heaven. They were dating girls freely, and in those days Istanbul was much of a European city. Dating was allowed and wasn't a closed society by any means. I don't know how it is now, but I'm curious to find out!

European Tourists

In my first year in Istanbul, I had time to mingle with many European tourists, most of whom were students. They came from Britain, Germany, France, Italy, and other European countries, and they all spoke English. I learned so much from them about European life. This was such a thrill for me to communicate with these students and enlarge my horizons in science, literature, social issues, and on and on. I also listened to their arguments about their politics, customs, traditions, and so on. Most of them were conservatives, and a few were socialists or communists. This interaction with these European students kept my fluency of English intact.

Fen Fakültesi

The school that I enrolled in was called in Turkish *Fen Fakültesi*. *Fen* is an Arabic word meaning "art," and *fakültesi* obviously means "faculty." The school was really similar to a college of arts and sciences in a US university. It was a beautiful building with nice auditoriums. When I showed Hikmat Sulayman, the former prime minister of Iraq that I previously spoke of, the building of the college, he said, "This college was built by Iraqi oil money, and I know about it."

Nonetheless, the main question at this time for me was whether to enroll in chemical engineering or astronomy. I agonized about this decision for quite a while, and finally I decided to enroll in chemical engineering with the knowledge that I could switch to astronomy anytime I wanted. I was told that my earned credit hours could easily be transferred between the two fields when applicable. This fact made making my decision easier.

It was time for me to go and visit the astronomy department in Istanbul and see what it was like. The department was about four miles away from the College of Science, so I took the bus. As soon as I saw the observatory dome, I knew I had arrived at my destination. I introduced myself to the professors in the department, and they welcomed me and asked me if I wanted to see the telescope. I said yes, of course. This was early in the afternoon, and I saw the students drawing sunspots on a piece of paper mounted at the focal point of the telescope, as part of their training. The department impressed me, and as I recall, the telescope was a twenty-four-inch refractor (i.e., lens) built in Germany. I should mention here that Turkey and Germany had a close relationship that went back to the First World War when the Ottoman Empire fought alongside Germany.

The astronomy professors asked me to come back at night and visit in order to see the moon and other celestial objects using the telescope. I accepted the invitation, and then I went one night and took a look through the telescope as they pointed it at the moon. The craters of the moon were impressive to see. I knew that the telescope was meant to be for student training and not for research, especially since it was inside the city of Istanbul where the sky did not get dark for viewing.

This activity was so impressive to me that I started thinking seriously about enrolling in the astronomy department. However it was not the time to make that decision since I was just entering the university as a freshman. Also I was discouraged when I learned that there were no more than twelve students in the department of astronomy. This made the decision to enroll in astronomy much more difficult.

Chapter 2

The End of the Royal Family in Baghdad

Affter the end of the academic year, at the onset of summer, I decided to visit my family in Baghdad. I still remember that I arrived on July 13 via the Orient Express, only one day before the revolution that took place in Iraq where the army killed the royal family (King Faisal the second and his uncle Prince Abdul-Illah). They also captured Prime Minister Nuri Al-Said as he was fleeing to Iran dressed like a woman and killed him.

By the end of August it was time to leave to Istanbul, so I took the Orient Express and got ready to start school. My freshman year was very interesting, filled with introductory courses in physics, chemistry, and math. I was surprised by the way the school functioned as there was no attendance (which is unlike Baghdad University) and no homework to be done. I was told that the University of Istanbul followed the same pattern as German universities; in other words there were no tests, not even midterms, except for one final test for each course. The rationale for following the German tradition was because Germany had a strong relationship with the old and vanished Ottoman Empire. After all, they fought together against the Allies in World War I, which in the end dissolved the Ottoman Empire. The Arabs rose against the empire under the leadership of King Hussein, who fired the first shot. The British helped the Arabs against the Turks with the help of the famous Lawrence of Arabia.

All these developments brought about the rise of Atatürk

(meaning "father of the Turks"), whose real name is Mustafa Kamal. Atatürk transformed Turkey into a modern country tailored after the European model. For example, he changed the writing of the Turkish language from Arabic letters to more like the English alphabet. He changed the weekly holiday from Friday to Sunday, so that Turkey could do commerce with Europe for more days of the week. He was so loved by his countrymen that they use to stand by his statues (there were many of them) and pray for him.

The school procedures that I talked about above were astonishing to me because it meant that I would be deciding my grade in every course with a two-hour exam at the end of the semester. I thought that this was really weird because they didn't really give you a second chance if you didn't perform well in the final exam. There were hardly any contact hours with the professors unless you asked to see them, so the interaction between the professors and the students was minimal. I asked other students why that was, and they said we were lucky, because in Germany the students went to the professors' houses to take exams. I don't know if that is true or not! However, my university did follow the credit-hour system. I don't know if Germany had a credit-hours system, but I know that this was the case in US schools. My university also gave the students the freedom to choose the courses that they want to enroll in, just like in the United States. I don't know if the German schools gave that freedom to students.

Turkey's Military Coup d'État in 1960

In 1960 I woke up in Istanbul one morning to hear that there were tanks in the streets and military personnel everywhere. I asked the people on the street what was happening, and they said it was a military coup d'état and that Prime Minister Adnan Menderes had been arrested. I was really surprised at that because Turkey was a member of NATO and I'd always thought that Turkey was a politically stable country. It was a bloodless coup, and the military declared a curfew in Istanbul for a day or two. They later held a trial for Prime Minister Menderes and hung him to the dismay of NATO countries, including the United States. This event reminded me of what was happening in Iraq in those days. The Turkish opposition leader at the time was **İsmet İnönü**, who I'd heard was behind the coup d'état by influencing the military. He later on was elected prime minister in 1961. This event put an end to the former slain Prime Minister Menderes, who was behind the formation of the Baghdad Pact, to oppose the communist threat from the Soviet Union. As I mentioned before, the scholarship I got to go to Turkey was established by the Baghdad Pact.

The most important thing that happened this year was that I made up my mind to move to the astronomy department. I felt that the chemical engineering department was focused on more chemistry than engineering. The name of the department was Kimya Muhendisi (both words are Arabic in origin; Kimya is Chemistry and Muhendisi is engineering), but as far as I was concerned, it was more chemistry than anything else, i.e., it was engineering in name only. That was a startling realization on my part that took a while to realize. As I indulged in taking courses and trying to succeed, I lost track of what this program was all about. I asked the professors about the department, and they told me that they were preparing courses that would involve chemical engineering. I realized then that this was a department that was destined to grow into chemical engineering in the future but was not ready yet. I was amazed of this belated conclusion. I think it took me so long to realize because of the enormous difficulty of having contact hours with the professors.

I decided to wait until the summer, when I would be visiting Baghdad, to tell my parents about my decision to move to the astronomy department. As I told them of my decision, my brothers started laughing because they thought I would be an astrologer. My mother and father were astonished with my decision and were a little worried because there were no astronomers in Iraq and they had never heard of anybody enrolling to become an astronomer. However, my father was very supportive of the idea and encouraged me to do that. As a famous historian, he knew about the history of astronomy in the old days of Arabia. He started telling me about some of the names of the stars and constellations that were Arabic in origin, such as Deneb ("tail"), Fomalhaut ("mouth of the whale"), Altair ("flying bird"), and Vega ("from the falling eagle"). My father was delighted with my decision because he wanted his son to be a pioneer in a new field. He also knew that in Arabia and Mesopotamia astronomy had thrived at one time and it would be good to have his son pioneering in this field.

The Turkish Border

I got the encouragement from my family to transfer to the astronomy department, and I took the Orient Express back to Istanbul. As I got the visa to enter Turkey in my passport, the Turkish embassy in Baghdad didn't know that there was an outbreak of cholera somewhere in northern Iraq. When we arrived at the Turkish border, we were shocked when the police told us that we had to leave the train and would be quarantined for five to six days by the Turkish army. This was a precautionary measure by Turkey to make sure that none of us had developed cholera. It was a routine policy to avoid the spread of diseases. Turkish army trucks came in and took us out of the train into the wilderness and then set up temporary tents for us. This was certainly an experience. I had to sleep in a bed in a tent in the wilderness surrounded by army personnel with automatic weapons. They dug two holes in the ground as makeshift bathrooms, which were horrible, to say the least.

The food they gave us was also horrible, more like rations. We had to eat the food, as bad as it was, but luckily some of the students with us had brought sweets (such as baklava) from Baghdad so they could give them to their Turkish girlfriends. They were kind enough to surrender those sweets and shared them with us. That helped fill us up instead of the army rations! Some students also had playing cards, so we started playing poker to pass the time and kill the boredom. The army personnel were guarding us from coyotes, wolves, dogs, and other animals that may stray into our camp. One time, I woke up in the middle of the night and heard animal noises that sounded like a wolf. I also saw that the tent was flapping as if the wolf is trying to get inside the tent. I screamed and woke up almost everybody, including the Turkish guard, who was supposed to be on guard. He started to shoot live ammunition in the direction where I was pointing in the pitch dark of a moonless night. There was no wolf near the tent but perhaps far away. The students all woke up at my screaming and realized what was happening and then started laughing since no animal was there.

The next day I gathered the students, and we had a meeting where I told them that the guard had been asleep, which was dangerous. We relayed our concerns to the army chief, and then he spoke to his superiors and came back and assured us that it wouldn't happen again. During this stay for five days or so in the Turkish army camp, I was worried about missing the deadline for transferring to the astronomy department. Luckily, I didn't miss the deadline, and everything was fine.

Communism in Iraq

In 1963 I was in Istanbul and heard that there had been an attempted assassination of the then-leader General Abdul Karim Kassem by members of the Ba'ath Party. Saddam Hussein was one of the assassins. The attempt injured Kassem but not fatally. Most of the assassins were caught by the government, with the exception of Saddam Hussein, who fled to Syria. Kassem reacted by punishing the Ba'ath Party, and he formed a kangaroo court headed by Al-Mahdawi, a judge who was a member of the outlawed Iraqi Communist Party. I saw some of the trials in his court during my visit to my family in the summer. Whenever the defendant spoke, he was spat at, slapped in the face, and called names live on TV, and they threatened them brutally. Several volumes of the proceedings of these trials were published in Iraq, and sometimes I wish that we could translate them into English because they are incredible example of lawlessness in justice! The court tried several of the king's men and hung them.

Kassem decided to unleash the Communist Party and give them free hand to punish their archenemy, the Ba'ath Party, and other Arab nationalist who followed the charismatic Nasser, the leader in Egypt at that time. Luckily I was in Istanbul when these things happened. I believe these events lasted about ten months. By some estimates the Communists killed about ten thousand people in the major cities of Iraq. They hung people on telephone poles and dragged bodies of others with jeeps. The people in Baghdad greatly feared the Communists.

The Communists chose different names for their organizations, for example supporters of peace, in Arabic "Ansar Al-Salam". My father told me that when he went every day to his job at the Ministry of Education for the months when the communists had a free hand, he always carried the Communist newspaper underneath his armpit when he went to his job at the Ministry of Education. He did that to avoid having been accused of being a reactionary! My mother also told me that sometimes Communist teenagers would ask her for monetary donations to the Communist Party and would follow her. She said she used to lash at them and tell them to go away. I asked her if she was afraid, and she said no, because she didn't think they would harm a woman, at least she hoped so.

The Return of the Ba'ath Party

In 1963 the Ba'ath party staged a coup d'état and let a soldier fire a bullet into the head of the then-leader Kassem on live television so that the people in Baghdad would believe that he was dead. They put on this display because Kassem used to say to the country that he was immortal and that the person who would kill him had not been born yet! Anyway, a few months later we found out from a Ba'athist friend that the Communist Party had put an X on our house. They had put an X on almost every house except the Communist houses in Baghdad. This fact was found from the documents that the Ba'ath Party seized at the headquarters of the Iraqi Communist Party. The X meant that all the occupants of the house would be killed, a very chilling thing to find out.

The reason behind the X mark was that reactionaries, and not friends of the Communist Party, occupied those houses and therefore should be eliminated. A couple of years later, I met some of the Iraqis I sort of knew who were Communist; they told me point-blank that slaughtering three or four million reactionary people was really not important for the success of Communism in Iraq! They said that in the course of human history this would be a footnote if anything!

Chapter 3

Life in Istanbul

Playing Poker!

Going back to the nature of the schooling in Istanbul, I thought to myself, *Hey, wait a minute; you don't have to attend classes if you study the text on your own. You just go for the day of the final exam and take it. That's all they care about.* This was really bizarre to me, but at the same time I felt this was a great freedom. I didn't have to be guided by anything; I was on my own. One time I thought that I could play poker or do anything unscholastic for almost two months of the semester and then study hard for one month and take the exam in each course. Actually, I did that for two semesters, believe it or not, in my junior year. A few of my student friends used to get together early in the evening, play poker till about eight o'clock in the morning, and then go home to sleep. By afternoon I would go with my friends for a big dinner in a restaurant. We did that for many days! Approximately one month before the final exam I did nothing but study very hard till late at night and almost put a curfew on myself at my home.

The Car Accident

The Iraqi government decided that Iraqi students in Europe were allowed to import a car to Iraq for only one time. An Iraqi businessman who I met through a friend wanted to import a van (a Ford Taunus) from Germany, put it in my name, and then sell it in Iraq. This way he could use my student-abroad privilege, and in return he would give me 500 dinars (equivalent to approximately $1,700). In these days this was a good amount of money. I thought about this idea and finally decided to do it. However, we had to make a trip to Greece, the closest European country, specifically to the city of Salonika (which was closer to Istanbul than Athens) where there was any Iraqi consulate so we could transfer the van into my name.

So we embarked on this trip. The van had no seats inside because the businessman was planning to install seats in Baghdad and make it into a passenger transportation van. A few miles before reaching the Greek border we came to an unpaved piece of road coming down from a hill. A drunken cab driver went ahead of us and started generating a lot of dust. The businessman, who was driving, weaved all over the road as he applied the brakes. The dust was so thick that we couldn't see ahead of us, but we knew we were going to crash somewhere. Finally he applied the brakes hard enough that the van tipped over on the road, spun around, and fell into a valley of enormous depth. As I was rolling inside the van, I thought that my life was going to be over if the van did not come to a stop soon. After four or five turns down the valley the van finally came to a stop.

I got out of the van and was astonished to see the van had been stopped by a single tree. Otherwise the van would have rolled all the way down the valley. I realized then that this was the miracle of miracles. I had only minor scratches, believe it or not, and my shirt was torn. The driver suffered two broken ribs, and another friend, who was traveling with us for the joy of the trip and to visit Greece, suffered cuts on his arm and his scalp but nothing serious.

The van was basically demolished, and after few minutes passerby cars stopped to see what had happened to us and came down the valley to check on us. One of them was a medical doctor who examined me and told me that I was fine. Then he examined the driver and the other passenger and recommended they go to the hospital. He contacted the Turkish army, and they sent an ambulance.

I visited them in the hospital, and they were doing fine and were being treated by the doctors. The people who came down the valley were astonished and said this was some miracle. If I hadn't survived this awful accident, I wouldn't be writing this book today of course. Whenever I remember this accident, I believe that a second life was written for me.

A few weeks after the awful car accident I got a letter from my family saying that they wanted to visit me in Istanbul. Of course I did not tell them about the car accident fearing that they will be worried about me, and I said to myself it is better to tell them when they are here with me. So I rented an apartment for them since they were going to stay at least two months. The visit was by my father and mother, my sister Amel, and my brother Naseer. My father was so excited about this trip to Istanbul because he's a historian and he wanted to visit all the museums and research some of the Arabic manuscripts that were taken during the reign of the Ottoman Empire.

My father also brought papers with him to show that he is also a correspondent for the same newspaper that I was a correspondent of. I was delighted with that because we both were journalists and we could use that status to visit many places that other people could not. We were also invited to news conferences and other functions. For example, my father and I were invited to a journalistic conference of Turkish correspondents. During the conference many of the Turkish correspondents clustered around us and they were asking us so many questions about Iraq and the Middle East and we had a great time talking to them. Of course my father didn't speak Turkish so I had to translate every question to him into Arabic then he answers in Arabic and I translate his answer to Turkish. After a while as you can imagine I was thoroughly exhausted but well entertained by the whole experience.

I must say here that the city is Istanbul and not Constantinople i.e. the famous old song that was so popular in the 1950's. The song emphasizes that when the Turks conquered the Byzantine Empire they changed the name of the city from Constantinople (which was named after the Byzantine ruler Constantine) to Istanbul.

In the last year, I worked very hard to finish all the exams and get good grades, but I had mixed feelings about the end of my journey in Istanbul. My speaking Turkish was very fluent to the degree were people use to ask me if I was from eastern Turkey since they detected a slight accent that sounds like Turks from the eastern part of the country. This was somewhat disheartening to me because I liked the smoothness of the Istanbul dialect of Turkish especially when women spoke it. I had established many Turkish friends and some of the Arab students there. I have also become Europeanized in my behavior, my thinking process, and my values. During my stay in Istanbul, I managed to keep my knowledge of English and even improve it. I did that by speaking to tourists and reading books and magazines. The reason for keeping my knowledge of the English language strong, is because I always realized that this is the first step to prepare myself to excell in astronomy, and eventually to complete my education in the US.

Notions of Staying for Good

The European atmosphere had such an effect on me that at times I felt like staying in Istanbul for good. But that was impossible since they didn't have a good graduate program in astronomy. Also the very few girls that I dated, who were typically Greek or Italian Christians, were not the type that I could see myself marrying and establishing a family with. If I stayed, it would be much more difficult to complete my education in the United States, especially with a family to take with me. As soon as I graduated, these notions almost disappeared, and I started thinking of going back to Baghdad and what my life would be like there. I'm glad that these notions disappeared because I recently heard from my friends who were with me in Istanbul that life there has changed dramatically from the one we knew.

Chapter 4
Going Back to Baghdad

M y final trip on the Orient Express headed back to Baghdad was very sentimental. I left behind many memories, many friends, and many things to think about and remember. I took with me the BS degree, issued by the University of Istanbul; later that BS degree would be much bigger in size than the PhD degree that I would get later in the United States. An Iraqi student who once was my roommate was with me on the trip, and he had gotten a PhD from the English department in Istanbul. We celebrated our graduation with a lot of wine and reminiscing about our memories of Istanbul.

I was worried about how to get employment in Baghdad, being the only astronomer in Iraq. I should note that there was one female astronomer before me, Dr. May Arif Kaftan-Kassim, but she had left Iraq and was in the United States. It was somewhat terrifying to be the only one in my field. Where would I work if there was no astronomy institution in the country? Aside from that I was annoyed by the constant reference to astrology whenever somebody asked me about my specialty. A lot of people in Baghdad used to ask me to construct their horoscopes and tell their fortunes! I don't blame them for that, since it was a growing country. Some women used to ask me to read their palms and not tell them if there was something really bad.

I felt miserable for about four months after coming back to Baghdad because I couldn't find a job. Luckily my father and a friend of his were visiting the dean of the College of Science at the

University of Baghdad to ask him a favor to help someone. During the conversation the dean asked my father about his children and their specialties. When my father told him I was an astronomer, the dean was excited. He told my father, "My goodness, I didn't know you had a son who is an astronomer." This was wonderful news to the dean because he needed an astronomer to help establish a planetarium in Baghdad.

I was delighted with this news, and I immediately went to see the dean, Dr. Wasil Al-Thahir. He immediately hired me and appointed me a member of the committee to establish the Baghdad planetarium. He also appointed me as physics lab teacher, since there was not enough work just to be on the planetarium committee. I cannot express the joy and excitement I had after this development.

Carl Zeiss Planetarium Projector

We had several meetings at the College of Science for the planetarium project, and the members of the committee emphasized to me that they were inclined to buy the Carl Zeiss planetarium projector from Jena, East Germany. They also told me to ignore any bids from the American-made projectors because Iraq didn't have good relations with the United States. They asked me what I thought of the projector from East Germany, because I was the only expert in the field of astronomy. I told them that after reviewing the literature and the bids that I preferred purchasing the Carl Zeiss projector from West Germany since it was highly computerized. I noticed the dismay on their faces and then realized that my input was politically incorrect. The Iraqi government had good relations with the Soviet Union and its satellites, and the committee members, including the dean, decided to buy the projector from East Germany even though that I told them it was inferior to the one from West Germany. They were looking for my blessings to buy it from East Germany since I was the only technical member of the committee and an astronomer for God's sake! In any case, I decided to go along with them for fear that I may harm my working relationship with the dean and the other members and who knows what else.

I told the committee that I concurred and agreed to purchase the projector from East Germany, a decision that was painful for me. The dean, who was the head of the committee, said that Egypt was buying the same projector for the Cairo planetarium. He also said that when the Cairo planetarium opened, I would go to Cairo to represent Iraq in the opening ceremonies. I felt that this gesture was meant to make me feel better about their decision.

My teaching assignment was enjoyable, and I was very successful at it. I enjoyed working with both male and female students, unlike primary and high schools in Baghdad, which are not co-ed. I also became friends with the other teachers in the College of Science. I still treasure those friends to this day. I became close friends with the chair of the physics department, Dr. Jassim Al-Husseiny, who received his PhD from Caltech. His wife was also a lab teacher in our group, and she was a very nice person. My best friend among the physics lab teachers was Rasool Abdul-Amir. Unfortunately Saddam Hussein ordered all Shiites who had family origins in Iran (they were called "Ajamies") persecuted. As a result Rasool's family was sent to the borders between Iraq and Iran, and he was forced to stay away from them. Because of this, his health deteriorated. This combined with his deep sorrow of being separated from his wife and children caused his premature death. This happened a few years after I was in the United States.

A Failed Coup d'État

Sometimes early in 1967, I was driving back home from the College of Science, and I saw a fighter jet in the distance. The pilot was coming down low and shooting bullets on the curbs of the street. There were hardly any people walking on the curbs, so I realized that this was a horrible scare tactic. I was immediately frightened and swerved onto a side street to get out of his way. The fighter plane looked so huge to me that I panicked, to say the least. I realized that something was seriously happening in Baghdad. The fighter plane then lifted up and went across the Tigris River where the presidential palace was. I continued on my way home with fast speed as you may expect!

When I arrived home, my mother asked, "Are you okay? You look pale." I said I was sort of all right. Most of my brothers were outside the house watching the sky and following a few fighter jets that were coming close to our house, which was across the Tigris from the presidential palace.

I shouted to my brothers, "Aren't you afraid? Get into the house!"

To my surprise they started laughing at me and said, "Why are you afraid? This is nothing!" They told me that I just wasn't used to these things and that this was hardly anything scary. I went inside the house and left them outside. I begun to realize that they had been hardened to these incidents because they saw so many of them. My living for several years in Istanbul, a relatively stable country, had changed me quite a bit.

My family followed the news on the one government channel on television, and they said that the coup d'état had failed and the president was unharmed. The president was Abdul-Rahman Arif, who was Abdul Salam Arif's brother. Abdul Salam Arif was the co-leader of the revolution that had killed the royal family and was also a former president of Iraq. He had been killed and burned in a helicopter accident in southern Iraq. We did not believe the government report offhand as usual; however, Baghdad became so calm that we realized that the coup d'état must have failed.

My TV Appearance

After a few months in my job at the College of Science, the word got out that I was the only astronomer in Iraq. At that time there was only one television channel run by the government. There was also a popular weekly TV program called *Science for All* anchored by a former physics teacher called "Kamil Al Dabagh". This show actually was the number one watched program, but sometimes loses to a program on sports. Both programs exchanged first place position. The anchorman Kamil heard that I was the only astronomer in Iraq so he contacted me. Later on I found out that he did contact the first female astronomer that I mentioned earlier (Dr. May Kaftan-Kassim) when she was in Baghdad and she appeared on his TV show also before I did.

The Thrill of Research

My First Simple Encounter with Research

My first interaction with research, if I can call it that, was very humble indeed. Remember, I was in Baghdad without a great research atmosphere, so cut me some slack!

Constructing a Star Finder for the Latitude of Baghdad

During my TV appearances I showed how to find stars in the sky using a star finder from the United States, which was designed for latitude 45°, or close to New York City. The anchor for the TV show asked me if I could design one for Baghdad with latitude of approximately 34°. I said yes and spent that summer designing the star finder, which, upon completion, would be sold to the public in Baghdad and distributed to students and whoever was interested. I spent a lot of time perfecting the design and making sure it was correct. I wanted to make sure that when people used this star finder, they would indeed find the right stars in the sky. Otherwise I would be in big trouble, and the embarrassment would be tremendous.

I finalized the design and checked it out myself many times, making sure that the star Canopus was just above the horizon in the summer. The Iraqi government gave us funds to mass-produce the star finder with my name on it. It was a satisfying experience for me to do that, and I felt as if I had accomplished something worthwhile. I have no idea what happened to it after I left Baghdad.

Building a Crude Portable Planetarium

Following my successful experience with the star finder, I got more ambitious and told the TV anchor that I could design a relatively simple portable planetarium. He asked me if there was one in Europe or the United States. I said I didn't know; I certainly hadn't seen one. The anchor was fascinated by the idea of people buying a cheap portable planetarium and learning the constellations.

My concept for this was simple, basically to make a dome out of metal and then drill holes for the stars with varying sizes according to their magnitude or brightness. The holes would be drilled based on their actual locations in the sky and in their constellations. A light source could then be put inside the dome to create the images of the stars. This could be done inside any room or appropriate place that the user chose. Of course, to be a perfect projection, the room would have to be in the shape of a dome. But in any case, the images would be reflected fairly accurately on the ceiling and walls of a typical room. This is why I called it a poor man's planetarium. At this point I didn't concern myself with the motion of the stars, because I wanted first to see how the dome succeeded in projecting the stars.

I went to a bazaar in Baghdad where they made tin and copper artifacts and antiques. I described what I wanted to an owner of one of the shops. He looked at me kind of strange and asked, "Why do you need this dome?"

I said, "It's a long story, and I can't get into it now."

He said, "Is there anything illegal about this, and should I worry about the police?"

I laughed. I tried my best to explain the project in a simple manner, but I don't know if he understood it.

He said, "Okay, I'll do it. I hope to God I don't go to jail for this."

He asked for a pretty high price, and I agreed. In any case he made a perfect dome that I was very impressed with. I couldn't help but think, *Do I consider this research?* Then I laughed at this notion.

My best friend at the College of Science, Rasool Abdul-Amir (God rest his soul), was very interested in this project and offered his help in drilling the holes for the stars on the dome. I asked him if he knew what he was getting into. There were a lot of stars and different sizes, so we would have to change the bits of the drill constantly. He told me not to worry. He said he had lots of patience and that we could do it over weekends and in the evening after work.

I spent a lot of time drawing the images of the stars on the dome with a pen so that we could drill the holes where they were supposed to be. I made a master for the different sizes of the holes of the stars according to their brightness magnitude. This was not an easy job, and my family said, "What are you doing for hours and hours? Are you doing God's work?" Often when people asked me what I did for a living in Baghdad, they would ask, "Do you do God's work?"

Finally I finished placing the stars, and then Rasool started drilling the holes. The drilling took several weeks to finish, since we worked on it after official working hours. The moment of truth arrived when I put the light source inside the dome in a dark room. Rasool and I were first amazed at the projection, and we celebrated the result, perhaps prematurely.

Upon close inspection I realized that I had exaggerated the sizes of the holes of the stars with respect to their brightness. For example the star Sirius looked like the size of 1/8 of the moon, and I was very disappointed after all that hard work. I realized that I'd made a major mistake: I should have done an early test of a few images before proceeding with the whole project. This realization caused me a lot of personal embarrassment, and I kept asking myself why I didn't think of that. I told Rasool that I wished I had some tiny lenses to concentrate the images of the stars. But then that would defeat the idea of making it cheap and simple.

I realized, too late of course, that the holes should have been pinholes, and the bits of the drill should have been very small. I told the TV anchorman the results. I said that I could fix it but didn't have the time or the patience to start all over again. He took the dome with the light and tried it himself. He realized it was useful but not realistic. He kept encouraging me to do it again, but I just couldn't see myself getting another dome and doing all of that work again. It was my first experience of pursuing a good idea but implementing it incorrectly.

It was really delightful to be on his TV show, and I enjoyed it so much. It lasted for four years, and my last appearance was on December 8, 1969, three weeks before I traveled to the United States. I appeared on the show at least once a month and sometimes twice for all of the four years. In the third year Kamil asked me to co-anchor the show with him. I started appearing every week, but that didn't last for more than a month and a half. I stopped co-anchoring the show because there were rumors that I was going to take the show from him, which was absolutely not true. Kamil and I greatly admired and respected each other. The show started with pointing out the constellations in the sky for each month, sort of like the Horkheimer show from the Miami, Florida, planetarium, the famous "keep looking up!" show.

Upon requests from the show viewers, I started telling the wonderful stories from Greek mythology behind each constellation. After that I concentrated on answering astronomy questions from the viewers. Later on Kamil asked me to choose topics that I would like to discuss, such as the planets in the solar system, nebulae, supernovas, black holes, and so on.

This activity made me a well-known person in Baghdad and in Mosul and Basra, where the show was shown one or two days later by video. There was only the one TV channel, so a lot of people watched. I didn't like that very much, because it put restrictions on my freedom and activities. For example, every time I went to the movie theater with my brothers, we had to enter when it was completely dark and leave before the lights came on, so I wouldn't be noticed. The other amazing thing was that I got phone calls from many females in Baghdad who wanted to marry me just because they saw me on television. My mother used to laugh every time the phone rang and a female, who I'd never met, asked me to marry her. Every time I met Kamil, he gave me a bundle of letters to read. I thought they were astronomy questions, and some of them were, but the majority were from females asking either to meet me somewhere or to marry me.

The Landmark TV Appearance on the Day of the 1968 Coup d'État

I will never forget this episode for the rest of my life. On the day that the coup d'état started for the Ba'ath Party to take over the government, their first goal was to take the TV station and the radio station. My family and I were watching the news on television and following the developments as they unfolded. It so happened that the day of the coup d'état was a Wednesday, the same day *Science for All* normally broadcasted. At about noon Kamil called and told me that he'd received a phone call from the leader of the coup d'état, General Hassan Al-Bakir. General Hassan Al-Bakir told him that in order to show the Iraqi people that the coup d'état was bloodless; the Revolutionary Council had decided to run the TV program as normal as if nothing had happened. Kamil asked me to come up with a subject to talk about for the show. He pleaded with me to choose any topic to do with astronomy. I asked him if any other people would be coming to the program, and he said it was just going to be the two of us.

I told Kamil that I would discuss it with my family and call him back. He said, "Please hurry it up. I am counting on you to appear with me." His voice was shivering as I'd never heard it before. I started panicking as soon as I hung up the phone, thinking about going to the television station at eight o'clock and driving myself with all the tanks in the streets of Baghdad!

My father thought I should go because if I didn't, they might come and arrest me and take me by force to the station, and then who knew what they would do with me after that. My mother thought I shouldn't go and should tell Kamil to find someone else to go with him. My brothers' opinions were all mixed, some agreeing with my father and some with my mother. I told my family that Kamil was desperate and was not going to take no for an answer. I suddenly remembered my roommate in Istanbul Asim Al-Tikriti, who knew Saddam Hussein (who was the head of the Revolutionary Council). So I told my family that if anything happened to me that Asim would bail me out because he was high up in the Ba'ath Party. This relieved some of their fears, and they told me that it was up to me to decide what to do and that they would accept my decision.

I was on my own in this, which put a lot of pressure on me. Soon after, I called Kamil and told him that I would be coming to the TV station before eight o'clock. He was so happy and relieved and assured me that everything would be fine and told me not to worry. I didn't buy any of his assurances, because I could tell he was worried himself. Anyway, I started scrambling to get a topic in astronomy to talk about that evening. I honestly don't remember what topic I chose that evening, though perhaps my notes are somewhere in the stuff that I left behind in Baghdad after I left to the United States for good.

The Mob at the TV Station

I embarked on my dangerous journey to the TV station. It was so crazy to maneuver through the streets, which were full of tanks and armored vehicles. I waved to the troops in the tanks and armored vehicles. I then crossed the bridge to the other side where the TV station was, checking my watch from time to time to make sure I didn't arrive late. The amazing thing was that none of the troops stopped me, asked me for identification papers, as I was carrying my Iraqi passport with me, or asked where I was going, which was completely surprising to me. To this day I still don't understand why they didn't stop me or ask me any questions. Finally, I arrived at the TV station and parked on the opposite side of the station. I sat in the car looking at the huge mob of teenagers waving their AK-47s and shooting bullets in the air. I waited for Kamil to arrive so that we could go together inside the station, as he requested when we spoke earlier on the phone. He arrived momentarily, and we both got out of our cars and started to cross the street toward the TV station. We spoke little because both of us were terrified of the mob and the bullets flying in the air. We both were saying to each other, "Keep your composure, and don't panic."

As we came to the gate, a few kids stopped us and asked what we were doing here. Kamil told them that we were doing the TV program on orders from General Al-Bakir. A few kids on the top of the building with their AK-47s recognized us and said, "Those are the guys from the *Science for All* program. Let them pass through." Some of them shouted, "This is Kamil and the guy who talks about the universe!" Kamil and I were both so relieved. The kids also shouted to us, "Long live the revolution!" So Kamil and I started shouting "Long live the revolution" as loud as we could as we walked through the TV station to the studio.

Talking about Astronomy in Front of an AK-47

Under normal conditions we used to go to the makeup studio first and then to the other studio to do the live broadcast. This time the producer came and said, "Don't go to the makeup studio. You're looking fine; you don't need it today." He laughed. We then went to the broadcasting studio, and to my surprise I saw two soldiers each pointing an AK-47 at the table where we did the broadcast. I was really worried now because I didn't understand what this was all about. In a whisper I asked Kamil about this arrangement, and he told me that it was a precautionary measure by the Revolutionary Council. I asked why, and he said so we wouldn't shout all of a sudden that the revolution had failed and then cause chaos in Baghdad.

Before we started the live broadcast, one of the soldiers said, "Now you behave; otherwise you will be dead instantly." We said we understood, and then we both did our parts of the show. The show lasted an hour, all under the threat of AK–47s, one pointed at him and the other at me. The experience was very nerve-racking for both of us. The hour went by very slowly, and we were so relieved once it was over. The two soldiers told us we did a good job, as if they knew what we were talking about!

As we were leaving the station, the kids on the roof of the building and everywhere else all started applauding us. They said, "Job well done. Long live the revolution!" We waved back to them. Kamil and I congratulated each other on our successful performance, and he thanked me for doing the show with him under these circumstances. I maneuvered back home between the tanks and armored vehicles, waving to the troops as I did going in. When I got inside the house, my family jumped up and down in joy to see me alive. They told me that they were so worried. I then joked, "Why were you so worried? It was a piece of cake!" I still remember that night because I couldn't sleep; I only slept about two hours in the morning.

A few months after the Ba'ath Party took over in Iraq, they decided to send the Jesuit fathers packing home to the United States. They took over Baghdad College, the American high school, and also Al-Hikmah University, the American university in Baghdad. I told my father that we should talk to the government and the Ba'ath Party about reversing this decision and letting the Jesuit fathers stay in Baghdad. This request was for the sake of the Christian minority, since the fathers' mission was to teach Christianity to the Christians in Baghdad. My father started some contacts with the government, and then a few days later he was told to leave this issue and not to meddle with it. This was a threat not to interfere in the government business and to stay away. We relayed those attempts to the Jesuit fathers, and they were disappointed they had to leave, because they loved living in Baghdad.

Chapter 5

Teaching Astronomy
in Baghdad

A PhD was worth everything in Baghdad in those days, since
you didn't have to do research and could just teach. This was
because there were no masters programs or PhD programs, in other
words no graduate school. Of course today in Baghdad they do
have masters and PhD programs, and I am sure they do research and
publish in local and maybe international journals. However, Saddam
Hussein changed the language of instruction at the university level
from English to Arabic. I don't know whether this change applied
to all disciplines, including astronomy.

The professors who had PhDs in the College of Science went to
some prestigious schools in the United States like Caltech, MIT, and
Stanford, to name a few, but these PhD graduates were teaching and
doing no research. The word in the college was out that the professors
who graduated from US schools were better teachers than the ones
that graduated from Britain. The reason was a heavier emphasis on
graduate courses in the United States compared to Britain.

At this time I decided that the best thing for me was to work for
few years at the College of Science until I could go to the United
States and stay there for good in order to do research. Nobody
was saying in Baghdad that a PhD must be followed by doing
independently conducted research. Also it was not thought of as the
first step in establishing yourself as a scientist. This fallacy in thinking
did a lot of harm to the science students in Baghdad because their

goal was just to get a PhD, period. The professors bragged about the schools that they graduated from and overlooked the fact that they never published one paper in an internationally recognized scientific journal.

The Status of the Sacred PhD Degree Today

It is very strange to me to see so many fields—from political science (which I fail to understand why it is called science!), education, library science, and on and on—giving out PhDs today. A PhD degree by definition means doctor of philosophy, and a few hundred years ago it was given to students of philosophy, mathematics, physics, astronomy, chemistry, and hard-core science in general. I personally prefer the doctor of science degree over the PhD degree, and I think it should be limited to fields of hard-core science. Anything beyond that should be called something else. This is just a thought, but I believe it is an important one.

Teaching Astronomy in Baghdad

In the second year of my employment in the College of Science, the chair of the physics department asked me to teach an introductory course in astronomy. He asked me to structure the course so that it would be one hour of instruction and then one hour of laboratory work. He asked me to use a telescope that the physics department had purchased recently from East Germany for lab work. The telescope was a simple one useful for instruction. It had no clock drive and was mounted on a tripod. The chairman also asked me to hold these lab sessions on the roof of the physics building and show the students the stars and other objects.

After approximately a month of teaching this course the chairman canceled it. That was unfortunate for me because I was enjoying teaching the course. When I asked him why he canceled the course, he said, "Haven't you heard the rumors?" He said that male students had been romancing the female students on the roof in the dark while

I was busy teaching. He also told me that some of the female students' parents were calling him or visiting him in his office asking to stop this course for fear of what may happen to their daughters. Of course I understood his reasons and decided to let it go, for fear that it may get even worse if I argued to continue teaching the course. As you may expect, I was deeply disappointed with the whole issue, and I lost a chance to teach what I loved to teach.

Chemical Weapons of Mass Destruction?

Many years later, in 2003, I heard on the news in the United States that international intelligence reports said that Iraq had started building chemical weapons as early as the mid-1960s. The reports also said that the research was being done in the College of Science in Baghdad. This piece of news astonished me because the department of chemistry was adjacent to the department of physics in the same building. So I started wondering if they had been building chemical weapons of mass destruction right next to me while I was teaching there. Obviously, we had no knowledge or even suspicions about it. It is scary to think about, to say the least, especially if something had gone wrong or an accident had happened. I don't know if these reports were true or not; however, I know that the best chemists in Iraq were in the building next to ours.

I started early in 1969 to apply for graduate studies in astronomy at major universities in the United States. I applied first to Caltech, MIT, Stanford, the University of Arizona, and other universities. Almost all of them said they would accept me, but they could not give me financial aid, except for the University of Arizona, which was looking into giving me an assistantship. Without a teaching or research assistantship it would be difficult to get through graduate school. However, in 1969 the first female astronomer from Iraq, Dr. May Kaftan-Kassim, visited Baghdad. She heard about me, so naturally she visited our family.

May asked me what my plans were for graduate study, so I

explained my applications to various US universities. She asked if I would consider coming to her university. May was an associate professor in the astronomy and space science department at the State University of New York (SUNY) at Albany. She said their department was new and could offer me either a teaching or research assistantship. She also told me the type of research the professors of the department were doing. She was in the field of radio astronomy, but I wasn't really keen on getting into radio astronomy. She told me that they also had professors specialized in stellar evolution, stellar atmospheres, and space science, in particular the interplanetary medium. I told her I would think about it.

On her second visit to my family she talked to the department over the phone, and they tentatively offered me admission at SUNY, Albany, pending the exchange of my degree and other necessary documents. I then accepted the initial offer and started preparing to go to Albany, New York. May also asked what fields I was interested in, and I told her everything from chemistry of the planets to stellar evolution and stellar atmospheres. She said that was perfect because they had Dudley Observatory with Dr. Jerry L. Weinberg and Dr. Curtis L. Hemenway (the chair of the department), who were doing research in interplanetary dust, one in stellar evolution, and another in stellar atmospheres. I was happy with this information and decided that this was the department I wanted to go to.

Relations between the United States and Iraq were deteriorating quickly, and I was told that perhaps I would be the last person to leave Iraq to the United States on official basis. In 1969 I applied for the Gulbenkian scholarship to come to the United States. Gulbenkian was known as Mr. 5 Percent because he was an arbitrator between the British and American oil companies and the government of Iraq. For mediating the agreement, they rewarded him by giving him 5 percent of the oil profits. Gulbenkian was an Armenian living in Iraq, and he became an instant millionaire if not a billionaire. In return Gulbenkian assigned a piece of his fortune to go for costs of sending students abroad to study, especially in the field of petroleum engineering.

I almost got the scholarship except the president of the University of Baghdad insisted on not giving it to me, citing that I would be just like my brother Lutfi, who got the scholarship and then never came back to serve in Baghdad. My brother got a PhD in biochemistry from the Imperial College in England. Of course as things turned out, he was right; I didn't return to Baghdad.

After the failure to get this scholarship the College of Science decided to give me a paid leave of absence to get a master's degree in astronomy in the United States. This meant that they would send me my salary every month so that I could study in the United States. Unfortunately my salary was so low in these days in Iraq so it only amounted to $120 a month, since the Iraqi dinar was close to three dollars at the time, and the standard of living in the United States was very high.

The problem now was how to get the visa to the United States with the political relationship quickly deteriorating. I also had to get my passport in order, which was no easy task in those days in Baghdad.

Fleeing from the Iraqi Defense Ministry

Before leaving the country I first had to prove that I had satisfied the condition of doing military service. So I went to the Ministry of Defense and went to the right office to tell them that I was exempted from the military service. When I was first hired by the College of Science in 1966, my father; Shakir Al-Tikriti, a close friend of my father who was also a relative of Tahir Yahya Al-Tikriti a former prime minister of Iraq; and I visited the minister of defense. He wrote an official letter saying that I was exempted from military service because I was the only astronomer in Iraq. He stated also that my services were needed more in academia and not in the military and ordered an official discharge.

When I went back in my preparations to go to the United States, the officer asked me if I did the military service. I told him I was exempted by the minister of defense and explained why. I told him he should have a copy of the minister's letter in my file. He said he didn't have a letter like that and said I was just giving him a story. He then told me that I was a deserter and that I should be arrested right now. I appealed to him, saying, "Please believe me; I'm telling you the truth." He then went on to call the soldiers to arrest me. I realized immediately that if I was arrested, I would be put in some prison. It would take my father at least two months to find where I was, and all the plans for the trip to the United States would be gone.

Realizing this predicament, I decided to run out of his office and get to my car. I ran as fast as I could with two soldiers running after me with their machine guns and ordering me to stop or else they would shoot. Luckily I made a right turn down a hallway and somehow managed to lose them. I succeeded in getting to my car and sped away so fast, thanking God for not being caught. My family didn't know whether to cry or to laugh about this incident.

The only way out of this debacle was with help from my father and his friend Shakir Al-Tikriti. My father said that the only person who could resolve this issue was the minister of state. He added that the minister of state was the one responsible for anybody leaving the country to a foreign land. So my father made an appointment with the minister of state and took his friend Shakir Al-Tikriti and me with him. I waited for an hour in the waiting room full of anxiety about what was going to happen. My father and his friend finally emerged. My father said everything was taken care of, and I started jumping in joy. I asked my father why it took so long, and he said the minister of state had called the minister of defense to verify the exemption from the military service and then they had talked about the politics of the day. The minister of state also told my father that I would be the last person to leave Iraq to the United States on official business. I don't know if that was completely true.

My father had mixed feelings about me going to the United States. He knew that he had to help me succeed. On the other hand, he knew that I probably wouldn't come back, and he knew that he might never see me again because he was suffering from diabetes and heart problems. Unfortunately that proved to be true. He died on April 11, 1971, from a heart attack. I was in Albany, New York, when the news came, and I cannot explain the sorrow I felt upon his death.

Chapter 6

Coming to the United States

O n January 2, 1970, I flew from Baghdad over Jordan, Lebanon, Austria, and Germany and to London, England. I had profound mixed emotions. I felt sad for leaving my family and my background since I knew for sure that I was not going to see my family or Baghdad again. I had made up my mind to stay in the United States for good. I also felt happiness since I was heading to the United States, with great expectations. I had a great feeling in the plane when the pilot said we had left the airspace of Iraq and were now in Jordan's airspace. The passengers started clapping in joy because we had been told that the Iraqi government could recall the plane as long as it was still in Iraq's airspace and arrest passengers for various reasons that could be political. Such incidents had happened in the recent past, so we were all worried.

Remember the Titanic

My brother was residing in London, and my sister and her husband were in Birmingham, pursuing their degrees. They were all glad to see me in England. I planned to stay for nine days in England to process my visa to enter the United States and visit with my brother and sister. I visited the American embassy in London to get my visa and then went to Pan-American Airlines to buy a ticket to New York City. The agent in Pan-American asked me if I wanted to fly on the new Boeing 747. He said it had just flown its maiden flight from New York to London and that Raquel Welch was going to be on the plane for the trip back to New York.

I immediately said, "Remember the *Titanic*."

He said, "Man, you are so pessimistic." I asked him to give me a ticket on the 707 airplane, and he said, "Even Raquel Welch doesn't sway you." I said no.

Frostbite in Albany, New York

I arrived at New York City and marveled at the skyscrapers and spent one week sightseeing and visiting all the major sites. The most important to me were Ellis Island and the Statue of Liberty. All this made me feel like my dreams had come true. Upon arriving at Albany, I visited the university and the professors in the astronomy department, and then I stayed at the International House for foreign students. On my second visit to the department, I left around five in the evening to go back to the International House. However, I missed the bus by almost one minute, and then I had to wait twenty minutes for the next bus. On that day the windchill temperature in Albany was 40° F below zero, and the wind was blowing furiously. I was well dressed, but my ears and face were exposed to the cold. After the twenty minutes the bus came, and when I got onto the bus, I felt that my ears were burning. By the time I arrived at a restaurant to eat dinner I noticed in the mirror on the wall that my ears were swelling and their shape had changed. I asked the owner of the restaurant what he thought of my ears, and he said, "Oh my God, you have frostbite!" He told me I should hurry to a hospital, and he called a cab for me. I was frightened to say the least. I had never heard of frostbite, and I thought maybe they would amputate my ears! Unfortunately in the hospital the doctors that examined me initially were interns and had no experience with frostbite. Finally they got the surgeon to examine me, and he said that the blood flow was still going to my ears. He recommended that I drink alcohol that night as much as I could, to keep the blood circulation going. The nurses bandaged my ears and then called a cab for me. The doctors also told me that if my ears turned purple, I should come back immediately to the hospital.

I asked the cabdriver to take me to a bar so I could drink as much alcohol as I could, explaining that I needed to keep the circulation of my blood going. He tried his best, but all the bars we went to were closed, since by then it was past midnight. The cabdriver told me that I should go back to the dormitory and that the students must have some beer or whiskey that I could drink, so I agreed. Unfortunately, none of the students had any alcoholic beverages with them at the time, though they sympathized with my situation. So I went to my room. I couldn't sleep all night because I was checking the color of my ears every ten minutes or so. By about six o'clock in the morning I heard the director of the dormitory entering her office. I immediately went to see her, and she was shocked to see the bandages on my ears. She also told me that she had noticed the swelling on my ears the day before. She had wanted to say something to me, but then she thought that I knew what was happening. I anxiously asked her if she had any alcohol. She was shocked at this request! I explained to her that the doctors wanted me to have alcohol to get my blood circulation going.

The lady was sort of embarrassed, but then she opened a drawer in her desk and said she had a bottle of sherry. I immediately screamed, "Please give it to me!" She did and wanted to get me a glass, but I said I would drink from the bottle. I drank the whole bottle in about two or three gulps just like an alcoholic! A few minutes later I sat on the chair and went to sleep.

At around two o'clock in the afternoon I was awakened by a flower tickling my nose. As I opened my eyes, I saw the wife of my graduate adviser, Professor Donald Schmalberger, tickling my nose with a flower. Most of the astronomy faculty professors were there at the dormitory. They'd heard what had happened to me, so they started cheering me up. Later on May Kaftan drove me to her physician. He examined my ears and said I had third-degree frostbite that would not leave lasting damage. He said that if I had waited another ten minutes for the bus, I would've had first-degree frostbite and my ears would have had to be amputated. He said, "My friend, you were very lucky, and it must be that God loves you."

The professors in the astronomy department brought me several earmuffs to protect my ears, and I witnessed for the first time the degree to which Americans are concerned when somebody has a problem. I really appreciated their help, and on top of that they also contacted a few student girls to come one at a time to the dormitory and keep me company (imagine that!). They did that because the doctor told me that I could not leave the dormitory for a whole week. Till this day my ears are sensitive to cold. Whenever I feel cold weather is coming, I wrap them with a band. However, since I now live in Florida, these days are rare, though I certainly take precautions when I visit the north.

I was advised to visit Dudley Observatory, which was part of the department but located in another area in Albany. It was a very old observatory, but it had recently been converted into a space science observatory. In other words the old telescope had been removed. There were two major groups in the observatory with nearly thirty employees and an advanced machine shop to make space hardware that would be space worthy to fly in satellites or human astronaut flights. Dr. Curtis L. Hemenway (the director of the observatory) headed one group, and Dr. Jerry L. Weinberg headed the other. I met Jerry and had a lengthy conversation with him about what he was doing. He was at the time involved in using the imager of *Pioneer 10* and *11* missions to Jupiter and beyond, which would send the first close-up images of Jupiter to Earth. Jerry proposed to NASA to use the imager to observe the zodiacal light. The zodiacal light is a cone of faint light that is seen shortly after sunset and shortly before sunrise (see photo on page 69). It can only be seen in remote, very dark areas without light pollution. The zodiacal light arises from the scattering of sunlight by interplanetary dust particles that orbit the sun. These dust particles are remnants from colliding asteroids and dust tails of comets.

NASA was looking for a way to use the imager of *Pioneer 10* and *11* which would have been idle for a few years before reaching Jupiter. Jerry suggested to NASA that it should be turned around to look at the zodiacal light from space. In the 1960s and '70s NASA was interested in interplanetary dust simply because it presented a hazard for astronaut suits and spacecraft. These dust particles orbit at a velocity of approximately twenty kilometers a second. This velocity can cause major damage even though the particles are smaller than one millimeter. If a particle hit the spacesuit of an astronaut during a space walk, it would puncture it, and all the oxygen and pressure would be gone, causing the astronaut to die instantly.

After a few visits with Jerry and more discussions, I showed great interest in joining his group. However, I told him that this was not a final commitment because I still had my love for stellar evolution and stellar atmospheres and also cosmology. He said he didn't have a problem with that and that I was free to decide what I wanted to do later on.

May Kaftan tried to get the department to give me a good teaching assistantship in terms of financial value, which was at the time $3,300 a year. So the department offered me the teaching assistantship formally, which meant I would be conducting astronomy laboratory exercises with astronomy undergraduate students. I told Jerry about the offer from the department, and he immediately offered me a research assistantship with the same salary from his NASA grants. I decided to go with the research assistantship from Jerry. May Kaftan naturally was disappointed about my decision. She told me she had tried very hard to get me the best teaching assistantship. I thanked her for doing that but told her I really wanted to do the research assistantship.

My decision to go with the research assistantship was really a turning point in my career and changed the course of my future considerably. I started working at Dudley Observatory at the end of February 1970 and stayed working there for several years.

Since I joined the department at the beginning of the spring semester, my adviser said we should go easy on the number of courses I took. He said some courses were two semesters anyway and started in the fall semester, so I couldn't join them in the spring. The late Dr. Donald Schmalberger was my graduate adviser, and his field was stellar atmospheres, so naturally he started guiding me toward courses that were necessary for the field of stellar atmospheres. So I took a course in complex variables in the math department to start with, and he wanted me to take modern physics in the fall with quantum mechanics, along with math methods for physicists. Both of these courses were two semesters.

The Airglow Atlas Project

I had a heavy load of coursework to catch up because my background was not up to snuff with graduate school level in the United States. Jerry told me that he would give me an easy project to work on. He had accumulated a vast amount of data from observations of the zodiacal light when he was at the University of Hawaii. He had an observing station on top of Haleakalā in Maui, Hawaii. The observing station was at about thirteen thousand feet altitude from sea level and was adjacent to an observing infrared telescope operated by the US military that was aimed to check on military activities in China, as rumors had it. My project was easy because it didn't involve real research. I was supposed to photograph observations made at Haleakalā of a phenomenon called airglow.[1] These photographs would be put together in the form of an atlas book so that researchers

---

[1] Airglow, briefly for those readers who are interested, arises from two spectral lines of emissions in the Earth's atmosphere: one green line at 5577 A° and one red emission line at 6300 A°

could look at them and do some theoretical interpretation of what they showed. The project turned out to be laborious and took about two years to complete with part-time work. It was the first work that I *helped* publish, with the emphasis on *helped*.

The *Airglow Atlas*, as it was called, was then sent to many observatories in the United States and around the world. The project was just the right one for me because my coursework ended up being very heavy, especially for quantum mechanics. I believe that the most difficult subject to study in this world is cosmology, followed by quantum mechanics. Actually both subjects are intertwined, especially when you consider quantum gravity.

In my first semester (spring of 1970), it so happened that there was a political upheaval in the United States. There was a shooting at Kent State University by the National Guard, and all hell broke loose at campuses all over the United States. Some final exams were canceled, and some grades were changed to satisfactory or unsatisfactory instead of letter grades. I was shocked by these events because I had just come from a country where there were a lot of political upheavals and now it was in the United States as well!

Soon it was the beginning of the fall semester when I took courses in modern physics and mathematical methods for physicists. Dr. Keith F. Ratcliff taught the modern physics course. He was a very good teacher and actually won an award for being the best teacher in New York State. Later Keith and I would work together on research. He taught quantum mechanics inside the course so vividly, and I was impressed. Even though Keith was a great teacher, his accomplishments in research were minimal.

There were about thirty-two students in the modern physics course, and the competition was intense. I mentioned before that a typical graduate astronomy course would have just a few students, maybe six or seven at most. Usually graduate programs in astronomy in the United States will have between ten and twenty-five students. When I was a graduate student in astronomy, there were six thousand to seven thousand astronomers in the United States. There were even fewer astronomers in Britain, Germany, France, Japan, Russia, and so on; on the high end of the spectrum, some countries had hundreds of astronomers while on the low end other countries had under one hundred. Bottom line: astronomers were a small community in the world, perhaps no more than twenty thousand.

My graduate adviser asked me to take an advanced quantum mechanics course in the physics department. The late Dr. Norbert Rosenzweig, a former student of Richard Feynman, taught the course … scary, yes. Quantum mechanics was enough, but advanced quantum mechanics was another story. He taught it using the bra–ket notation. I always got a kick out of the naming of bras (i.e., <) and kets (i.e., >) for an obvious reason! The famous physicist Paul Dirac, who was at this time spending his retirement years at Florida State University, first used this notation. I did rather well in this course and impressed Dr. Rosenzweig. He used to tell me that one day he'd hear that I had discovered a belt around some big object in the sky somewhere and it would be named the Misconi belt.

He repeated this from time to time, and I really enjoyed hearing this because it undeniably boosted my ego a lot. God rest his soul, as he died about a couple of years later from a strange cancer of the bones. He used to go to Argonne National Laboratory every summer working on the N–Body problem. The N–Problem is a very difficult dynamical problem to solve, since it has to track and predict the motion of many bodies or particles at the same time.

The Death of My Father

I took my father's death pretty hard. I wasn't told about it until a month after his death. My mother knew that I was in the middle of final exams preparation, and she didn't want me to be affected by it. The mourning of my father's death was a big event that involved the Catholic Church and their school in a mourning parade. Many of the leading members of the Muslim community in Baghdad participated in the funeral ceremony. Many of them gave speeches on the fortieth day, which was published in a book by the Ministry of Information.

My Marriage to Irene Donohue

During the first two and a half years after I came to the United States, I was fortunate to have several relationships with women I met at the dormitory and outside the dormitory. My friends called me a playboy, and my student teammates often wondered how I was going to get a PhD in astronomy while being a playboy. I used to tell myself, "This is not Istanbul; this is the United States and the dawn of the sexual revolution in the early 1970s … Make the best out of it!" In any case I had several affairs. Some lasted months, and some lasted weeks or days. Some were even one-night stands!

Aside from all these activities, I met one woman whom I became serious about. Her name was Irene Theresa Donohue. Irene had an MS degree in library science and was a student at the University of Albany. She graduated in 1970 and then became the base librarian at Plattsburgh Air Force Base in northern New York. We continued our relationship during this time. I would travel to Plattsburgh, and she would come down to Albany, so we could see each other on weekends. She then moved and took a job in Albany for the sake of being near me. We then fell in love with each other. We decided to get married on August 31, 1972. We could not have a honeymoon because school was just starting. Though Irene and I would later get divorced, our life together was wonderful. We decided not to have children until I finished my PhD.

Jack Sulentic was a classmate of mine in the graduate school, and he became my best friend. We used to eat lunch every day together outside the department, and also he joined me in my daily swimming exercise at an indoor pool. You bet it was indoor, considering the weather in Albany! Jack and I shared many views on internal politics and world affairs. We also shared similar views on social issues, and in a nutshell we had a very good friendship. Jack became a PhD student of May Arif, and he did his PhD thesis on galaxies using radio astronomy observations. In an attempt to keep Jack closer to Albany I introduced him to Connie, the sister of our neighbor Paula Begley. Jack married Connie and had a great wedding ceremony, and after his graduation he went to California and worked with Halton Arp, a well-known observer of galaxies at Caltech. After a few years Jack got a position in the astronomy department at the University of Alabama in Tuscaloosa. He stayed there till he retired a few years ago. The last time I saw him was when he invited me to Tuscaloosa to give a colloquium on one topic of my research.

Astronomy and Car Mechanics

I need to discuss here a strange phenomenon in my schooling at SUNY. Most of the graduate students, including myself, were interested in fixing our cars and discussing car mechanics. One of our professors was even building his own dune buggy and took me for a ride to show me how it cornered so well on exits. I was frightened during that ride but had to endure it! Other students and I kept wondering why there was a connection between car mechanics and astronomy. We even tried every now and then to fix our professors' cars if you can believe that! Once I planned to miss attending a class which I was supposed to give a presentation and did not think I was ready enough. I pretended along with a classmate that my car needed fixing! The professor insisted on the phone to drive and pick us up. He did and I had to give my presentation and it was good to my surprise. The mystery of the relation between astronomy and car mechanics will continue on and on for the rest of my life, and I will never figure it out.

Incidentally, the university was built in the 1960s. Architect Frank Lloyd Wright created the design for a university to be built in South Florida, I believe Miami. The story was that they didn't come up with enough money to build it. At the same time the governor of New York State, Nelson Rockefeller, knew about the situation and offered to buy the plans from Florida and build it in Albany (see photos of the University at Albany). This is perhaps why the University at Albany looks like it was built for a warm climate. There are long and wide outdoor hallways, and it is decorated with huge chandeliers with artificial fruits hanging on them.

An aerial photo of the campus of the University at Albany, New York. This photo was taken by photographer Gary D. Gold, and we appreciate his providing it to us.

Frank Lloyd Wright's design was such a masterpiece that it encouraged the officials at the university to hold international conventions to showcase the university. I remember several scientists from Europe marveling at the unique design of the university. However, the design was not practical for a university in a cold climate. We mostly used the underground heated walkways to go between one department to the other. A huge computer center was at the heart of the university and housed the Univac 1108 system at that time. The cafeterias and dormitories and other facilities looked like a Hilton Hotel. The furniture at the university also was magnificent.

Photo of part of the podium of the university taken
by an unknown photographer to us.

Unfortunately, and I don't say that lightly, all of these amenities were fully or partially destroyed by the students during the Kent State anti–Vietnam War demonstrations. I saw so many couches that had been ripped by knives, and the four towers of undergraduate dormitories were full of graffiti, starting with the elevators. It was really so sad to see these things happen to an otherwise beautiful university.

The Fallout from the Anti–Vietnam War Movement

As a result of the antiwar demonstrations several rules and regulations of universities were changed. One of them that struck me as odd was that there had to be a student representative sitting in on all faculty meetings at the department to make sure that the students' rights were not violated! Our student representative would come out of the meetings and tell us about how the professors were interacting with each other and what the chairman said to other faculty members.

In other words it was mostly gossip and issues that had nothing to do with the welfare of the students and their rights. The student representative to attend the faculty meetings changed on a rotational basis.

When the next rotation came, almost all the students pressured me to become their representative. I refused strongly because I didn't believe in the concept and didn't think I should waste my time on such a useless effort. I asked my friend Jack who had been the representative before if he really defended any rights for the students, and he said absolutely not. I always felt a deep respect for the faculty. Maybe that is old-fashioned, but I thought that was the way we should conduct ourselves.

Another student that I was also close to was Gopal Sistla, who was from India. Gopal was a good friend to both me and Jack and a good fellow with whom to exchange views and opinions on things that mattered to us in our mission. He joined the university I believe two years before us, and he had a lot of experience with how things were going with the department. We always enjoyed his advice.

Star Trekkies

This was an interesting phenomenon: every once in a while we would have students come to our graduate office and ask us how to go about joining the graduate school in astronomy. However, after we asked them some questions about their background in physics and math, we realized they lacked a whole lot. Furthermore, when we asked them why they wanted to join the astronomy department, they started talking about how the episodes of *Star Trek* motivated them. They didn't stick around much, because they left pretty quickly once we started telling them what astronomy was all about and the physics and math that they needed in their background.

In the mid 1970s, NASA realized that they didn't have the budget to finish the Apollo missions to the moon as planned. So NASA canceled the Apollo missions after Apollo 16. NASA then decided to convert one of the Saturn V rockets into a space laboratory and called it Skylab. Jerry saw a great opportunity and started traveling to NASA headquarters and lobbying for an experiment to be put on Skylab to observe the zodiacal light and the dust environment. NASA was still interested in the dust environment in orbit for reasons I mentioned before, and they granted Jerry a multimillion-dollar contract to build a small telescope to do the observations. There was, however, one catch that proved to be a disaster: the telescope had to be extended away from the main body of Skylab whenever observations were to be carried out to avoid viewing obstructions from other experiments.

Jerry was apprehensive about this situation, but he could not do anything about it. I remember he kept worrying about astronauts operating the extension mechanism and orienting his telescope, which they had to be trained to do. The astronauts had to be trained for operating most of the experiments on Skylab, and there was too much for the astronauts to perfect. This was what worried Jerry a lot. In any case, I was extremely happy because now we had two major experiments, one using *Pioneer 10* and *11* probes and one making observations from Skylab. I couldn't ask for more than that. This was actually a researcher heaven, even though at this juncture I wasn't involved in the two experiments because I was busy with my PhD preparations. Nonetheless, I could see myself involved in both later on in my research. Martin Marietta was assigned to do the extension mechanism of the telescope, and Jerry and his helpers made numerous trips to Martin Marietta to participate in the design.

Skylab was launched, and it was a success in orbit. The astronauts started operating Jerry's telescope, and he started getting data. However, shortly after, the extension mechanism jammed, and that was the disaster that I spoke about earlier. NASA and the astronauts tried hard to correct the problem, but they failed. The telescope was idle and had to be ejected from Skylab, if I remember correctly. This was certainly a down ↓ thrill-of-research moment.

Attending the Sixth Texas High-Energy Astrophysics Symposium

The astronomy department paid for the expenses to send me and my classmate Jack to New York City to attend THE SIXTH TEXAS HIGH-ENERGY ASTROPHYSICS SYMPOSIUM. They wanted us to have the experience of seeing how the big boys operated in a symposium. The attendees were famous astronomers and astrophysicists, including Stephen Hawking, Robert Dicke, Charles Misner, Geoffrey and Margaret Burbidge, Sterling Colgate, and on and on. The first night of the symposium there was a cocktail party, and I saw a ring of many astronomers around two astronomers telling jokes and making everyone laugh. I asked my professor Stefan Temesvary, who also came down for the symposium, who the two astronomers in the middle were. He said it was the Burbidges, the married couple Geoffrey and Margaret Burbidge.

It was truly a great experience for me to witness such a gathering, and luck had it that I sat for dinner at one table with Robert H. Dicke from Princeton University and Charles Misner from Caltech. I got to sit with them because Stefan Temesvary used to be at Princeton University and knew Robert Dicke. Dicke asked Jack and me what type of astronomers we were. I told him we were in solar system, and he said that was good because most astrophysicists were either in stellar evolution or stellar atmospheres. For the rest of the dinner, we listened to Charlie Misner talk to Bob Dicke about his experiments, which were very interesting. Dicke, who passed away in 1997, was a brilliant theoretician and experimenter.

Research could be a thrill, providing an uplifting feeling that could last for quite a long time if not forever. However, research also had its ups and downs, though in my experience the down feeling was never a lasting one, simply because I knew I had accomplished something that had not been done before or had done better than before. Basically, I started out with an idea and didn't know whether it was going to pan out or not, and I hoped that the research funding agencies would give me the money regardless of the outcome. So sometimes it was an up ↑ thrill, but other times it was a *down* ↓ thrill, if there is such a thing as a down ↓ thrill. Even none other than Robert Dicke experienced down thrills.

Robert Dicke vs. Albert Einstein

Dicke decided that the precession of the perihelion of Mercury was not due to general relativity as Einstein postulated but due to the oblateness of the sun. Dicke set out to do another classical test of general relativity to prove his own theory. It so happened that the result would be given at this symposium in New York City. In the symposium they had a black shroud over a huge photo of Albert Einstein. Then after Dicke finished his talk, they removed the black shroud, and Dicke admitted that the prediction of general relativity about the planet Mercury was correct and that his postulate was wrong. This must have been a down ↓ thrill-of-research moment for him I assume. The applause after Dicke finished his remarks was deafening; it was a great historical moment.

Stephen Hawking

Then Stephen Hawking was introduced, and he gave his paper about the second law of thermodynamics. His speech was difficult to follow due to his disability. We all were given copies of his paper to read in case we could not understand what he was saying. I had the great joy of seeing him after he finished his talk. I shook his hand and said hello, and he answered hello back. The symposium proved to me that the thrill of research is out there and is so important and enjoyable.

Sterling Colgate

I also saw Sterling Colgate, a brilliant astrophysicist and an expert in supernovae research, in the elevator with some of his colleagues. He'd had a few drinks and had just taken his colleagues on a tour in his own helicopter. Sterling was still talking about his research to his colleagues in the elevator regardless of the drinks he'd consumed, which fascinated me!

Comet Kohoutek and the Trip to Green Bank, West Virginia

In 1973 amateur astronomer Kohoutek discovered that a big comet was coming and would be visible to the naked eye in about four months. It was estimated that it would be the biggest comet in modern times to pass near the Earth. NASA and solar astronomers got excited to study this comet and thought it was a great opportunity since the passage of Halley's comet in 1906. At the Space Astronomy Laboratory (SAL) we had a meeting, and Jerry asked us all what we could do to participate in studying this comet. There was little to do in four months to prepare for major observations of the comet. I proposed an idea to study the free-free emissions from free electrons in the nucleus of the comet since this would give us an idea of how much ionization was happening on the surface of the nucleus of the comet.

This emission could be observed in the centimeter wavelengths of the radio spectrum, and for that I suggested we team up with May Arif and my classmate Jack Sulentic since they were doing radio astronomy research. Jerry and I wrote a small proposal to NASA for $30,000 to fund my part of the project. It was my first experience writing a research proposal for soft money! The term "Soft Money" means that you don't have a job in a university or any other institution, i.e. nobody pays your salary. So you are a free-lance researcher having to acquire your salary and research costs from a funding agency. However, you have to be associated with a university or research institution with a "courtesy appointment".

The money I requested in the proposal would finance my trip to the National Radio Astronomy Observatory in Green Bank, West Virginia, and my time spent making calculations on where to point the huge radio telescope during daylight to observe the comet. The fund would also pay for my time spent analyzing the data with May and Jack. May Arif would ask for the time to use the three-hundred-foot radio telescope, since she was a known radio astronomer.

Jack and I set out to travel to Green Bank in, I believe, April 1973. We flew over the mountains surrounding the radio telescope in West Virginia in a small propeller plane. The flight was scary to me and was very bumpy. At Green Bank, I was astonished to see the "big ear," as they used to call it, i.e., the radio telescope, sitting majestically in a valley surrounded by many mountains. They chose this site for the telescope because the mountains protected it from radio noise. I noticed that we had to either ride a bicycle (they had several) to the telescope or drive one of their special cars that has no spark plugs to avoid creating any noise for the telescope. These cars had diesel engines in them.

We arrived at dinnertime, and before we ate dinner at the cafeteria, Jack suggested we go to the booze room, as they called it, where they had all kinds of complementary alcohol for visitors. This was one of the fringe benefits that researchers got from the government for doing research! It was timely for me to have a scotch and soda after the tension of the bumpy ride of the flight.

The next day I worked very hard using the computers at Green Bank to try to find where the comet would be during our noontime observation slot, because we could not see it with the naked eye during daytime. I had to give the operators of the telescope the coordinates so that they could steer the telescope and aim it at the comet without being able to seeing it. Therefore, my calculations had to be extremely accurate. I remember I couldn't sleep almost the whole night before doing the observations, going over all the equations and making sure I calculated it right. The idea that these operators could be steering the telescope to the wrong spot was frightening to me to say the least. Perhaps scotch and soda would have helped, but I couldn't do that, because I had to stay alert. Jack was sympathetic to my problem, but he couldn't help in any way, because that wasn't his field. He only wished me luck.

We met some of the radio astronomers that were also visiting to make their observations of galaxies and other objects. There were other relatively smaller telescopes that were called the *ballerina telescopes* because they had to be oriented the same way and move the same way, a technique called radio interferometry. The radio astronomers I met asked me what I was doing, and I told them we'd come to observe Comet Kohoutek. They got excited. Some of them were using the ballerina telescopes, and they asked me for the coordinates so that they could point their telescopes to Comet Kohoutek too. I gave them the coordinates, and I was so excited and felt proud that I was a student and supplying these professionals with my data. This was one of the up↑ thrills of research moments. As small as it was, it was nonetheless important to me.

After returning to Albany, it was time to analyze the data. However, this did not materialize since the data was noisy. If there was any information, it would be difficult to discern from the noise. I had no experience at all in analyzing radio astronomy data, so I relied on May and Jack. May told me that there was no meaningful data, which meant that the ionization of the atoms and molecules on the surface of the comet nucleus was not significant enough to be above the noise in the data. Finally, I had to write the final report on the project, and I said we had little data and that it was too noisy so we were not sure that there was anything there. This was perhaps the correct conclusion since we learned later that Kohoutek did not live up to expectations and, so to speak, fizzled out. This meant that no major ionization on the surface of the nucleus took place and was not easily detected.

Chapter 7

Research on Soft Money

The department got a new chairman from Rensselaer Polytechnic Institute, the late Dr. Mayo Greenberg. He was a well-known astrophysicist specialized in interstellar dust (cosmic dust in the universe). I took several courses from Professor Greenberg and did well in them. He was interested in my knowledge of quantum mechanics because he was teaching us a course in astrophysics and quantum mechanics was a big part of it. He wrote equations on the board and did derivations. He didn't prepare for these derivations, doing them from earlier memory. He sometimes got stuck, and I used to help him out. His understanding of quantum mechanics was solid; he just didn't bother to prepare before the class and relied on his memory and his intuition. Mayo told us in one of his classes that he used to do calculus at the age of twelve. Mayo Greenberg was a force to be contended with if we were to pass the PhD qualifying exam. I liked Mayo very much because he was interested in research more than anything else, and his publications attested to that.

After hard work for three years of coursework, in May 1973, I finally had to face the PhD qualifying exam. It so happened that my best friend, Jack Sulentic, and I were eligible at that time to take the PhD qualifying exam. Normally that would be great competition with two students taking the qualifying exam at the same time, but we were such good friends that we didn't feel that way. We both wished the other good luck. The rules of the department were that if we were to fail the qualifying exam, then we would earn a master's degree without the need to write a master's thesis. To me this option was no less than a disaster; I had to pass the PhD qualifying exam or bust.

The faculty used to tell us that when we prepared for the qualifying exam, we had to know more about astronomy than any member of the faculty. To me passing the qualifying exam and getting my PhD was the passport that said I could do independent research in astronomy. The preparation for the exam was really painful and consumed me completely. Different astronomy departments have different setups for these tests. Ours was sort of difficult because they asked for two written tests, the first for observational astronomy and the second for theoretical astronomy. There was also a third oral test that could cover any topic each faculty member chose, and there were seven of them[2] … God help us!

The first test was on a Monday for observational astronomy, and Jack and I went at noon to take the exam. Without any exaggeration, it took me till eight thirty that day to finish it. It was a lengthy exam and difficult. When the other students in the department saw a copy of the first exam, they made a comment to the effect that the faculty members were trying to show off, that each one of them could ask a harder question than the other. The next day, Tuesday, we went at noon again to take the theoretical astronomy test, and it was more or less the same level of difficulty. This time I finished the test at six o'clock in the evening. I was exhausted and worn out. My wife, Irene, told me to take it easy and rest for the oral exam that would be on Friday.

I went first for the oral exam at nine o'clock in the morning and fielded questions from seven professors on every field in astronomy you can imagine. The test lasted two and a half hours, after which I went down to the graduate students' office waiting for the verdict. After a long and arduous twenty minutes the phone rang, and they asked me to go upstairs. As soon as I opened the door to the department, I saw them all gathered there cheering and congratulating me for passing the qualifying exam with flying colors.

---

[2] May Arif was on sabbatical leave that year, so she was not involved in my qualifying PhD exam.

I was glad I went first for the oral test, because now everybody knew that I had passed. As for Jack, he was getting nervous about what would happen to him because the prevailing wisdom at that time was that one student could upstage the other in the exam, causing the faculty to flunk the other. I kept telling Jack that he would pass too and not to worry about the exam. I told him once he got there he would do well, but he didn't believe me. Jack passed too, but he wasn't happy at all as I was. Apparently he thought he didn't do well in the oral exam, and he was miserable the rest of the day. I, on the other hand, was very happy and took my wife to a restaurant and almost got drunk in the middle of the day. Later on that day I heard that the students had organized a poker game, so I went and played poker till midnight.

Now I realized after passing the qualifying exam that I needed to decide on what field I would do a PhD thesis on. I visited my previous graduate adviser Dr. Schmalberger and asked him if he had a research project that he could suggest for me to do a thesis on in stellar atmospheres. He did not seem to have a specific problem to suggest. Then I visited Dr. Stefan Temesvary, who was in the field of stellar evolution, and asked the same thing. He also didn't have anything specific enough to suggest. I was not that concerned about this outcome, since I had developed an interest in interplanetary dust and the interplanetary medium in general. Around the time I finished my PhD qualifying exam, Jerry decided to leave Dudley Observatory and establish SAL. He moved to a different location also close to the university. So I met with Jerry and told him that I would like to do a thesis in the field of interplanetary dust. Jerry was happy because I would be the first PhD student he would be advising, and he offered me his extensive library of observations that he did at Haleakalā, Hawaii. I appreciated his offer and thanked him for giving me this opportunity.

Shortly after I went on a mission by reading more than one hundred papers published in the field of interplanetary dust. It gave me such a feel for the field and what had been done in it. I also read a few theses that other scholars had done before me. From this extensive reading, I developed a good background in this field and a special love for interplanetary dust dynamics, their motion in space, their orbital dynamics, and so on.

Supporting a Small Organization on Soft Money

The most important thing that I learned from Jerry Weinberg was how to do research on soft money. It was certainly difficult to support a small organization, roughly ten employees, sometimes less or more, like SAL on soft money. He had to write proposals, submit them to NASA and other organizations, and secure the funding to pay the engineers and scientists and the students at the laboratory. It was a rare operation in the country, and we heard that there was one other laboratory in Arizona that did the same thing. Jerry had to make budgets, determine salaries of each person, pay overhead to the university, pay the rent of the space occupied by the laboratory, pay the utilities, and so on and so on. This operation was somewhat similar to a small business, but the only customer was the government because no private sector was going to fund basic research in astronomy at the time. This was indeed a major undertaking that few people could really perform, and I know that because later on in my career I did a similar thing. Later I will talk about several things that involve doing research on soft money.

In some cases the PhD adviser suggests topics for the student to do a thesis on; in others the student comes up with his or her own topic or problem. In my case, I wanted to choose the topic myself. After a lot of thought I decided on a topic and then went to Jerry to tell him about it. I wanted to do a thesis on the effects of solar flares emanating from the sun on the zodiacal light or basically interplanetary dust. Jerry was happy with the topic, but then he asked, "Aren't you going to use my observational data bank?" I said of course. I also told him that half of my thesis or more would be on theoretical topics involving interplanetary dust dynamics and the dust-plasma interactions near the sun. Plasma means a rarefied gas that is made up of free electrons and free protons and some ionized nuclei, and that is basically what a solar flare is.

Zodiacal Light

Zodiacal light is sunlight scattered by interplanetary dust orbiting the sun. It appears after the end of astronomical twilight as the sun sets (about an hour and a half after sunset) and also an hour and a half before sunrise. I researched if the Arabs had ever seen zodiacal light and, if so, what they called it. I found a mention of it in a book written around 500 AD, and they called it *Amoud al-Subh*, "the morning pillar." I don't know why they called it the morning pillar, since it appears twice each day. Zodiacal light is a cone-shaped light that is slightly yellowish like the color of the sun, and you can see it if you are away from city lights and in the wilderness, preferably on top of a mountain. Members of the Society of Amateur Astronomy of Central Florida told me that they had seen it in Central Florida in remote areas.

Among the staff of SAL, Dr. Martha Hanner was working on the analysis of the zodiacal light data from *Pioneer 10* and *11* probes to Jupiter and beyond. Martha heard of my decision to do my thesis on solar-flare effects on the zodiacal light, and she was interested in talking to me about it. Previously I'd read a paper published by two French astronomers about the enhancement of the zodiacal light due to the onset of a solar flare. They also published a photograph taken by a telescope of that brightness enhancement.

I told Martha about this paper and explained it to her, and then she said, "Don't you want to know which part of the dust cloud contributes the most to the brightness of the zodiacal light?"

I said, "Yes, of course."

Then Martha said, "I have a computer program that you could use to do that kind of calculation."

Photo of the Zodiacal Light: Astrophotographer Steve Zigler created this image in Death Valley during the new moon on January 30, 2014. At center, stretching up, shines an intense display of Zodiacal light. Several other notable features gleam forth, including the winter Milky Way, the Andromeda Galaxy, Jupiter, the Pleiades, and the Orion Nebula.

I dove into the computer program and altered it to do what I wanted to calculate. The results were fascinating, and I had an up ↑ thrill-of-research moment when I discovered that the zodiacal light close to the sun arose from dust close to the sun and not from dust close to Earth, as postulated years before. My next assignment was to put the methodology and the results together in a drafted paper and show it to Martha. She read the draft and had some suggestions to improve the paper.

Martha suggested that we submit the paper "On the Possibility of Solar Flare Effects on the Zodiacal Light?" to *Planetary and Space Science*, which is based in Britain, and we did. The reviewers made minor changes to it, and it was approved for publication (see the reference to this paper in appendix B). This was a major feat for me because in many cases PhD students don't publish papers until they finish their PhD thesis.

I believe it was late June 1974, and the American Astronomical Society (AAS) held a meeting at the State University of New York at Rochester, New York. I decided to submit an abstract of the first paper I did with Martha to present at the meeting. It so happened that my mother was visiting me for the first time. My mother, Kolomba, my wife and I went to Rochester so my mother could attend my presentation. It was my first appearance in front of astronomers in my field. The presentation was pretty good, and I fielded many questions. My mother was so happy with the presentation (though she of course did not know what I was talking about), and she said to me later, "You're just like your father." She said I was eloquent and brave just as he was.

Many colleagues told me at the time that it was important to present papers at the AAS. This would help me get to be known pretty early. At the meeting I met Dr. Philip Lamy, a French astronomer who had just graduated from Cornell University. I chatted with him, and he was the first foreign astronomer that I got to know.

President Nixon's Resignation

My mother was still with us, and we were touring Upstate New York, near one of the Finger Lakes, when we heard on the car radio that President Nixon had resigned. My mother did not speak English and asked me what was going on. I explained, and she said, "Oh yeah, in Baghdad people are saying that he stuffed the ballot boxes in the election with false ones bearing his name, and that's how he won the election." At this point I asked my mother if she'd heard of the Watergate scandal. She hadn't, so I explained what went on in Watergate. She was really astonished because she had never heard of it, and she said most of the people in Baghdad hadn't heard of it either. So much for world communication in those days!

Mayo Greenberg, the active chairman of our astronomy department, was about to get on a plane to Leiden, the Netherlands, when a member of the astronomy department gave him a slip of a no-confidence vote of the department in his chairmanship. So I said jokingly to my classmates that the way the department did this reminded me of when Brutus and his associates stabbed Julius Caesar with knives on the steps of the senate on the Ides of March. The graduate students in the department laughed so much at this analogy! Mayo then decided to accept a prestigious position in Leiden that had been offered to him before this incident. I was disappointed with that because I really respected Mayo and liked him as a teacher and more importantly as a pioneer researcher in cosmic dust and the interstellar medium. He later passed away in 2001 of pancreatic cancer.

I realized it wasn't easy to put a thesis together, and it took a lot of hard work. As I finished my thesis, it was time to choose an outside member for my thesis committee. The outside member must be from a different university. Jerry said to me that perhaps the best person was Professor Martin Harwit, the chairman of the astronomy department at Cornell University. Martin was a well-known researcher in the solar system and the interplanetary medium, and he was a perfect choice for my committee. However, my classmates warned me that I was playing with fire to bring somebody of Martin Harwit's caliber on my committee. I brushed all of these warnings aside because I really wanted the challenge. I'd also used, as other students did in other departments, Martin's famous book *Astrophysical Concepts* to prepare for the PhD qualifying exam.

I called Professor Harwit and asked for an appointment and asked him to be my outside member for my PhD thesis committee. He accepted initially, but he wanted to see me first before he made his final decision. I drove up to Ithaca, New York, to meet with him, and that was an interesting experience. I gave him about half of my thesis at the time to read and make suggestions. He flipped through the pages and saw some equations that I put in that were not derived, so he asked me to go on his blackboard and derive them.

I derived some of them, but I couldn't remember how I derived others, so I told him that I would get back to him later in another visit. He agreed, and we set a date for another visit. I was pleasantly surprised to discover that Professor Harwit had been in Istanbul and finished his high school there. We spoke some Turkish together and exchanged memories of places in Istanbul. I told him that I used to walk by the high school that he attended, and that was really wonderful. I never asked him how he ended up in Istanbul, but his family was from Czechoslovakia, so I assumed they decided to go there to escape the Nazi rule. I went again to see him in Ithaca and derived the rest of the equations. Martin said he enjoyed reading my thesis and thought it was good, so that gave me a great relief. In these two visits to Martin, I felt as if I was a student back again for the qualifying exam. I felt gratified that an astrophysicist of his caliber and a chairman of the department at Cornell University, which was more prestigious than my department, approved of my work.

During my second visit Martin told me that I didn't need to come back anymore. I could just mail him the rest of my thesis, and we would talk on the phone. And so we did, but I was always nervous during every phone call I made. He made a few suggestions but kept praising the thesis, which was very gratifying to me. He also told me that he would travel on the day of the thesis defense to Albany in a small plane (because there were no big airliners flying between the two cities) and that he wanted to give a colloquium after I finished my thesis defense.

On September 5, 1975, I did my defense. The defense went well, and I passed and was granted the PhD degree. Professor Harwit gave a wonderful talk on his new research, and while I was driving him to the airport, he asked me what I thought of his presentation. I said it was wonderful and very philosophical. He said, "Oh no, I wanted to avoid giving the impression that it was philosophical." He also told me that the professors' comments after I finished my defense were good. He finally told me that he usually kept student theses for a year or two on his bookcase in his office but he thought mine would stay for about ten years. I thought that was a great compliment from him, and I thanked him very much.

Pluses and Minuses of Soft Money

If you have a mind like Richard Feynman's, then you don't have to read this book.

First and foremost I have to mention here that I have conducted research on so-called soft money for twenty-six years (1970–96). During this period, I succeeded in acquiring my annual salary strictly from research grants, and that is where the expression *soft money* comes from. Obviously, this is not by any means easy to do, i.e., you do not have a guaranteed income for yourself and your family. Therefore, the pressures you put on yourself can be enormous sometimes, if not most of the time!

From 1996 until I retired in 2009, I was a professor at the University of Central Florida (UCF), and I had teaching duties and therefore a tenure-track position. What all this means is that I was on hard money, i.e., guaranteed salary, and in six years I could apply for tenure status. Prior to this appointment, I was a research professor at the Florida Institute of Technology, or Florida Tech, but I was still on soft money at that time.

When you are on soft money, you can't work from home! You have to be affiliated with a university or some other research-conducting entity that is recognized as prestigious by the funding agencies. For example, in my case I worked at the Space Astronomy Laboratory, which was associated with the State University of New York at Albany.

The research-funding agencies are numerous, and they can be federal, state, or private entities. I solicited grant money from the following agencies on the federal level: NASA, National Science Foundation (NSF), Air Force Office of Scientific Research (AFOSR), US Natick Army R & D Center, Defense Advanced Research Projects Agency (DARPA), US Army Tank-Automotive Command at Warren, Michigan, Naval Research Laboratory (NRL). On the state level, I contacted Technological Research and Development Authority (TRDA), a Florida state agency, and Florida Spaceport Authority (FSA).

It is noteworthy to mention here that acquiring research grants from federal agencies is more difficult than acquiring grants from state agencies. This is due to the fact that at the federal level the competition is much more severe because of the sheer number of proposals and the higher quality of the proposals. For state funding agencies, the quality and number of proposals is lower. It is also noteworthy to mention that you are competing with scientists working in your own state. Also some of the research problems are confined to that state and do not have immediate implications on the federal level. One good example is a research proposal submitted to the state on studying traffic conditions on a congested state highway.

Another difference between state and federal research funding is the amount of funding. More often than not, the amount (in dollars) of funding from the federal agencies greatly exceeds that from the state agencies. In some cases, researchers get millions of dollars from NASA for their space-research instruments on major space missions. On the other hand, many scientists submit highly complicated proposals to federal agencies only to compete for funding at the $50,000, $100,000, and $150,000 levels. In many cases, for example, NASA and NSF may receive over two hundred proposals and then choose less than ten proposals to fulfill, for levels of funding of $50,000, $100,000, and $150,000. This is really a pretty sad situation considering that many good proposals are thrown out and never see the light of day. I myself at times experienced that with NASA's funding agencies, the difficulty of being one out of hundreds of proposals to be funded. I even at times regretted writing the proposal and submitting it.

The problem mentioned above arises from the fact that the federal agencies send out solicitations for proposals in a certain area, and the proposers know the total amount of budget allocated for the solicitation in that area of research. They are also told the range of funding for each winning proposal. What submitters do not known is the total number of competing proposals. I don't know how one can go about providing this important information because the total number of proposals is not known until the deadline for submission had arrived. By that time, it is too late for the proposer to know whether he or she should write a proposal or not bother. Ultimately, if there was a reliable projection of that number, and I don't know if that is possible, then it may help. If such information can be given, it will save a lot of wasted time and efforts that goes into the preparation of proposals, which often have little chance of acquiring funding.

It is no accident that in football each team aspires to be number one. The winner of the Super Bowl is embraced and revered while the defeated team is treated by the fans as unimportant and considered a loser. Most people in the United States have heard that being number two is not important and in actuality is a little shameful! Being number one is everything in America, and the hard reality is there are no places for second place. This mental attitude is often helpful in arguably keeping the United States number one in the world in research, technology, and as a superpower. In order to keep the United States in this unique position, US researchers must continue to be in this mind-set or all is lost.

In most universities across the United States, the university administrators ask their professors to include in their annual activity reports research proposals that they submitted but were declined for funding. This way the university will know that their professors have tried but did not succeed. This procedure acts as a reminder to the professors that they should improve their writing skills and practice more on how to sell their research ideas to the federal and state funding agencies, corporations, and so on. It also informs the administration that the professors are putting forth the effort. If they don't have declined or funded proposals, it means they were not trying at all, and that is the kiss of death for tenure and promotion. In a university you cannot get tenure or promotion if you just teach, no matter how good of a teacher you are. I am saying this from my experience in the sciences and engineering; I have no idea how tenure works in other disciplines.

It is important to note here that for success in research, university professors should have special capabilities. These special capabilities are more often than not different from the ones needed to be successful in teaching. Seldom will you find professors who can successfully do both. For research, you have to have creativity, imagination, and the capability to generate new ideas. You must have a solid foundation, for example, in physics and math if you are an astronomer. In other words you need to have the tools necessary to carry out your research. You also need the capability to sell your ideas in a proposal; you need to make your research ideas sexy—yes, this is talked about a lot by scientists who review proposals.

Using the Weapon of Fear

Some researchers use the factor of fear to sell their ideas by, for example, doing research in global warming or dangers from orbital debris in space. Anytime you can make sound arguments of what will happen if your research is not carried out, you may win the decision for funding. For years I and many others have talked about the dangers of junk particles in space destroying satellites, the space shuttle, and the international space station. Global-warming researchers talk about the loss of land from rising seawater and now climate change. I wrote a proposal with Dr. George Blaha about retrieving and getting rid of dead satellites in the geostationary ring. The geostationary ring (at approximately 22,300 miles above Earth's surface) is the altitude at which satellites orbit at the same rotation rate of the Earth and therefore remain fixed in the sky. Each satellite must have 3 degrees to broadcast, and the geostationary ring is 360 degrees. So we can only put up 120 satellites, and the United Nations divides that number among different nations. Efforts have been made to reduce the broadcast to 2 degrees, and that way we can have 180 satellites. So in my proposal with Dr. Blaha, we used these argument and others to sell our proposal. Sometimes the danger could be real, and other times it may not be. It's important to not exaggerate the fear too much. One fear that I believe cannot be exaggerated is the possibility of the human race being eradicated by a collision with a large asteroid or a big comet.

By writing proposals to seek funding for my research ideas, I realized important characteristics that one must have to succeed in doing research on soft money.

What Does Not Matter

1. It does not matter which university you graduated from.
2. It does not matter how good your grades were in graduate school.
3. It does not matter how good of a teacher you are.
4. It does not matter if you have engineering design and construction skills. You can always hire engineers to do what you need. This is not meant to downgrade what engineers do; actually to succeed in research you have to have first-class engineers on your team.
5. It does not matter what kind of relationships you have with the fair sex!

What Does Matter

1. You must have creativity.
2. You must be able to generate new ideas.
3. How you communicate your research ideas to others matters.
4. It does matter if you have established a good reputation as a researcher in your field of research.
5. You should have established a good network of friends in your field.
6. You should know how to sell your ideas to funding agencies.
7. Good writing skills matter.
8. You should have a great drive and be a crusader for doing research.
9. It does matter if you are working on soft money. This way you have no notions of getting into universities for the sole purpose of getting tenure, which would be hard money.
10. Funding agencies and their reviewers do look at what university you are associated with, and in some cases this could be the kiss of death!
11. You need to have good skills in presenting your research ideas in front of those who are going to fund or not fund your research.
12. You must have expertise in your field and associated fields so that when you speak to funding agencies you are looked upon as a competent researcher who knows what he or she is talking about. For example, if you have to fly your experiment on a satellite or the space shuttle, then you need to know quite a bit about the space environment and the orbital dynamics and so on and so forth.
13. It does matter early on to attend conferences and present papers at the AAS meetings, especially after graduating. Attending other meetings, domestic and international, to get exposure and meet other astronomers to exchange ideas is highly important.

These two lists are by no means exhaustive, but for now this is what I see as most important. The numbering sequence of these two lists does not reflect the importance of each item; they are just ordered in the manner that I thought of them. I want the reader to keep in mind that doing research on soft money is much different from doing research on hard money. Tenure-track professors do not have to struggle for their salaries for six to seven years. Research is still important for them, though, in order to get tenure and then promotions from assistant to associate and into full professorship, in addition to earning a good reputation. Nowadays I cannot picture professors getting tenure without doing profound research first; excellent teaching is not enough. It is a rough world out there these days, especially in science and engineering fields!

Moguls and Mafia Heads in Research

There is an interesting view of some of the personalities in research. When I was a graduate student, we used to talk about the mafia in research! For example, we considered Alastair G. W. Cameron, a brilliant astrophysicist at Harvard, to be the mafia head researcher in solar-system studies. He also had several PhDs working with him. This was not fair to a brilliant astrophysicist like Cameron. The reason we called him that was because whenever he proposed to NASA his research was funded. So we were sort of jealous of Cameron because he was so successful and drained the money allocated for basic research in the solar system. I am sure that some scientists may have also looked at Jerry Weinberg the same way. One time Jerry told me that when he used to go to NASA headquarters asking for funding, some of the people there used to say, "Here comes Weinberg with his photopolarimeter," which was a name for his small telescope.

Another Research Mogul: Fred Lawrence Whipple, "Comet Man"

The reputation of being a mogul was good to have in research, and it was good for young PhDs to be associated with scientists like that.

Another mogul was the famous Professor Fred L. Whipple, director of the Smithsonian Astrophysical Observatory, well known as "Comet Man" for his great work in cometary physics. Whipple received the Distinguished Federal Civilian Service Medal from President John F. Kennedy for his accomplishments. Whipple was also a good friend of mine, and we used to talk over the phone. My first acquaintance with the late Fred Whipple was when I was a graduate student and he came to attend a symposium on interplanetary dust at my university. I was shocked the first time I saw him because he was wearing a cowboy hat and two fake guns at his belt. I asked Jerry who this man was, and Jerry said he was the famous Fred Whipple, otherwise known as "Comet Man."

My next meeting with Fred Whipple was when I presented my paper at the American Astronomical Society (AAS) in Philadelphia, Pennsylvania. He was the chair of one of the sessions in which I gave my paper. When my turn came, he gave a nice introduction to my work to the audience. We chatted after the end of the session, and he asked me about my future research plans. Another time I met with him was when I presented a paper at the AAS meeting at Austin, Texas. This time he came and sat in the front row to listen to my paper. The session was held at the President Lyndon Baines Johnson Auditorium at the University of Texas. After I finished my paper, Whipple asked several questions, and I sat with him afterward. We chatted about my research for quite a while.

Fred Whipple was really an amazing astrophysicist and astronomer; he published so many scientific research papers that the Smithsonian Astrophysical Observatory put them together in two big volumes titled *The Complete Works of Fred L. Whipple*. He was still publishing papers when he was sixty-seven years old! I still remember one incident, many years later in my career, when I was talking to Dr. Baloga, who was in charge of funding proposals at the American Geophysical Union. He asked me to see if Fred Whipple would vouch for funding my proposal. I then called on Fred Whipple to make a phone call to Dr. Baloga, and he did. A few days later I called Whipple and asked him about his call to Dr. Baloga. Apparently Dr. Baloga had asked him, "If you think so much of Misconi's proposal, why don't you give up on funding your proposal?" Whipple said that funding should not be like this. I thanked him for his effort.

Me as a Research Mogul ... No!

I am sure that I had some reputation like a mogul later on in my career when scientists in NASA would say, "Here comes Misconi with his laser-spin experiment."

Chapter 8

The Concept of Laser-Particle Levitation

After my graduation Irene and I took a month for our belated honeymoon. We visited Kennedy Space Center (KSC). Then Irene told me how great Disney World was, and so we went to Disney World too. Now looking back at our honeymoon, I say, "Isn't that what athletes do after they win the Super Bowl or other titles in other sports?" I was stunned at what I saw at Disney World and Epcot Center; it was fascinating to say the least. I thanked my wife for suggesting it and talking me into going.

Jerry earlier offered me a position as a postdoc in his Space Astronomy Laboratory at SUNY. He offered me the highest salary at the time for a postdoc, which was *$12,000 a year*, can you believe that! My main assignment was to analyze the data on zodiacal light that Jerry took in Hawaii under a grant from NASA for $150,000 a year (to be renewed for a few years depending on results and NASA's needs). I also was working on publishing papers from my research that I did for my PhD thesis. The accepted wisdom was that if you didn't publish the research in your thesis, then it wasn't officially published, even though it had a Library of Congress number and a copy on a microfiche film.

Since one important goal among others of this book is to explain to the readers the nature of doing research on soft money, I need to include all my activities to continue on this course. Sometimes, I had to consider this line of work, as hard as it was, as making a living for my family and me. Doing research on soft money to earn your own salary is a perplexing experience. Here are some of the things you have to do:

1. You have to continuously come up with new ideas and write many proposals. Some of them will be funded, and others will be rejected.
2. You must assemble the necessary teams to do the research.
3. You must make budgets to pay yourself and others on the team and present it to the university with their overhead included.
4. You have to allow for the university overhead that could be anywhere between 30 percent or 40 percent up to 60 percent of the total budget (not including payments to students), depending on which university you are associated with.
5. Sometimes you have to prepare a list of suggested potential reviewers to help the funding scientist, since he or she more often than not is not in your field. The funding scientist may pick names from your list or may ignore them all.

As I said earlier, this is by no means all of the responsibilities. I will include other duties as I go along.

The most terrifying prospect in doing research on soft money is that if you don't have any funded research for a few months or a year, then you're out of salary, and how do you support your family and yourself? The university you are associated with is not going to help you monetarily; in fact they keep asking you when the next grant is coming because they want the overhead money. This is a terrifying situation to be in; nonetheless I did it for approximately twenty years. Sometimes I would lie down in bed at night thinking, *Where is the next money going to come from, and which proposal is going to make it?* When the phone in my office rang, I never knew if it would be good news or bad news! With all these hardships, you may ask why I did it. The answer is simple: I loved it.

The uncertainty can be wonderful, and perhaps sometimes it resembles a poker game, though not in the strict sense. In poker you have to bluff; in research you can't bluff your way through. Well, maybe you can. I certainly did not do that, nor did I see it in the proposals of other scientists that I reviewed. But I suppose it can happen, and it could happen more than I think. All in all, I still loved working on soft money, and I still fondly remember it. I would do it again and again if I had to and would do it all over again.

So Jerry asked me to participate in writing the proposal for the continuation of his NASA grant titled "Physical Properties of Interplanetary Dust," which meant I had to explain what I was going to do with his data. Jerry explained to me clearly that this was training for me on how to write proposals since in the near future I would be doing my own proposals. He was the principal investigator (PI) on this grant, and he appointed me as a research associate, which was the fair thing to do.

Jerry had amassed the most zodiacal-light observations of anyone in the history of the world. He collected his data from his observing station on top of Mt. Haleakalā, Maui, Hawaii, some thirteen thousand feet above sea level, from 1964 to 1968. It is a magnificent collection of observations done very accurately, and now it is housed in Snellville, Georgia (near Atlanta, Georgia). Jerry was a PhD student of Professor Franklin Roach (who looked so much like Benjamin Franklin that we called him that). We also called Franklin Roach the pope of zodiacal light! The only other smaller set of observations of the zodiacal light was done by my great friend the French astronomer Rene Dumont from Mount Tenerife, in the Canary Islands. Jerry's observations were registered on green waxy charts, and I used to call them the green wonders. The wax would burn when the somewhat hot pen contacted it. Jerry used to spend hours measuring the deflections (magnitude of brightness) on these charts, which I had no patience to do. The deflections on those charts were analog and not digital. There were no digital capabilities in those days.

Jerry, however, had heard of a company in Palo Alto, California, that used a laser beam to digitize the deflections on these charts. It was expensive since the technology was new, and Jerry used $30,000 from his grant to digitize approximately thirty charts that we selected together. The data therefore now was computerized, and I used it in my PhD thesis and for many years to follow. This data was instrumental in several scientific papers I published.

The time arrived to work hard on publishing my second research paper from my thesis, titled "Solar Flare Effects on the Zodiacal Light?," which I submitted to the *Journal of Astronomy and Astrophysics* (see the attached list of publications). The reviewers accepted and published it.

Seeing the Light in 1977

It always amazes me that I did a PhD thesis on zodiacal light without actually seeing it! The problem was I had to be on a mountain away from cities in order to see it. My chance came in January 1977 when I went with Jerry and other SAL astronomers to present my paper at the AAS meeting in Honolulu, Hawaii. Jerry suggested we go to Maui to visit his observation station on top of Haleakalā after we finished presenting our papers. Jerry drove us to the top of the mountain, and I was petrified by the turns he made on the narrow road. It was a clear, beautiful sky, and soon after sunset there was a majestic cone of light with the color of the sun. Everyone in our group shouted, "Nebil has seen the light!" It certainly was a moment to remember. I also marveled at the dormant volcanoes. The volcanic rocks scattered everywhere make me think of the surface of Mars. All these enjoyable things that we did in Hawaii were dampened as we faced the snow in Albany, and reality sat in.

The Birth of My Son

After I graduated in September 1975 my wife, Irene, started talking about leaving our apartment and buying a house. She preferred to live in a house, and I agreed, especially since we were planning to have a child. So we bought a medium-size house, and Irene got pregnant. On August 27, 1977, Michael was born, my only child. This was a great year: visiting Hawaii and seeing the light for the first time and having my first and only child.

A Great Honor Bestowed on Me Early On

In 1977, Jerry asked me to apply for membership of the International Astronomical Union (IAU), which he was a member of. I told him that this would be risky since I didn't believe I had secured the necessary credentials to get the membership. Jerry told me it didn't hurt to try. The problem was that the United States had about 650 members in the IAU, the largest membership in the IAU at that time. As a result, other countries like France, Germany, and Japan were complaining that the United States had too many members. Well, this disproportion was fair because the United States had over six thousand astronomers and astrophysicists, whereas the other countries that were complaining had below one thousand and some even way below five hundred.

I have to mention here that many countries had fewer than ten astronomers, and therefore they all become members of the IAU by default! If I'd asked to be a member from Iraq, I would have been a member instantly with no questions asked. However, to be a member of the IAU from the United States meant tough scrutiny since only about six hundred astronomers and astrophysicists made it out of about six thousand at that time. A couple of months passed by, and then I got a letter from the IAU congratulating me for becoming a member of Commission 21 of the IAU. This was based on a nomination letter they'd received from the US committee that nominates IAU members. The letter said that I had done enough high-class research and was expected to do more in the future to deserve the nomination. I was jubilant to say the least, and it was definitely an up ↑ thrill-of-research moment. I still consider this membership to be a great honor and a high point in my career. Later on, I was also asked to join Commission 22, "Comets, Asteroids and Meteors," which also made me proud.

While I was doing my PhD thesis, I read a PhD thesis written by Dr. Stephen Paddack, who was a senior engineering manager at NASA's Goddard Spaceflight Center (GSFC) in Maryland. His thesis was interesting because he did a study on the rotation of small bodies in space due to solar-radiation pressure. He called this phenomenon the *windmill effect*. His methodology was unique because he selected some rocks with irregular surface-shape features (ordinary rocks have that feature) and dropped them in a swimming pool. He then dove below them with his scuba-diving gear and measured their rotation as they went down to the bottom of the pool. This to me was an intriguing analogy of rocks or dust particles in space being bombarded by photons from the sun. In his analogy he replaced the photon field with molecules of water. The rotation was caused by the uneven transfer of the momentum to the rock (or from the analogy a dust particle in space) due to surface shape irregularities.

I immediately thought after reading this that dust particles in space could spin like a windmill and there was nothing to slow down (dampen) this spin due to the hard vacuum in space. The dust particles would also accelerate until the particles burst due to the tension from the spin. In other words the centrifugal force from this spin would overcome the internal cohesion of the particle (tensile strength), and therefore the particle would break apart or burst. I wrote my ideas about this in my PhD thesis and derived an equation to predict how high the spin needed to be to cause any particle to break apart. The equation that calculates the bursting spin rate for a spherical particle is:

$$\omega_b \fallingdotseq \frac{1.22}{2\pi s}\sqrt{\frac{T}{\delta}} \tag{1}$$

Where ω_b is the bursting rotation rate in rotations per second, s is the radius of the particle in cm, δ is the specific density of the particle in g/cm^3, and T is the tensile strength of the particle in dynes/cm^2, i.e. the internal cohesion of the particle.

The spin rate is staggering, around 10^6 to 10^7 rotations per second. There are many consequences to this phenomenon that I cannot get into in this book but that are detailed in several of my published papers.

Working Together with My Teacher

I heard that my teacher of modern physics, Dr. Keith Ratcliff, needed to do some research for his promotion to associate professor. He contacted me, and we had a meeting about doing research together. I told him about my ideas to study the spin of particles in space, and he was also intrigued by it. We needed to study this spin in a laboratory experiment where we could simulate the conditions in space. Keith told me that Bell Labs physicist Dr. Arthur Ashkin succeeded in levitating silica particles using a laser beam inside a vacuum chamber. To me that meant by using this technique we could simulate the conditions of space and replace solar light with laser light. The laser light would neutralize the gravity, and the particle would float slightly above the focal point of the laser beam, as if it was floating in space ... perfect. Keith and I wrote a proposal together as co–principal investigators and submitted the proposal to a funding program at NASA's GSFC. In the meantime I was in touch with Stephen Paddack about doing this research, which he was supportive of and interested in. We were awarded $45,000 to do a laser levitation experiment at GSFC at the optical site. The GSFC people also assigned a scientist and a graduate student to work with us to build the laboratory experiment.

The Concept of Laser-Particle Levitation

We placed a highly pure silica spherical particle of typically twenty micrometers (20×10^{-6} meters) in size on a glass plate inside a cubic glass chamber. We then vibrated the glass plate where the particle was sitting via a piezoelectric crystal, which would break the Van Der Waals forces (electrostatic forces) that was keeping the particle stuck to the glass plate. The laser beam was focused using a lens, which had a focal length of about four to five centimeters. The particle would jump and get caught in the laser beam above the focus of the beam (magic, yes).

The radiation incident upon the particle served the dual purpose of both levitating the particle by providing photon pressure to balance the weight of the particle and providing the radiation that accelerated the particle's rotation. The momentum transfer balanced the weight of the particle, hence levitation. It also provided confinement of the particle in the transverse direction. Arthur Ashkin at Bell Laboratories at New Jersey developed this methodology in 1971. The explanation of confining the particle inside the laser beam is provided in figure 1 (a and b) below:

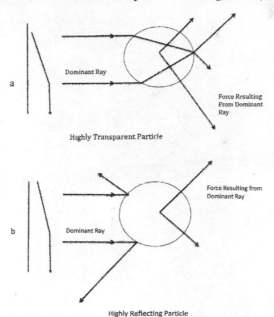

Figure 1. Momentum transfer and the resulting transverse confinement of a transparent sphere in a Gaussian beam (a) and an opaque particle (b).

To understand this confinement mechanism, note that in figure 1a the transparent particle is in a Gaussian-shaped beam, where the higher laser intensity gives rise to the dominant ray that forces the particle to stay in the middle of the Gaussian beam. For an opaque particle the force from the dominant ray is directed away from the middle of the laser beam.

Visiting the Bell Laboratories at New Jersey

We needed to duplicate Ashkin's experiment at Bell Labs first and then modify it so it could do the research that would prove that particles in space can break apart because of this phenomenon. We visited Ashkin at Bell Labs and witnessed a spherical pure silica 20 μm particle levitated by a laser beam. We were fascinated. For almost half a year Keith and I were flying to GSFC almost every week to conduct the experiment. We succeeded in levitating particles, and the director of GSFC at the time was invited to see it. This was definitely an up ↑ thrill-of-research moment or even moments.

Photo of a levitated particle at my laboratory, on a
Florida Tech student catalog, front cover.

The Challenge

The biggest challenge we had in this experiment was to levitate an *irregularly shaped* particle of pure silica. We were levitating spherical particles, but those don't resemble real interplanetary particles, which are irregularly shaped. So far we had succeeded in levitating pure spherical silica particles inside an air- or nitrogen-filled chamber. The particles usually rotated at a modest rate. However, that was due to the uneven heating of the particle by the laser beam and not due to the windmill effect. So the challenge remained to levitate irregularly shaped particles inside the chamber in a hard vacuum. This was the only way to simulate particles in space subjected to the rays of the sun.

I thought the first step toward that goal was to split the laser beam into ultimately four beams, thus creating an optical bottle to contain the particle. I also thought that it was best to photograph these particles while they were levitated and rotating. I started using my 8 mm Kodak film camera and started making movies of the levitated particles and their motions, which were fascinating to say the least.

Incidentally, I showed these movies to Arthur Ashkin (who pioneered this technique) from Bell Labs during his visit to us at SAL a couple of years later. Arthur was fascinated by these movies and said he wished he had photographed his levitation in the form of movies. In any case, I asked the technicians at Goddard to split the beam into three beams because that is easier than four beams to start with, and they did. I spent the next visit to Goddard trying to levitate an irregularly shaped particle, and out of hundreds of tries I succeeded in levitating one particle and took a movie of it. This obviously was a down ↓ thrill-of-research moment.

From the above results, I realized that we were up against a tough challenge. However, research in general always confronts you with situations like that; it is never easy. We had not yet tried levitating a particle in a hard vacuum chamber, which posed one more difficulty: the particle tended to oscillate on top of the focal point of the laser beam and then leave the laser beam at around one Torr pressure. The reason for these oscillations was that at one Torr pressure, the mean free path of the air molecules approached the size of the levitated particle. This caused the air molecules to collide with the levitated particle, causing these oscillations. Once the pressure went below one Torr, these oscillations would stop, because the mean free path of the molecules became larger than the size of the particle. The methodology to remedy this was to manipulate the power of the laser beam to neutralize these oscillations of the particle and eventually stabilize it. This methodology is called *servo system* or *feedback system*.

Chapter 9

Miscellaneous Research Ideas

Research on Soft Money with No Final Results

Keith and I realized that we need a long-term research grant if we were to get results from this research. The funding we got from GSFC was under the GSFC Director's Fund for one year to fund high-risk research. High-risk research implies, as you may have guessed, no guarantee of the desired or any other results but the potential of a big payoff. In any case even though we did not get results, we learned a lot on how to do this research, and we succeeded in creating a lot of publicity about it. We wrote a final report and submitted a research paper to the International Astronomical Union (IAU) Commission 21 meeting "The Light of the Night Sky" at Montreal, Canada, in 1978. To our dismay the experiment apparatus had to be dismantled and some parts of it mothballed. I asked my colleagues how we could do research with no final results, and they said for $40,000 we learned a lot on how to do this research for a relatively cheap price. They also said we should seek other funding agencies to continue this research.

The Importance of Research into the Spin of Particles

Our universe is made up mostly of gas and dust. As dust particles coalesce, they make boulders, which are the basic building blocks for forming planets. This process is known as accretion. Mayo Greenberg, who is an expert on interstellar dust, told us in one of his classes that the process of accretion does not account by itself for the number density seen in the interstellar medium. There have to be other mechanisms to account for the observed totality of the abundance of interstellar dust. This fact attracted my attention and suggested to me that perhaps this spin mechanism breaks up the dust into smaller fragments. These fragments would break up again by their spin and eventually become so small that the sun or any other star could not hold them by gravity. The fragments then would be blown out into the interstellar medium by the star's radiation pressure. The spin-and-breakup mechanism could contribute to this deficiency in finding mechanisms to form the interstellar dust.

I explained why my research on the spin of interplanetary dust particles is important during a meeting with Professor Martin Harwit, Professor Mayo Greenberg, and Dr. Jerry Weinberg. We chatted about the old times of my schooling and my PhD thesis defense, and it was a pleasant evening. I gave Martin and Mayo a brief synopsis of my research plans, specifically the spin problem that I was investigating. They listened with interest to what I had to say, specifically to my idea that a high spin rate, approximately 10^6 to 10^7 rotations per second, would cause these particles to break up into smaller pieces.

To me this explained why there was a difference in the size of dust particles in the interplanetary medium over the dust particles in the interstellar medium (beyond the solar system). The size distribution in the interstellar medium is considerably smaller than the size distribution in the interplanetary medium. Furthermore, since all stars (including the sun) have dust shells around them, then starlight will spin these particles to the degree of breakup. The particles therefore reduce in size until they are blown out from the vicinity of stars by the stars' radiation pressure and become interstellar dust. Interplanetary dust is larger than interstellar dust because it has been relatively recently released from comets. Also the grinding from collisions of asteroids generates dust particles, and these particles have not had the chance to become small enough to leave the solar system. More on that below.

The So-Called Beta (β) Meteoroids

To continue this explanation of my ideas, I need to explain the interesting phenomenon of the β *ratio*. This ratio is between two forces: the radiation pressure force from the star divided by the gravitation force of the star. If the β ratio is greater than one (>1), then these particles would leave the star and populate the interstellar medium. These particles are called (β) meteoroids.

Proof from Space

Earth–orbiting satellites have observed dust particles moving in a perpendicular direction to the satellites' sensors, which means the particles are leaving the solar system and heading into the interstellar medium. I had an up ↑ thrill-of-research moment when I read about observing and confirming the existence of the beta meteoroids. This gave me an added assurance of my postulate. However, all this was the theoretical part of this whole problem. The more difficult part was how to prove this mechanism experimentally. This challenge would continue to haunt me throughout my career, as you will see in the remaining pages of this book.

The Lifetime of a Dust Particle Orbiting the Sun

How long do these dust particles last orbiting the sun? Is there enough time for the spin to accelerate to the degree of breakup and then for the fragments to spin and break up too? Well, as far back as 1905, Poynting, an astrophysicist, theorized that photons emanating from the sun would shrink the size of the dust particle's orbit ever so slightly. Due to this drag Poynting suggested that dust particles couldn't orbit the sun as long as the sun existed (about another five billion years). This drag is now called the Poynting–Robertson drag, since Robertson added the effect of Einstein's theory of relativity on this mechanism in 1937.

To understand this drag in simple terms, let me use this analogy: Assume that you are driving your car and heavy rain is coming down vertically to the ground. You will see the raindrops hitting your windshield at a vertical angle. Dust particles orbiting the sun will absorb the photons at a radial direction, but when they emit the photons, they emit them at a slightly different angle. This will cause a loss in angular momentum of the dust particle, and the photons will shrink the orbit of the dust particle slightly. After one million years or more (depending on the size of the particle), the particles' orbits will shrink so much that they will reach the vicinity of the sun. Because of the sun's gravity, they will then sink into the sun. Considering this very long lifetime, there is ample time for this spin mechanism to work on these particles to break them up.

Doing Research with No Funding

Doing research on soft money doesn't mean that you are limited in doing only the research you have funding for. Since my whole salary was covered via the research grant that Jerry was administrating, I could still do extra research on my own time with Jerry's knowledge. Also I could still do research without funding and then write a proposal asking for funding. Writing a proposal for research you've already done was somewhat common in those days. If I had gaps in my salary payment, I still continued to do research for the hope that I would be funded for it later. These are some of the tricks of this trade! It was interesting to write a proposal on research I'd already done and knew the results of, while telling the funding agency that I was seeking funds for doing this research. This easily can happen in theoretical research, where you have developed the equations, but it is not likely to do with experimental work. How about that? I don't think I did that at all. Well, maybe partially, I don't remember. I know others who have done it, though.

On the subject of dust in the interstellar medium, I met a Swedish graduate student who was a doctoral student of Mayo Greenberg. His name was Bo Gustafson, and he was sent to SAL to do his doctoral thesis. Bo and I had numerous discussions on dust in the interplanetary and interstellar mediums. I suggested to Bo that we do model calculations to find out how much interstellar medium dust is being swept into the solar system. As our solar system rotates around the center of our Milky Way galaxy, it attracts interstellar dust in the galaxy, simply by its gravitational pull. These dust particles enter the solar system and take an orbit around the sun.

We did this research in SAL using a new computer built by Digital that was as big as a cabinet, so we no longer relied on the UNIVAC 1110 at SUNY. We got exciting results from this research, and we rushed a research paper to the prestigious British journal *Nature*, known for publishing important scientific discoveries relatively quickly.

Professor Donald Brownlee's Appraisal of This Paper

Many years later Professor Donald Brownlee, NASA's principal scientist of the Stardust mission, read this paper. The Stardust mission approached and collected dust from comet Wild 2 and then ejected a capsule containing the dust collected from the comet into the Great Salt Lake Desert in Utah two years later. The capsule was recovered successfully by a US helicopter.

Professor Brownlee wrote a letter (see a copy of this letter in appendix A) in support of my tenure application at the University of Central Florida (UCF). He said, "One of Dr. Misconi's most significant publications was his 1979 Nature paper on streaming of interstellar grains into the solar system. The paper predicted that interstellar dust should stream into the solar system from the direction of, the then detectable, interstellar gas and it also described the interaction of the extra-solar particles with the solar wind and the interplanetary magnetic field. The paper was timely and highly prophetic as the stream of interstellar dust was detected just a few years later by instruments on the Ulysses and Galileo spacecraft."

Seed Money for Research

Researchers can also acquire seed money or hard money to pay for time spent in writing proposals. Universities supply that kind of money to researchers on soft money in most cases, depending on the researcher's reputation of success in acquiring funds. In other cases universities give seed money to younger researchers to help them get started. For example, during my tenure at the University of Central Florida (UCF) in later years, I was a member of the research committee to distribute seed money to young faculty and established faculty, not on soft money, for a modest amount of $7,500 each.

Research Seed Money from the
Gators Football Team!

I was at the University of Florida (UF) in Gainesville, Florida, in later years because SAL moved from SUNY to UF. SAL had established such a good reputation in acquiring research funds that the administration of UF was impressed and decided to give us seed money for writing proposals. These funds, we were told, came from profits from UF's football team, the Gators. So I became an ardent Gators fan! This was a remarkable case of strange bedfellows. If I remember correctly, this seed money sometimes was about $250,000 for SAL. So I say, *"Go Gators!"* However, since I joined UCF later on, I am now torn between UCF's Knights and the Gators. At this time of writing this book, the Knights have won the Fiesta Bowl, and the Gators have had their worst season.

Chapter 10

The gravitational Effect of the Planets on the Dust

Another area of research that I got extensively interested in was the gravitational effect of the planets and how they can attract dust particles. The dust particles are mainly populated around a *symmetry plane* that seems to dissect the dust–cloud cone into two symmetric halves. The prevailing belief was that the symmetry plane coincided with the *invariable plane of the solar system*. I started my research in this area. The invariable plane is a calculated plane that takes into consideration the total masses of the planets and the sun and the inclinations of their orbits around the sun. The invariable plane of the solar system is a theoretically calculated average plane, which is dominated by the orbital plane of the planet Jupiter, due to Jupiter's huge mass. So basically at that time the prevailing thinking was that Jupiter was the most effective gravitational influence on the orbits of the dust particles around the sun.

Using Jerry's data taken from Haleakalā of the zodiacal light, I started making models of the dust cloud and compared them to the observations. The results confirmed my earlier suspicions that this could not be true. Since Venus, with a mass close to that of Earth, was close to the inner part (inside the Earth's orbit) of the interplanetary dust complex, I thought it should gravitationally affect the dust. After making theoretical models and comparing them to the observations, I concluded that the symmetry plane of the zodiacal cloud is close to the orbital plane of Venus. Professor Seung Soo Hong, a prominent theoretician, a former classmate at SUNY, and a former chair of the department of astronomy at the National Seoul University in South Korea, mentioned my discovery about Venus (see letter in appendix A).

I quickly rushed a research paper to the US journal *Science*, which publishes the latest discoveries with a rapid review process. To my big surprise, after the paper was published, many people requested a reprint. There was nothing strange about that until I looked at who was requesting the reprints. I didn't recognize any of them as known scientists or astronomers. I asked Jerry why these people were requesting the reprints, and he said they were people collecting anything published with a title that has Venus in it. So they were collectors. Some did the same thing for Mars and Jupiter and other things. This was something that I didn't know anything about. It was surprising and pretty flattering to me.

One Research Result Led Me to Others

The result that I found for the gravitational effect of Venus led me to believe that perhaps there was no single symmetry plane for the zodiacal cloud. This conclusion was simply based on the fact that if Venus could pull the dust to its orbital plane, then certainly Jupiter could as well, more effectively too, due to its huge mass. This led me to believe that we have at least two symmetry planes. Since I knew that there was definitely a symmetry plane associated with Jupiter, then the next thing to look for was whether Mars affected the dust also. This was a long shot since Mars has approximately one-eighth of the mass of the Earth.

To solve this problem I looked for data that Jerry took from Skylab before the small telescope was ejected into space. To my surprise the data showed that Mars was affecting the dust also and that the symmetry plane of the dust cloud was skewed to the orbit of Mars.

The International Astronomical Union (IAU) Meeting at Montreal, Canada

I first presented my results on the skew of the symmetry plane of the dust cloud to the IAU meeting at Montreal, Canada, for Commission 21, known as "Light of the Night Sky." The name of Commission 21 was recently changed to "Extragalactic Light," meaning the faint light between galaxies, which is reflected by interstellar dust. This was the first time I had left the United States since I'd come in 1970, and I had an uneasy feeling about leaving, even for a few days. I felt so secure being in the United States because of its political stability and the freedoms we had. It was the kind of feeling that you couldn't invent; it just came upon you.

SAL rented a limousine to take us from Albany to Montreal since it was so close. Among the passengers were Mayo Greenberg, Jerry, and others. Mayo kept questioning me about his teaching of quantum mechanics as part of his astrophysics course. I told Mayo he understand quantum mechanics well but didn't come prepared for the class. This was a typical syndrome of hard-core researchers like Mayo. Mayo thanked me for my candidness and thought my opinion was fair.

After I presented my results in Montreal, Anny Chantal Levasseur-Regourd, a French astronomer, suggested that perhaps I shouldn't call the plane a *symmetry plane* but rather call it a *symmetry surface*. I immediately agreed with her. Following Anny Chantal's suggestion, I started referring to the symmetry plane as symmetry surface whenever I could. Sometimes I also said in my papers that there was a multiplicity of symmetry planes. Using the word *surface* was better because it could show changes in the inclinations of the symmetry.

A few years later, I published another paper in the prestigious American journal *Icarus*, named after the asteroid Icarus. In this paper I did model calculations and compared them to observations on the position of the optical center of the *Gegenschein*, which is a German word meaning "counterglow." This was a brightness enhancement in the zodiacal light directly opposite to the sun; in other words, this sunlight scattering was like a mirror, except the mirror was made of loose dust particles. I also concluded that Jupiter gravitationally affected the dust that was opposite to the sun. I had a good relationship with the editor of *Icarus*, Professor Joseph Burns at Cornell University, a brilliant scientist of orbital mechanics and other fields of astronomy and astrophysics. I asked him several times to move to Florida, especially since his wife did not like the cold weather. He said he would think about it, but he never did, although the University of Florida would have loved to have him.

May Arif Kaftan-Kassim attended the IAU meeting at Montreal, and by then she had moved back to Iraq after accepting an astronomy directorship position. She brought with her to the conference about four or five young Iraqi astronomers who had graduated with PhDs from Manchester, England, under the advisement of Indian radio astronomer Kopal. May wanted me to meet them, and so I chatted with them. I also met an Egyptian astronomer who was also working in zodiacal light research, Assad. Assad made observations of the zodiacal light from a mountain in Aswan, Egypt. He told me that he was following my research closely and was impressed with my results. I thanked him for his compliments and wished him well in his research.

Major Discovery from Pioneer 10 and 11 Space Probes

One of the most important results that Jerry and SAL found from the *Pioneer 10* and *11* space probes concerned the origin of the Gegenschein. The result was that the Gegenschein did not arise from dust accumulated *gravitationally* behind the Earth (i.e., Earth's tail), which had been theorized before in several published research papers. The new discovery was that the Gegenschein arose from normal distribution of the dust beyond the Earth and all the way to the asteroid belt, i.e. the cumulative column density. So no more major effect of dust tail from the Earth. This certainly was one big up ↑ thrill-of-research moment for Jerry and others at SAL.

The Ottawa Dust Symposium

After the meeting in Montreal we all traveled to Ottawa, Canada, for a dust symposium of IAU, Commission 21. I need to mention here that I used to joke with my colleagues that we are dusty people and should shake away the dust from our clothes before presenting a research paper so it would be clean! A few people know that interplanetary dust is inside our bodies and that all the inner planets (Mercury, Venus, Earth, and Mars) were made from dust. The outer planets are made of mostly gas, with the exception of some of their moons.

At the Ottawa meeting, Keith Ratcliff and I presented a paper on our experiment with laser levitation that we did at Goddard Space Flight Center. Our colleagues received the paper with some skepticism because they questioned whether the dust particles had enough irregularities on the surface to spin as a windmill so fast as to break apart. I argued with them that the irregularities were so tiny; it was found experimentally by Paddack (1970) to be one part in ten thousand of the size of the particle, i.e., a few angstroms. Nevertheless, they were not convinced, something that is common among scientists.

My further argument about this mechanism was that I believed the dust particles spun like a gyroscope, free from gravity, and therefore the spin would accelerate continuously with nothing to dampen it in the hard vacuum of space. However, the critics of this mechanism pointed out one other problem: how to keep the particle facing the sun in one position continuously. My response to this criticism was to do some more calculations using gyroscope dynamics. I soon found out that the force needed to change the direction of the particle from the sun was minuscule. This did not satisfy me until I did more calculations assuming that the particle did rotate its faces around the sun. I found out that the lifetime of the dust particle orbiting the sun was long enough (million and more years) to get it to break up from the tension of the fast spin. I did not publish these calculations but mentioned the results in my papers on the subject. My main reason for that was because we had not shown experimentally that the particles spin fast in the laboratory.

Moving SAL from Albany, New York, to Gainesville, Florida

In early 1979 Jerry started talking about moving SAL from Albany to either North Carolina or Florida because the taxes in New York were getting high and moving south would put us closer to "NASA's corridor," as he put it. Jerry meant that Florida is where Kennedy Space Center (KSC) is, and North Carolina is close to Washington, DC. We had several meetings with Jerry about this issue, and there was unanimity on this decision except for our chief engineer, Dick Hahn. Jerry made two trips, one to the University of North Carolina at Chapel Hill and the other to the University of Florida at Gainesville. He negotiated with both universities but realized that the University of North Carolina was not equipped with the proper purchasing department for instrumentations that SAL needed. Jerry argued that we were going to build instruments to fly in space and needed an efficient and rapid purchasing department to meet NASA's deadlines. He was absolutely right in that respect; UF had a huge purchasing department and had a big building that housed at least fifty or more employees. Jerry also maintained that Florida did not have income tax, only federal tax, so that would be a major savings for us. Believe me: when you work on soft money, that's a major plus. In any case, after consulting with all the members of SAL, he decided to move to UF at Gainesville.

My wife, Irene, was so disappointed with this decision because she hated the humidity in Florida and also because her family lived in

Greensboro, North Carolina. Her family was disappointed with the decision also because obviously we would have lived just a few miles from them. I have to admit that I was delighted with this decision simply because I hated snow. I loved the snow for two to three weeks but no more; beyond that it became a pain! Moreover, I was born and lived for many years in a hot climate.

We put our house in Albany up for sale, and it sold earlier than we expected, by September 1979. Jerry told me that SAL would move by the end of the year, so he said I could help establish SAL in Gainesville. I bought a house in Gainesville and moved by the end of September.

In the remaining months of 1979, I was in touch with Jerry by phone almost every day. UF did not have enough space on campus for us, so they asked Jerry to rent a place near the campus. Jerry and I looked at several places and then decided on one. My research at this point was halted since I was doing administrative work. I had several meetings with officials of the university to process our move, and I met several times with the department of astronomy chair and astronomy professors, since we were going to be affiliated with them. For the first time in my life I had a taste of what administrative work was like. I did not enjoy this kind of work, but I had to do it. I missed doing research because it put me in a completely different world. Sometimes I almost forget what was surrounding me.

SAL had a relatively big budget that paid salaries for a secretary, an accountant, computer programmers, and two engineers at that time. This whole operation was on soft money, believe it or not! The funds came from research grants from NASA and the US Air Force. The reader might wonder about the connection between interplanetary-dust research and the US Air Force. The Air Force Office of Scientific Research (AFOSR) was interested in the effects dust particles (orbiting the Earth) had on military communications. Also AFOSR was concerned about the threat they posed to hitting military satellites and disabling them, since the dust acts like orbital debris. The difference between the two is their orbital velocity, which is approximately twenty kilometers a second for the dust compared to orbital debris velocity of approximately eight kilometers a second. The air force routinely monitored orbital debris of one centimeter in size and bigger using infrared telescopes on Earth. However, they could not monitor particles smaller than one centimeter at that time.

So basically the budget of SAL was over $1 million for personnel only, not including the costs of acquiring instruments, hardware, computers, and so on. At that time SAL had four PhD astronomers, including Jerry. This kind of budget was lucrative for universities to have, since they charged overhead at 30 percent and others up to 50 percent. In appendix B, please see an example of one of the budgets I made for a proposal. Universities also liked this kind of operation since there were a lot of research papers published in the name of the university, enhancing their national ratings. To maintain this operation, Jerry used to remind us to write proposals and get our own grants in order to ease the pressure on him to financially support the whole operation.

Enjoying the Freedom of Working on Soft Money

This topic is enjoyable for me to write about, and that is the feeling of freedom. Suffice it to say that you are your own boss when you work on soft money. You decide what research you want to do and what funding agency you want to write your proposal to. You also have the freedom to choose whoever you want to work with and can decide which journals you want to publish your papers in. Jerry used to discuss salaries and raises with us and decide on them, which was no problem at all. Here is why: if you are going to lobby for a higher salary, then you have to make sure that you can bring in the money to cover the raise. Besides, my salary was not important to me as long as it was sufficient to comfortably cover my and my family's expenses. For example, I was never involved in the family budget; I left it to Irene, which made her complain sometimes. All I wanted to know was what the bottom line on the balance of the budget was!

Fortunately, and unfortunately, when you are a researcher, you lose any passion to make money. You feel more like a dedicated scholar, and you are more concerned about your scientific reputation. Money becomes the vehicle to sustain living comfortably and not much else. This is not to say that making money is not attractive anymore; you will just be busier with research and survival, so you won't have time to think about it. Let's face it: you are not going to be a millionaire doing academic research! There are exceptions, of course, like anything else in life.

Many specific things contributed to how wonderful this freedom of working on soft money was. For example, SAL provided me with an office space and a supporting research cast, i.e., computer programmers, engineers, and a supporting director who gave me advice from his own experiences but did not interfere in my research plans. Occasionally, some delightful parties took place during Thanksgiving and Christmas holidays and other occasions. I call those fringe benefits! In addition, every time I was awarded a research grant, I had this great feeling that I was partially paying for the expenses of the supporting cast. Of course, with this great freedom came responsibility. The most important one was the responsibility to support my family financially. This of course was one of many other responsibilities to my family. Acquiring research grants eased the responsibility I felt toward supporting my workplace and helped to keep the organization going. However, all of these responsibilities did not outweigh the great feeling of freedom I felt.

Developing Phone and Mail Phobias

The most up ↑ and down ↓ feelings came when I got a phone call from the granting scientist at a funding agency. He would either tell me that my proposal had been accepted or denied. This is a yes or no situation if you are a gambler for each proposal. This made me develop a phone phobia. After a few months of submitting a proposal, every time the phone rang, I thought maybe it was the funding agency. The worst thing was in those days we didn't have cell phones, so if I was out of my office for one reason or another and missed the call, I got a message on my answering machine. If it was a rejection message, I don't have the chance to argue with the scientist about why I wasn't funded. It would take several phone calls to talk to the scientist, sometimes resulting in playing phone tag for days!

A few months after submitting a proposal, I also began to develop a fear of the mail that came every day. In many cases the director scientist may not call but instead send a letter. In most cases if a letter comes, it's a denial of funding. An organization would only send an acceptance letter if they had too many proposers being funded to call. When I had submitted more than one proposal, then the mail phobia became stronger. I always used to say to my associates that no news was good news and at least we hadn't gotten a denial letter yet. In this kind of business I didn't feel apprehensive for myself alone but also for my associates who were to be funded. I asked some researchers on soft money whether or not they had the same feelings, and most of them said yes.

In this case there would be many up ↑ and down ↓ thrill-of-research moments. The high of getting a proposal funded could last me at least a week or more. The downward feeling with denial of funding could last just as long, especially when I thought about all the time I spent in coming up with the research ideas, structuring them, writing the proposal, revising many times, and getting it ready for submission. However, after the initial disappointment of the denial of funding, I'd start to feel that I had accomplished something even though it wasn't successful. This, believe it or not, would give me an up ↑ thrill-of-research moment.

The Process of Evaluating a Proposal

The first step you take in submitting a proposal is to look for proposal solicitations from funding agencies that will fit your research ideas. Once you find the announcement that fits your research field, you start writing the proposal within the time frame given by the funding agency. The next step is to get all the signatures from the university to submit your proposal, which involves having the university accounting department approve your budget. For me, sending the number of copies required by the funding agency was always a problem. For one reason or another, I was never on time, and I always ended up having to FedEx them to get them there by the agency's deadline. In later years of my research I opened up an account with FedEx, believe it or not!

Once the proposal is received by the director of the program (who is always a scientist in the particular field of research), he or she starts a reviewer's selection process. Usually, the director selects about five reviewers from the field of the proposed research. The director has to avoid selecting reviewers that are known to be friends or close associates of the proposing scientists for fairness. The reviewers usually take their sweet time reading the proposals, in many cases months, because they are busy with their own research. Sometimes I had to call the director of the program many times to remind him to push the reviewers to read my proposal and evaluate it.

Usually, the reviewers (I was a reviewer many times) write a few paragraphs about their feelings on the proposed research on a form provided by the funding agency. At the bottom of that form there are grades to be checked. The grades are similar to the one students are rated with, i.e., from excellent, very good, good, fair, and finally poor. The proposals that are funded usually have two grades of excellent, two very good, and one good grade, or better than that or slightly lower.

The director of the program does not adhere to the grades very closely; sometimes he uses his own judgment. In some cases, you can get excellent and very good grades, and then one reviewer gives you a poor grade. The director of the program has the right to ignore the poor grade. Sometimes the reviewers may suggest improvements to the proposed research and ask you to resubmit the proposal. In the case of funding or denying funding of the proposal, the director of the program sends copies of the reviews to the proposing scientist. The proposer also has a chance to write rebuttals to the reviewers' summaries in the case of a no-funding decision. The rebuttal seldom reverses the decision, though, sort of like football. In football when a play is under further review by officials, sometimes they reverse the call on the field, but other times they don't. However, in football I think the chance for reversal is much higher.

Being the director of the funding program is usually an unattractive position that some scientists agree to do only grudgingly. In my later years of research I was offered a job like that at the National Science Foundation (NSF), which is a highly prestigious organization, but I declined it, even though it was on hard money! It's an unattractive job because you end up disappointing your colleagues by declining funding for their proposals, although you reward others. However, the nature of this job is that normally you get about two hundred proposals and you end up funding approximately ten to twenty. So there are a lot of rejection letters and phone calls to be made, and that is really difficult.

Some programs may have more money, and they could possibly fund half or one-third of the proposals that are submitted, but that's the exception, not the rule. As director you have to reject a lot of very good proposals. These proposals are for basic research, and therefore their budgets are low, of the order of $100,000 to $200,000. For these kinds of proposals NASA allocates a budget of roughly $2 million to $5 million. There's clearly much competition to get funded under those programs. Also when you accept a job like that, you really forget about your research; you have no time for it.

Proposals that ask for $5 million, $10 million, or $20 million are usually proposals for an instrument to be flown on a space mission, a big land-based laboratory instrumentation, and so on. SAL had one of these, which was the small telescope that was flown on NASA's Skylab mission. Usually, such a big grant on soft money will result in the hiring of a lot of scientists, engineers, and other supporting cast. This hiring results in exposing more and more people to the idea of working on soft money. I may be wrong on this, but I heard about ten years ago that Georgia Tech had about 750 scientists, engineers, and others working on soft money! This is a huge number. If it was true, then it was really something.

Our relationship with the astronomy department at UF was quite different from the one with SUNY in Albany. Jerry negotiated a tighter relationship with the department. I started this effort when I was working to help us make the transition. I met several times with the late Professor Heinz Eichhorn, the chair of the department, who told me that the research efforts of the department were somewhat subpar. He was hoping that our move would create collaborations and research between our staff and some of the professors in his department. This made some of the professors dislike our move. They thought that there would be friction and competition between the two organizations. I tried to smooth the relationships as much as I could, and the chair appreciated my efforts.

The tighter relationship encouraged us to attend colloquiums at the department and even give some of them. I had two colloquiums at the department on my research. We were welcomed to attend all their departmental meetings but seldom did so.

My First NSF Grant

After a year of settling in at Gainesville and SAL, I began to think about breaking out and having my own grants. By 1980 I had gotten one NASA grant, and I had been working on Jerry's NASA grant, which was renewed every year for five years based on the science that I was doing. Now I wanted to have my own grants independent of anybody else. This was how I could swim on my own on soft money. *Yeah!*

Getting an NSF grant is considered a milestone in one's research career and is prestigious. So I started writing a three-year proposal to the NSF titled "Can Cometary Dust Perturbed by the Inner Planets Explain the Observed Distribution of Interplanetary Dust?" I asked Bo Gustafson, the Swedish graduate student mentioned earlier, to be a coinvestigator on it. Bo was happy to join me, and after a few months I heard that I got funded as principal investigator. This event by far was a great up↑ thrill-of-research moment that called for a big celebration at SAL. So most of us got high on booze, and we all had a good time.

Flying a Telescope on the Space Shuttle Columbia

Well, Jerry struck again with the shuttle program. He proposed to NASA to fly a small telescope to study the optical environment of the bay of the shuttle and named it the *Shuttle-Induced Atmosphere experiment*. The goal was to study whether or not investigators could observe very low-light astronomical objects with their optical instruments in the bay of the shuttle. In other words, would the shuttle-induced light contaminate these astronomical observations, or would the sky be dark enough for astronomical observations? Jerry told me that this would be a fantastic opportunity for me to study the inner zodiacal light from the space shuttle, far away from the Earth's atmosphere. Space shuttle *Colombia* was scheduled to fly on March 22, 1982. Jerry had a year and a half to build the small telescope and get it ready for flight, and it was a tight schedule. I participated with our former chief engineer Dick Hahn in the calibration of the instrument. Dick left us because he did not like Florida's weather and so did not want to move with us. Dick traveled to Gainesville a number of times to work on the instrument and kept complaining about the humidity in Florida.

The telescope was designed to scan the sky back and forth from the bay of the shuttle. The instrument was programmed to stop when it reached the astronauts' cabin and stop again when it reached the tail of the shuttle. In NASA jargon, we wanted to know if the bird was dirty or clean optically. The space shuttle did a lot of maneuvers, including the *barbecue maneuver,* to keep the heating from the sun even on the space shuttle. Thrusters fired all the time, almost every minute or less, to keep the desired attitude. These maneuvers meant our telescope would get all kinds of look angles. If the instrument looked at the sun, then it would automatically shut down to keep the optics from being overwhelmed, and then it would turn back on when it was farther away from the sun. This opportunity excited me because I would have the chance to observe the part of the zodiacal light that was closer to the sun, which was impossible to do from the ground due to twilight.

Months passed by, and finally Colombia launched. Soon we started getting data. A couple of months later NASA sent us the x-, y-, and z-coordinates of the shuttle at all times in flight. They also sent us a computer program that changed these coordinates into ecliptic coordinates (coordinates that are based on the ecliptic plane between the sun and the Earth). I started using this program to try to find out where the telescope was looking at all times during the flight, and that was not easy to do. In the end, after thorough investigation, I determined that the data was contaminated with light from the thruster firings and a glow from the paint of the shuttle's bay. Later on, other space scientists studied the glow from the paint and determined that it was a chemical reaction (outside the scope of this book) between the gases emitted by the thrusters firings and the paint.

Jerry wrote and sent a final report to NASA saying that the bay of the shuttle was not suitable for astronomical observations (the bird was dirty!) unless a long extension mechanism could be attached to the observing instrument. So this was a down ↓ thrill-of-research moment for me, since I didn't get any information on the zodiacal light close to the sun. However, I learned a lot on how to analyze data from the space shuttle, which was interesting, so in that sense I did have an up ↑ thrill–of–research moment!

Years later the shuttle *Columbia* disintegrated in the atmosphere upon reentry. With it the astronauts died, and I was very saddened. When you use a spaceship to acquire data for you, you develop a strong attachment to it. When I saw the images of it disintegrating, I had a bad sinking feeling in my gut.

International Solar Polar Mission (ISPM)

In the 1980s the European space scientists, astronomers, and astrophysicists began to think about doing joint space missions with NASA. This initiative was welcomed by NASA administrators for several reasons: politically it was attractive and would lessen the pressure for the US Congress to fund NASA, and scientific collaborations with allies was always beneficial. One of the first suggested joint missions was a solar polar mission. NASA and the European Space Agency (ESA) felt that the sun has been studied extensively from satellites in the Earth–sun plane (ecliptic plane) but had not been studied in higher latitudes, specifically the poles. So the consensus was to send a NASA spacecraft to go over the sun's north pole and an ESA spacecraft to go over the sun's south pole.

This was a golden opportunity for SAL to join this mission so that we could probe the interplanetary dust complex from above and below the Earth–sun plane,. A view that we don't have data on. Jerry led the effort for SAL. He attended several meetings at NASA and succeeded in getting SAL involved in this mission. The experiment was called the *Zodiacal Light / Background Starlight Experiment*.

I was appointed as a coinvestigator on the NASA spacecraft, with Jerry as the principal investigator. I was excited for the science I was going to do on the spacecraft and started making outlines of what I wanted to do and get from the data. I would like to mention here that the easiest way to work on soft money is to join a team that is doing a major experiment on a spacecraft. But that's not enough; you have to make sure the science being done is up your alley. Such space-mission experiments can last at least ten years funding-wise, which gives you financial stability. You still have to write proposals to cover the remainder of your salary, though, because the mission will not pay for your full salary, only part of your time.

I contributed as a co-investigator and member of the NASA team for the science definition and design of the telescope/photopolarimeter to observe the zodiacal light. Our instrument was built in the Federal Republic of Germany to fly on the NASA spacecraft of the ISPM.

Unfortunately, this instrument was not flown because the US Congress or NASA had to cancel the spacecraft for lack of funds. This decision created a storm inside NASA and ESA because it left only the European spacecraft to be built and launched by an American rocket. Most European scientists did not like the idea, though others did like it for nationalistic reasons. In SAL we were all devastated at this news. The work we'd done so far was just wasted, but that's part of the space business, which is full of ups and downs. NASA said that the American investigators should try to team up with scientists on the Europeans experiments. This event proved that these collaborations between NASA and ESA would not always make funding for NASA from Congress easier.

In Europe there were about fifteen to twenty astronomers who were dusty (so to speak), and they had their own experiment on the ESA spacecraft of the ISPM mission. This did not leave us with good arguments to establish the need for an American experiment. Among those European astronomers was Gerhard Schwehm, a young German astronomer who had visited SAL in the mid-1970s. At Jerry's request, I had accompanied Dr. Schwehm during his visit. We had discussed what we were doing in research and established a good collaboration relationship. As it turned out, a few years later, that Dr. Schwehm became the principal investigator of the ISPM Zodiacal Light/Background Starlight Experiment.

Chapter 11

Considering some Spin-Off Military Research

The Expansion of SAL

The associate dean of the college of arts and sciences at UF contacted Jerry and said that the physicist Carl Rester (now deceased) wanted to join SAL on soft money. Carl Rester had another younger physicist and a female graduate student with him. Jerry asked those of us who were senior members what we thought of this idea. Jerry also said that we needed to expand the horizons of SAL. He said these two physicists were working on building a gamma-ray detector and could give us entry into the field of gamma-ray astronomy.

Carl Rester and his group ended up joining SAL. Jerry gave Carl Rester and his group one year to get grants. If they didn't get any funding by that time, they would leave SAL. Their salaries were partially funded by the college of arts and sciences, and the rest came from SAL. Carl worked hard on getting research grants but realized that the most likely use for his gamma-ray detector was perhaps with the military. There were quite a few detectors and even a satellite dedicated for gamma-ray astronomy.

By this time we needed to enlarge, and we rented a building about couple of miles from our office building, that was originally a movie theater and we converted it to a laboratory building. The laboratory was basically a theater for studying far infrared wavelength scattering by several cm size bodies. The ratio of the size of the body to the wavelength would then scale to the same ratio of visible light wavelength (much shorter) to micrometer size particles. This is a clever way to study light scattering, but it requires a large building with high ceilings. Bo Gustafson and Ru Wang, a Taiwanese scientist, carried out this experimental research. Bo Gustafson became interested in cometary dust and made a replica of it that he called *bird's nest* because fluffy cometary particles are formed by accretion in the same manner as a bird forms its nest.

US Worry about the Soviet Union Orbiting Nuclear Weapons in Space

Carl Rester was counting on this issue, and to use it to get funding from the Defense Department. Nuclear weapons flying in orbit around the Earth would emit gamma rays, and if the United States flew gamma-ray detectors on US satellites, they would be able to detect the gamma rays and know if the Soviet Union was flying nuclear weapons in space. This got President Reagan's attention. Reagan asked the Department of Defense to take care of this issue and proposed the Strategic Defense Initiative (SDI). Carl submitted a proposal to SDI about building his gamma-ray detector for this purpose. There were other physicists and astrophysicists in the United States who were also proposing to build their own detectors to do the same thing.

Saved by the Bell

Carl Rester had two days left in his employment and hadn't gotten any decision on the funding. I remember passing by his office and seeing him packing his stuff. I felt sorry because I didn't want to see a researcher get this kind of disappointment. By noon of that day, Carl Rester got a phone call from the SDI program, telling him that the Department of Defense had awarded him $1 million to build his gamma-ray detector. Saved by the bell, yes! Celebrations ensued, and Rester stopped packing and returned his things back to where they were. We all celebrated with him, as this was an up ↑ thrill-of-research moment for Rester and his group and SAL as a whole.

Soon after this event, Rester quickly hired a couple of engineers and established his operation at the new laboratory building that had been added to SAL. Now it remained to be seen if this new group was willing to do any research in gamma-ray astronomy and not just defense matters. After all SAL was not a military operation.

Getting Involved in "Star Wars"

Reagan's SDI program was initiated in the second half of the 1980s because of the threats to American satellites in space. The media dubbed this program "Star Wars," from George Lucas's *Star Wars*. Some say that the media and opponents of Reagan's new idea used the Star Wars name to mock the program. In any case, I got interested in the whole idea and thought it was an opportunity for me to expand my research. The so-called Star Wars emanated from the fact that laser weapons were getting very strong. I heard that the pulsed infrared Nd–YAG laser and the CO_2 laser had achieved high wattage and pretty wide laser beams. This development created a real threat to satellites in space. A laser beam from a satellite in space could obliterate or melt other satellites and destroy them. This poses a huge security threat to the US. This is how Star Wars idea was born.

Laser weapons were not the only threat; there were also the idea of kinetic guns on orbiting satellites that could shoot rock-size projectiles to destroy other satellites. There were also talks about threats from powerful ground–based laser weapons. It had been shown that when lasers were focused using lenses, they could drill a hole in a thick steel wall. A little story is in order at this point. I was working on a snowy day in 1978 at the Goddard Space Flight Center in Maryland. I was using a 15–watt argon laser and focusing it for particle levitation as I explained earlier. At day's end, Keith Ratcliff and I were rushing to our cars to face the snowy streets, and we forgot to shut down the laser. In our hurry we also knocked out a prism that was diverting the focused beam away from the wall. Another worker at the optical sight noticed this a few minutes later and shut down the laser, but not before the laser had made a big hole in the wall. We were very lucky it didn't start a fire! Since that incident I have feared and respected lasers!

Protecting Satellites from Laser Weapons

It so happened that my former teacher and research colleague Keith Radcliff was visiting me in Gainesville, Florida, to discuss doing research together and writing proposals. I told him about my idea of scattering laser light and not absorbing it using a layer of small particles (microns in size). Keith got excited immediately and thought it was a good idea. He then encouraged me to write a proposal to the Department of Defense under their solicitation for proposals for the SDI's instrumentation program. This program was aimed at funding scientists to purchase instrumentations only for the purpose of doing research to protect satellites from these threats. Keith then went back to Albany. I still remember it was Thanksgiving week of 1985 when I started writing that proposal. It was the thinnest proposal I had ever written, less than ten pages. At times I laughed after I submitted this proposal, thinking there was no chance in hell it would be funded, especially with a price tag of $155,000!

A few days before Christmas of the same year, we were having a party at SAL for the holidays. Jerry asked me if I had called the Department of Defense to check on my funding, and I said, "No. You must be kidding. I don't think I'll be funded."

Jerry then said, "Well, why don't you give it a try? What the heck!"

I slowly dragged myself over to the next building and called the Department of Defense to ask if I was funded or not. The lady who answered asked who I was, and then after a few moments she came back and said I was funded and gave me the amount of the award. I jumped in the air and ran to the other building and told Jerry and others that I was funded. This event was one of the most memorable in my career and certainly an up ↑ thrill-of-research moment.

In early 1986, I attended a meeting in Washington, DC, that included all those who were funded by this program. A scientist that I didn't know approached me and said he had approved the funding of my proposal because he thought that my idea had a good chance to succeed. He also told me that after I built the laboratory setup, I should ask for multiyear research money from the Air Force Office of Scientific Research (AFOSR). I thanked him and told him I'd do my best.

A large room was partitioned inside the SAL laboratory building, which was about two miles away from our office building. I immediately started purchasing equipment: an 18-watt argon laser, a large optical isolation table (to absorb vibrations), various pieces of optical equipment, state-of-the-art computers, and special plumbing to cool the laser. I also started talking to Dr. John Oliver, associate professor in the UF astronomy department, a good experimentalist who was looking for research to do. I told him that he was welcome to join my team in my research, once I got funding from AFOSR.

The University of Florida came up with titles for strictly research scientists (i.e., dedicated to research on soft money): research scientist, associate research scientist, and assistant research scientist. When I joined the UF they gave me the title of assistant research scientist. In 1982, I applied for associate research scientist and the committee at the department of astronomy approved it.

The dean of the college of arts and sciences, Dr. Charles Sidman, succeeded in building a strong physics department, as he said he would in a speech that he gave to the university senate, which I happened to be a member of that year. He said that he traveled all over the country and placed bids on hiring prominent physicists with severe competition with other deans to bring them to UF. He also sought to bring well-known astrophysicists to the physics department. These astrophysicists formed their own place in the physics department and changed the name of the department to the

Department of Physics and Astrophysics. The dean also managed to acquire the famous French cosmologist Pierre Ramon. Among this group I met the cosmologist Professor Jim Ipser, and we became friends. I learned from him some of what's going on in cosmology, which is, in my opinion, the most difficult subject in the world.

Colloquium at the University of Alabama in Tuscaloosa

My friend and classmate Dr. Jack Sulentic asked me if I was willing to give a colloquium at the physics department of the University of Alabama at Tuscaloosa. He then was a professor at the department. I was happy to do that and took my family with me. We went on a Friday and stayed the weekend with Jack and his wife, Connie. My colloquium, "Interplanetary Dust Dynamics," was received well, and I fielded many questions from curious physicists. At that time I was not into American football as I am now, so I didn't know about the Crimson Tide at the University of Alabama.

Teaching a Graduate Course at UF

The chair of the UF astronomy department, Dr. Eichhorn, asked me if I wanted to teach a graduate-level course for one semester on the physics of the interplanetary medium. He offered to pay 25 percent of my salary for doing that, and I have to admit that this offer was attractive since I wouldn't have to write a proposal for it! I accepted his offer immediately and liked the idea of teaching for a change, especially at the graduate level. I taught the course in the spring semester and had about six PhD students. The low number of students was normal for an astronomy department.

My First PhD Student

The course was popular, so the chair asked me to teach it again the following year under the same financial arrangement. However, an interesting thing happened during teaching the course. One of the students, Tom Rusk, wanted to do his PhD thesis in the field of the interplanetary medium. He wanted to be my first PhD student. Tom was interested in cosmology and was a student of Professor Guy Omer, a famous cosmologist. Tom was frustrated because he didn't get much attention from Professor Omer.

After Tom's request to become my PhD student, I attended the next astronomy department faculty meeting. In that meeting I asked the faculty to approve me as Tom Rusk's advisor, and they did. Tom had a good foundation in physics and math, and I told him that his thesis should be on the interplanetary magnetic field and the solar magnetic field cycle, especially the region near the sun, because we didn't know a lot about it. Tom worked hard on his PhD thesis. It was a good thesis, and he defended it well. So Tom Rusk became Dr. Tom Rusk to the delight of many!

I asked Jerry if Tom could join SAL, so he and I could work together on getting grants and doing research (on soft money of course). Jerry agreed, and so Tom started his job as postdoc at SAL. This whole experience with Tom got a lot of the graduate students' attention. A year later I had three PhD students, this time all of them from China. Their names were S. Yu, S. Wang, and S. Mi. This was exciting for me because a scholar's scientific reputation depends, among many other things, on how many PhD students he graduates, because that will give him more prestige in the research arena.

Swimming at the O'Connell Center at UF

Completing my PhD thesis at SUNY was stressful. To counter this stress, I started thinking about doing serious exercise, since health officials have numerously said that exercise can help stressful situations. In my early years in Baghdad I used to go to public swimming pools, and I loved swimming. So I started lap swimming at the indoor pool at the University at Albany. Soon after that Jack Sulentic joined me in this swimming exercise with other professors during lunchtime. I continued doing this exercise in the next five years when I was working as a postdoc and later on as a research associate at SUNY.

The stress after doing the PhD thesis continued, though now the stress was related to doing research, writing proposals, trying to acquire research funds, and making a living out of it all. This life was by no means a walk in the park. However, this didn't mean that I couldn't live stress-free. There are all kinds of stress in today's lifestyles. Some stress is good for you and is necessary and healthy; however, too much stress is bad. To me exercise was a vehicle to reduce the stress and have control over it. All in all it felt good all around.

After we moved from Albany to Gainesville and joined the University of Florida, I found out that they had a big Olympic pool at the O'Connell Center. They also had a dedicated one-hour time at lunch for professors who wanted to swim laps. This sounded like heaven to me since I enjoyed this exercise so much. As long as I was at UF, I was swimming at the O'Connell Center pool. I got so used to exercising every workday that when the pool was closed for some reason, I and a few other professors found an alternative.

We discovered that there was one small door left unlocked to the Gators' football field, which was well known as the Swamp. So we used to go to that field and climb up through the stands all the way to the top and then come down. How is that for a good alternative exercise! Field-goal kickers, punters, and a few other players used to be there practicing, and they would look at us going up the stands with bewilderment. I was afraid that they might think we were somehow crazy!

Since I swam almost every workday for an hour at lunch, I would bring a sandwich, yogurt, or other food with me from home and eat it while I was working. I used to amuse myself by adding up the accumulated distances I swam every day. I was shocked to discover that my swimming in Albany added to my swimming in Gainesville was like swimming from New York City to Chile in South America!

My exercise was not confined to swimming, I used to jog in the morning and shoot some baskets at the hoop in my driveway. I also had a lot of fun biking the hills of Santa Fe where my house was. All my exercise kept me healthy and in control of my weight.

Doing Unfunded Research While Doing Research under a Closely Related Grant

A good example of this is what I did with the instrumentation grant from the Department of Defense. I designed the apparatus in such a way that it would also do laser-particle levitation, even though that was not in the plan of the funded proposal. However, it was justifiable from the point of view that we needed also to study light scattering by a single particle. This would help us understand how light scattering by a layer of particles takes place. I would like to say here that the US military funds a big piece of the pie of basic research in the United States because the US military believes (and correctly so) that you never can tell what comes out of basic research. Without military funding, a limited amount of basic research would be carried out.

Let me explain here how you can do your own unfunded research while being funded by another grant. Once you work completely on soft money, you must have multiple grants or one big multiyear one. An example of the latter is if you are involved in a NASA space mission to the outer planets, which sometimes takes fifteen years or more to complete. If you don't have that, then you have to get multiple grants to support yourself financially. I had multiple grants over the years as opposed to long-term grants, and then I would lump together what I charged the grants in direct labor.

An item of concern in the budget is direct labor, the time the principal investigator (PI) estimates he or she needs to complete the research. This amount determines the principal investigator's salary and is usually at best an estimate. It could be underestimated, overestimated, and in some rare cases just right. In most cases the direct labor for the principal investigator is underestimated simply because the PI does not want to make the total cost of the grant too high and lessen his or her chances of being funded. For example, when the PI decides that he will spend three months of his time on the grant that means approximately forty hours of work a week for twelve weeks. This is by no means binding. The PI could spend many hours in the evening at the office or at home working on the research.

This situation unfortunately enhances the possibility of you getting divorced from your spouse for lack of attention and puts you between a rock and a hard place!

The Importance of Accuracy in Estimating Direct Labor

However, sometimes you can estimate direct labor accurately, based on a forty-hour week. If you do that on most of your grants, then you will end up having extra time to do your own unfunded research that is dear to your heart. The other challenge that the PI has is to estimate the direct labor of his or her associates, and that can be problematic, especially when building an instrument. The PI must come up with time numbers for direct labor of the engineers on his or her team. This is usually done by negotiating with the engineers. If they ask for too much time, which translates to more salary money than the total budget allows, the bottom line will be increased beyond what the PI is comfortable with. This almost always threatens the possibility of getting funding.

The PI's negotiations with his or her team members are often difficult and sensitive, and the PI must handle them delicately to avoid hard feelings. Otherwise some of the team members may decide to leave and work with somebody else. Writing the budget is a difficult job. The PI must balance the importance of the research he or she wants to do with how the funding agency sees it. The PI must also consider how much money the agency has for that particular program, how much competition there is, and how many research papers that he or she anticipates to be produced by this research. All in all, the PI must ask, how intriguing is the research, and what impact will it have on the scientific community in the United States and abroad? Finally, the question on the reviewers' minds is how much progress will be made in the particular field by the proposed research.

In my own experience, I underestimated the direct labor many times and overestimated it or got it just right only a few times. The accounting departments at the universities make the payments for everybody. They also oversee any purchasing of equipment and pay for all machine-shop work inside or outside the university. These services that the university provides are part of the overhead they charge, which is substantial, anywhere between 30 to 60 percent of the total budget, with the exception of the cost of instrument purchases and students' pay. Universities like to have research funds because the overhead pays part of the salaries of their accountants and purchasing employees. It also pays hourly rates for graduate students who happen to be working on the research grant and for any expenses for using their machine shop. All these university actions have to have the PI's signature and approval.

The remaining money of the overhead is at the discretionary use of the university administrators, which could be substantial depending on the size of the grant. They usually spend that money on things unrelated to the research grant. When I objected to these actions, university representatives said, "Well, we maintain an office for you, air-conditioning, and janitorial service." I had to pay for my own phone service, domestic and international; copy paper; pencils; erasers; and so on. The university administrators often overlook the fact that the publications that come out of the research bear the name of the university, and those research publications help give the university its prestige and reputation.

This is really sad, in my opinion. It's a heavy price tag to pay for being associated with the university. After all, these funds come from brilliant ideas generated by the scientists!

I find it exciting for any scientist, including myself, to be able to generate spin-off ideas and get funding from the military or other agencies and still do unfunded research in his or her own field.

I believe that the most opportune time to do your own unfunded research is when you get seed money to write proposals. This is the perfect opportunity to develop your own ideas and do some of your unfunded research. Like I mentioned before, we got this opportunity when UF diverted seed money from football proceeds to SAL for writing proposals and getting grants. The most suitable way to do your own unfunded research is if you're doing a theoretical research paper. Developing theoretical work usually does not require instruments and experimentation or a team to work with you. You can do such research on your own, and all you need is a computer. Depending on the theoretical research that you are doing, PCs can be all that you need, especially now that they are so fast, but in those days we used the powerful mainframes at the university.

I often used computers to do theoretical work. One time Dr. Bo Gustafson and I wanted to track dust particles orbiting the sun and have multiple perturbing forces on them. Bo was complaining to me about the necessity of more computer time to do these calculations. Luck had it that I got a phone call from the astronomy department at UF about a small mainframe computer that they didn't need anymore. Since they knew that Bo and I were doing theoretical calculations, they offered this computer for us to use solely.

I jumped on this offer and accepted it right away, and Bo was ecstatic. Two weeks later, Bo told me that the computer had been working 24-7 for the past two weeks and had finished tracking one dust particle until it sank into the sun. He also told me that he was worried about the computer catching fire because it was getting so hot. I told Bo that it was really unbelievable that it took so long. Unfortunately, that same day I got a phone call from the astronomy department saying that they didn't want us to use the computer anymore, because they couldn't afford the electric bill!

Years after this, the PCs with the Intel chip became so fast that a similar calculation took less than a minute to execute. This was the kind of advancement that took place in the second half of the 1990s. Go figure … so to speak.

Chapter 12

How to Defend US Satellites from the Threats of Laser Weapons

Following the advice that I got from the reviewer that funded my instrumentation proposal, I contacted Major Joseph Hager, who was in charge of funding proposals for AFOSR. He told me to send him a proposal for a three-year period to do the research. I wrote the proposal and formed my team, which included Dr. Keith Ratcliff, Dr. John Oliver, and my postdoc Dr. Tom Rusk. I also allocated some funds for Dr. Gunther Eichhorn, who came to SAL from Germany to write the computer software for this research. The total cost for the three-year proposal came to $650,000.

To do this defense contract, I had to study some material science on the characteristics of silicates and other materials. Silicate particles were a good candidate since they reflect visible light and absorb radiation at the edge of the infrared wavelength 1.6 microns and beyond. To get perfect reflection of visible light, we needed extremely pure silica particles. If they had other elements in them, they would absorb the light. The first thing that came to mind was using optical lenses that were made of quartz, which is a form of pure silica. So we bought several lenses and asked the material science department at UF to crush them into tiny particles with their powerful crushing machine.

Sand from the Beaches of Florida

My team and I thought that this was the best material to do the job. We started taking measurements with the laser beam using these micron-size particles. The results from the various layers of these particles reflected the laser light satisfactorily. I wanted to explore more possibilities, so I went out of the laboratory and picked up some sand from the dirt and looked at it in the microscope. The sand particles looked like crushed glass, especially after cleaned with water. I told my team that we should test those sand particles, and all of them laughed and asked why I wanted to do that. I said we should try to do everything possible, but they were shocked by the idea of using sand particles. The laboratory tests we did showed amazing results. The sand particles from the backyard were competing with the crushed quartz from the lenses. Everyone wondered how that was possible.

With these results I started thinking about going to Fort Walton Beach in the Florida Panhandle because I remembered from a vacation there that the sand was very white. I also remembered that the sand wasn't hot when I walked on it either. This suggested to me that the sand there was pure silica. Finally I convinced Dr. Keith Ratcliff (my former teacher) to go with me and collect sand samples. Keith joked, "I can't picture anybody other than you using air force funds to go to beaches and collect sand samples." We both laughed very hard, but I was serious in this endeavor. The tests from the samples from Fort Walton Beach were shocking to say the least. They reflected the laser light better than the particles of pure quartz glass from lenses!

Keith did not feel comfortable with these results, and kept saying to me how we can tell the Air Force that we found beach sand particles doing better than quartz. He thought that that would be humiliating for us to say that. I kept telling Keith that scientific results should be respected no matter what they are. He agreed and got used to the idea later on. I also suggested to Keith that we should go to Daytona Beach and test their beach sand also. As it turned out that the sand from Daytona Beach was very pure also. Later on I heard (and I don't know if it is true) that the Silicon Valley in California get there pure silica for making computer chips from Daytona Beaches. This was fascinating for me and Keith to know.

Keith and I wondered a lot about why the sand particles were reflecting light better than the quartz particles from manufactured lenses. Keith and I both agreed that perhaps in the process of making lenses, the crystalline structure of the sand was destroyed. Unfortunately, we did not pursue this issue with material scientists to see if what we thought was correct. We didn't pursue the issue because the air force had told us that although this research was not classified officially, it was sensitive, and we should be cautious in talking about it to others.

Presenting Our Results in a Conference at Albuquerque

Major Joseph Hager from AFOSR organized a conference for two days in Albuquerque, New Mexico. All the principal investigators under this program were invited to attend and present their early results, along with team members that the PIs deemed should be present. I made traveling plans for Keith and myself to go to Albuquerque. Keith was apprehensive about how I was going to present the results about the sand particles from the beaches of Florida being the best candidate to use for the defense of satellites! Keith's fears started creeping on me too, and I started to get nervous for the first time about a presentation. It so happened that my presentation was scheduled to be the last one in the conference, and I still remember getting more and more nervous about the presentation. In any case, it went okay, to my own thinking and Keith's, and I fielded many questions from the audience, which showed good interest. Surprisingly, we both thought that the results were received well, and no one questioned the fact that the candidate particles were taken from beaches in Florida. There was no laughter, thank God!

Till this day of writing this book, I still cannot understand why one would be embarrassed about using materials from beaches. I asked Keith several times about this point, and he kept saying to me it was human nature. The most interesting observation I made looking at sand particles with the microscope was that the particles had very sharp edges. I couldn't help wondering how I didn't get wounded by those sharp edges when I lay on the beach. The answer is trivial and that is the microscope exaggerates those sharp edges by its magnification. Still though it seems odd!

Silicate versus Carbon Particles

I felt that the conference was basically a confrontation between using carbon material vs. silicate material for protecting the satellites. Carbon can stand very high temperatures (~ 4000 degrees centigrade) from the heat from the laser weapon, while silicate particles will reflect the laser light thus keeping the satellite cool. That explained why there was so much interest in my talk. The biggest question that remained in this research was if the air force was to use our method, then how would we adhere the particles in a layer form and then adhere it to the satellite skin? Luckily, Major Hager told me earlier to concern myself with the basic research and leave the applications for later.

This issue came up when a scientist who worked for the SDI came to visit my laboratory as he was touring all the investigators' facilities in this program. He brought up the issue of applications with me and asked, "If you adhere this layer to the skin of a satellite, how do you keep the satellite from heating up after some time?" I told him I didn't know at this time but that it depended on what kind of adhesive was being used. For example, does it let heat go out, or does it keep it in? I said further that it should be an adhesive that would absorb the heat from the satellite and vent it back to space. He nodded in agreement and said, "Keep working on it, my friend."

Achieving Laser Particle Levitation for the Second Time

As I said before, one can do unfunded research using other funds from a grant that is preferably related to the research or a spin-off from it. So we geared up to levitate a pure silica particle in the laser beam as we did before at Goddard Space Flight Center (GSFC). This time, though, we wanted to levitate the particle in a hard vacuum, thus simulating space conditions (more on that later).

We had many distinguished visitors to my laboratory, and they witnessed laser particle levitation. Actually, I have a notebook where the visitors wrote their names with some flattering comments. Among those visitors I remember Nasr Al-Sahhaf, a young Saudi who was a friend of the Saudi prince who flew on the space shuttle. Nasr Al-Sahhaf asked if we could train him on the controls to levitate a particle. We did train him for about half an hour, and he succeeded in levitating a particle and was fascinated.

A Tragedy at SAL

A fellow coworker at SAL was Dr. Don Sheurman. He worked on the analysis of data from *Pioneer 10* and *11* space probes when he joined SAL in 1975. When we moved to Gainesville, Florida, his office was across from mine. We used to chat a lot and were good friends. On one ordinary work day, a Wednesday, it was getting to be ten o'clock in the morning, and Don hadn't shown up to work. As I was thinking that, Jerry gave me a call and told me that Don Sheurman had been killed in a traffic accident in Gainesville. We were all shocked and didn't work at all. We all sat in the conference room consoling each other and talking about what had happened. The suddenness of losing a colleague was, to say the least, very shocking. A city truck made an illegal turn on a red light at an intersection on Thirty-Ninth Street and struck Don. I attended a memorial at UF where Jerry eulogized him.

The ESA Giotto Space Mission

I was lucky enough to be around for a visit of Halley's comet to the inner solar system. Halley's comet returns every seventy-six *years* to go around the sun. The comet appeared to the naked eye in 1910, again in 1986, and will appear next in 2061. The European Space Agency (ESA) decided to send a space mission to come close to Halley's comet and study it. The mission was named Giotto after the Italian Renaissance painter Giotto di Bondone. He had observed Halley's comet in 1301 and was inspired to depict it as the star of Bethlehem in his painting *Adoration of the Magi*.

NASA decided not to send a mission for financial reasons, but they encouraged American astronomers to collaborate with European ones on the Giotto mission. Jerry took this opportunity to contact his European colleagues and team up with them. As I recall, he was only able to connect Dr. Frank Giovane of SAL to work with the Europeans on the design of their instrumentation. I was not involved in this mission at all. It is interesting to mention that the results from the Giotto mission confirmed what Fred Whipple, "Comet Man," had said about the nuclei of comets being made of "dirty ice." Giotto was the first mission to come as close as 596 miles from the nucleus of a comet.

The Challenge of Laser Levitating a Particle in a Hard Vacuum

Laser levitating a silica particle in a hard vacuum is not easy. The procedure starts with levitating the particle with the chamber full of air or sometimes nitrogen to avoid humidity. When you start vacuuming the chamber and reach a pressure of one Torr, the particle will start oscillating and fall from the laser beam, as explained earlier. The remedy to that is to manipulate the laser power so that it will dampen these oscillations and keep the particle in place (servo system). Once the pressure goes below one Torr, the oscillations will disappear, and the particle will be stable in its levitation.

Dr. John Oliver designed the servo System and got it to work in manipulating the laser beam power. I had purchased a state-of-the-art (at that time) turbomolecular pump with an ion gauge for this phase of the experiment. This system was capable of achieving 10^{-7} Torr of vacuum, somewhat close to the vacuum in space. For one reason or another, we kept losing the particle at pressure of one Torr (more on that later). While this problem was going on, there were other problems happening at SAL.

Observing the 1987A Supernova from the South Pole

If there is any gift for a scientist, it is what happened in 1987. Astronomers detected a supernova in the Large Magellanic Cloud (a neighbor of the Milky Way). NASA asked astronomers to try to observe this supernova. Carl Rester of SAL was very excited for this once-in-a-lifetime opportunity. NASA funded many observers for this unique opportunity, and among them was Rester for an expedition to the South Pole to observe the supernova with his gamma-ray detector. The large amount of funding for this expedition brought a lot of overhead to the university and to SAL. A NASA airplane flew Carl and his team to the South Pole where they carried out their observations.

The SOHO Space Mission to Observe the Sun

NASA decided to build a spacecraft that would observe the sun and named it the Solar and Heliospheric Observatory (SOHO). There is no relation to the Soho in London where most pornography is found and sold … ha-ha. SOHO was to be a joint project between NASA and ESA. NASA launched the spacecraft in 1995. SOHO was to orbit slowly around the first Lagrangian point (L1), where the combined gravity of the Earth and sun would keep SOHO in an orbit locked to the Earth–sun line. The L1 point is approximately 1.5 million kilometers away from Earth (about four times the distance to the moon), in the direction of the sun. There, SOHO would get an uninterrupted view of the sun.

The SOHO location arrangement was similar to what the famous Dr. Bob Forward suggested in a scientific paper that I had the privilege to review and approve for publication. He suggested this arrangement and called it a *statite*, meaning a static, unmoving satellite, because it orbited the sun together with the Earth and at a fixed distance from Earth (approximately 1.5 million miles). The only movement the statite made was to orbit the L1 point. All previous solar observatories have orbited the Earth, so their observations were periodically interrupted as the satellites went into the night side of their orbits.

The famous mathematician Joseph-Louis Lagrange discovered six points of equal gravity from his solution of the restricted three-body problem, e.g., Earth-sun-spacecraft in orbital mechanics. Astronomers sometimes call these points space parking lots! This motivated Gerard K. O'Neill of Princeton University to suggest building space colonies in these parking lots. These Lagrange points exist at the moon–earth system, the sun–Earth system, all the other planets and the sun, and all the moons and the planets they orbit.

At this point in my career my colleagues knew that I had established and published research papers concerning the interactions between the solar wind and interplanetary dust at the region near the sun. So Jerry suggested Dr. Frank Giovane and I join the SOHO team of scientists as co-investigators. Jerry, Frank, and I traveled to attend a SOHO meeting at Goddard Space Flight Center in Maryland. Frank and I were approved as co-investigators on the mission along with other European astronomers. This was a very long project, since the launch of the spacecraft took place in 1995 and the data would not be coming for perhaps a year or so after. This was the kind of project that would take a long time before we could get any funding for it, and who knew if our SAL would still be in existence. This was the tough thing about doing research on soft money when I couldn't count on any financial support for many years to come. However, that is the nature of the beast, long-term space probes in this case. So I scored a victory by becoming a co-investigator on the SOHO mission, which carried a lot of prestige but no immediate financial support.

Jeb Bush and the Idea of Establishing the Florida Space Science Institute

Jeb Bush, who later on became the governor of Florida for two terms, was the head of the space science committee, which was formed by the then-governor of Florida, Lawton Chiles. Jerry started going to the meetings of this committee and established a good relationship with Jeb Bush. Jeb came up with an idea of forming a space science institute in Florida that would oversee all the activities in astronomy and space science in the entire state. Jeb wanted all researchers in Florida in these two fields to work their proposals under the umbrella of this institute. Also this institute would have a major part of the overhead generated by the research grants. Jerry was interested in this and told us if we got this opportunity, it would give all of us a great measure of stability.

Jerry started spending a lot of time on preparations to form such an institute. I believe that he even suggested calling it the Florida Space Science Institute. Jerry filled me in on a lot of the details along with other senior members of SAL. To my great relief, Jerry maintained that SAL would stay as a core unit inside this institute.

Becoming an Associate Director of SAL

Shortly after Carl Rester and his team returned from the supernova observations at the South Pole, Jerry called me one day and asked me to be associate director of SAL. He said that he was overwhelmed with all the things he'd been doing and he wanted to dedicate more of his time to prepare a large proposal for the institute to submit to

Jeb Bush. I told him to give me at least one or two days to think about it.

My main purpose in my career was to be purely a research scientist. I never ever liked administrative work at all. I thought of it as a waste of time that would keep me from satisfying my research curiosities. I then talked to my wife about this offer, and she was against it because she knew I was primarily a researcher and didn't like administrative work. She reminded me how I hated to do administrative work when we first came to Gainesville. I told her that Jerry said he trusted me 100 percent to be his associate. If I refused, then he couldn't devote more time for the institute proposal. My wife said, "You know better; it is your call." I decided to accept the position and told Jerry over lunch. After lunch Jerry called for a meeting of all SAL members in the conference room and announced that I would be the associate director. He said that I would be doing all the signatures for purchasing and whatever else instead of him.

After reading so far in this book, would you rather do research or administer research? Well, I don't know what your answer is, but here is the story: Some researchers do very good or even excellent research for a long time, and then something happens. They might tire out or lose interest; sometimes they run out of new ideas. So what is the alternative? Since they did very good or excellent research, they will have attracted a lot of other beginning researchers. So then they can decide to administer research. This will still keep them in the game, since now their names will be included on their associated researchers' publications, not as first or prime author but second, third, fourth, and so on.

This modus operandi does not appeal to me at all; that is why I would rather not be an administrator. Those who administer research almost never do it in the beginning of their career, because they don't have the other researchers with them yet or the reputation. Researchers who administer research must have worked very hard for years in their career.

Life as an Associate Director

My style of working at SAL changed considerably when I became associate director. I was signing about fifty documents a day, and the accountants, clerks, and office managers were constantly knocking on my door all day. The only time I was able to do my own research was after five o'clock when most of the administrative people were gone. My research suffered, my ability to get grants suffered, and I was miserable all around. I still remember Don Ely, a young engineer, saying whenever he saw me, "Dr. Misconi, I never see you at the laser laboratory. It is your research, and we are stuck with levitating particles in a vacuum. Why don't you have a look and help us?"

I told my team at the laser lab that I'd be coming for a full day to help out. I told the administrative staff that they could only come to the laser lab if they needed very important signatures. I spent all day talking to the team about the problem and trying to diagnose what was going wrong. The only conclusion I came up with was that perhaps the servo system designed and built by Dr. Oliver was designed to manipulate a very strong beam, namely a total of 18 watts continuous wave laser. Dr. Oliver did not agree with my suggestion, but that was the only thing I could think of. We never found out what the problem was.

The Future of the SAL Operation

Carl Rester and Jerry's relationship started to deteriorate. They didn't see eye to eye on many things. I still don't know what it was all about, but in any case it got so bad that Jerry suggested to Carl in a letter that it would best if he left SAL. Carl did leave. In a nutshell the relationship between SAL and UF began to sour, and then even the provost of the university sided against SAL because our funding from grants was dwindling. That always rings a bell in everybody's mind, and we started getting criticism from the dean and the provost.

A year or less before this all happened, the physicist Mohammed Katoot joined SAL without any salary. He was a Palestinian who had lived in Syria, and he wanted to work in cosmology, another new branch for SAL. I met Katoot at some point and talked to him about his interest in cosmology. I pointed out to him that it was difficult to get grants in cosmology. He agreed with me and said he was hoping to get funding for something else and then maybe still do cosmology on the side, like a spin–off.

The Saudi Connection

Katoot told me that he knew of Saudis who were interested in space. The best example was the Saudi prince who flew on the space shuttle. He asked me if he could invite a Saudi friend of the prince to my laser laboratory to see the laser particle levitation. I said yes, of course, and that was how I met Nasr Al-Sahhaf, mentioned earlier. According to Katoot, Saudi Arabia had about $15 million left over of their investments in the United States for that year. He said they were willing to give this money to us if we formed an institute that would train Saudi students in space science and eventually fly Saudi experiments on the space shuttle. He also told me that the Saudi prince who flew on the shuttle was back in Saudi Arabia and would support an initiative like that.

I relayed all this information to Jerry, who got excited and thought this could help shore up SAL. Katoot wanted a salaried position at SAL. Since our funds were dwindling, Jerry went to the provost and asked him to hire Katoot for one year, explaining the proposal on the Saudi project. The provost agreed and hired Katoot in the hope that he may deliver on this project. Katoot also asked Jerry to hire a young (like Katoot) cosmologist to work with him. So I advertised, and we got three young cosmologists. They each came down and made their presentations. All of them were brilliant cosmologists, and we chose Dr. Charles Torre, who is now at Utah University. The astrophysics group in the physics department at UF hired one of the other candidates.

Shortly after, Katoot started his contact with Saudi Arabia, and the Saudi prince who flew on the shuttle invited him to visit. Jerry and Katoot asked me to write a major proposal for the new institute that would train the Saudis. I wrote this proposal and even gave it an Arabic name: Al-Haytham Institute for Space Studies. Al-Haytham was an Arab scientist and was born in AD 965. He made discoveries concerning the nature of light and other things.

Katoot left to Saudi Arabia, met with the prince at Al-Fahd University, and gave a speech to the professors in the prince's presence. He got promises of continual contacts and a lot of good will but no concrete plans. This up-in-the-air result spelled doom for SAL. I was worried about our future and what the university was going to do about us. An operation on soft money is always on shaky ground with its associated university. It does not matter how much money you've gotten in the past. They are always asking, what have you done for me lately? The other thing they look at is if you can support yourself independently of the university. If the answer is no, then you better think about leaving to go somewhere else. It is always an unhappy marriage between scientists on soft money and the university administrators! In any case, what ensued after was unfortunate.

The Closing of SAL at UF

The news of the result of Katoot's visit to Saudi Arabia reached the provost, and shortly after, the provost gave Jerry official notice that he was going to close SAL. The laboratory would be closed June 1989, giving us some eight months to find other universities to affiliate with if we wished to continue working on soft money. The provost also said that he would pay our salaries for that period of transition.

The Instruments in My Laboratory

Following this unfortunate incident I started worrying about my laboratory. Because I was working on soft money and was associated with a university, these were the rules:

1. The grants I acquired from funding agencies belonged to the university, and the contracts were made with the university. I, as the PI, could only administer the grant, i.e. purchase the equipment and hire the people that I needed to help me with my research and write the midterm report to the funding agency and the final report.

2. The university had the right to accept my grant or refuse it. For example, the university might refuse if the amount of money was too small and did not justify the involvement of university personnel to process the grant. This happened to me once with one of my research grants.

3. I had to lie awake at night whenever there was a problem with one of my grants, e.g., not being adequate to fund everybody, as often I didn't account for everything when I made the budget. I also lay awake at night when my research wasn't going well, when I had arguments with my coinvestigators on which direction to take, when I had problems with the engineers who were doing my experiment, which in my experience was quite often, and so on.

4. This one is a biggie; get ready for it. Your laboratory and all your instrumentations belong to the university, not to you! In most cases the university will ask their professors to visit the laboratory and ask for any equipment they feel they need for their own research. It's like a fire sale except it's not a sale but a grab!

This last item of the list worried me the most because now I had to find another university and I needed to take my laboratory intact with me to that other university. If I lost the laboratory, then I couldn't do my spin research. With all these terrible rules, why did I work on soft money? I did it because of the freedom that was associated with it. I could do any research I wanted to do, and I felt like my own boss. Plus I enjoyed the emotional ups and downs that

I got from thrill-of-research moments. My research also gave me recognition among my peers. Research is the engine of progress. Please believe me when I say I still loved working on soft money and everything that came with it.

Lucky Again

While all these unfortunate things were going on, my postdoc, Tom Rusk, kept suggesting we get in touch with the Florida Institute of Technology (FIT). Later on I found out that the students joked that FIT stood for *forget intercourse totally* because the university had predominantly male students. Rusk was friends with Dr. Bruce Rafert, a professor at FIT who had graduated from the University of Florida and had been Tom's roommate. Tom kept asking me again and again to contact Bruce Rafert to explore the possibility of Tom and me joining that university. I was not sure yet what I wanted to do, so I kept telling Tom I would think about it. Shortly after, I decided to have Tom contact Rafert.

Rafert invited Tom and me to come down to FIT in Melbourne, Florida. I'd never heard of Melbourne, Florida, until Tom told me about FIT. So Tom, Katoot, and I traveled to Melbourne. I met Rafert in his sailboat, since he said that he liked to do business on his sailboat. I thought this was a cool idea. We had a pleasant meeting, and he welcomed us with open arms. We actually talked about working at FIT on hard money, not soft money- -shocking surprise, yes. They were in the process of forming the Space Research Institute (SRI) and had gotten funding for it from the state of Florida.

Jeb Bush and the Space Research Institute (SRI)

Jeb Bush's space science committee had allocated $2.5 million dollars in startup money to form an institute to oversee space-research activities in Florida. Before the committee was to allocate this money to Jerry Weinberg, Jeb Bush went out of town for a week.

It turned out later on that that was a bad week for Jerry Weinberg and our operation as a whole. According to what I learned later on that FIT had a vice president for communications the late Mr. Tom Adams who was a former Lieutenant Governor of Florida in the early 1970s. He knew very well the members of the space committee and lobbied them to give this money to FIT. He argued that FIT is already forming their Space Research Institute (SRI). He also told the committee that FIT had just renovated a large building to house the SRI, and therefore they should allocate the funds to FIT instead of giving it to Jerry Weinberg's SAL. In the end, the space committee did allocate the money to FIT during that week **when Jeb Bush was away.** Jerry tried to change the decision but he was told it was too late.

Joining FIT

After the visit to Melbourne, I wrote a letter to Dr. Rafert accepting his offer to join FIT. I wanted to bring with me Tom Rusk, Mohammad Katoot, and Charles Torre, and I wanted FIT to give stipends for three PhD students of mine. They agreed to all of that. Bringing three PhDs with me was a mistake on my part. Several people, including Jerry, cautioned me against it. I also asked to get an offer letter from FIT's Vice President Dr. Allen Mense, a well-known and very bright physicist.

I set up a lunch meeting with Jerry to tell him about my decision to move to FIT. He sensed immediately that there was something important I wanted to tell him that he would not like hearing. Well, he was right. He didn't like the idea and cautioned me about FIT double-crossing me. This meeting was very difficult for me because I'd spent almost two decades working with Jerry. However, I didn't see any future for SAL and had doubts about Jerry succeeding in turning things around.

Jerry asked me why I didn't seek a position at the astronomy department at UF regardless of the Provost letter banning such action. I told Jerry that Dr. Eichhorn, the chair of the department, told me that he couldn't force the issue and get me in the department.

I couldn't understand this part of the provost's letter at all; I thought it was completely unfair.

Jerry kept asking me why I was rushing to leave when we had six to seven months to turn this thing around. Finally, though, he accepted my decision and wished me well. He warned me that the university was going to give me problems in moving my laboratory to FIT. As I said before, all equipment purchased on soft money belonged to the university. Knowing that, I set up a meeting with the director of research, Bill Walsh, who told me that they couldn't let me take a laboratory that cost a quarter of a million dollars to build. He said it was against the university's rules. I argued with him that nobody could use the laboratory for the experiment I was doing simply because they don't have the knowledge to do so, moreover it is not in their field of research.. He agreed but said they could use parts of the laboratory.

It was time to use my trump card. I told Walsh that with my early departure to FIT I would be saving UF six to seven months of salaries for me and the three PhDs in my group who are going with me, namely Tom Rusk, Charles Torre, and Mohammad Katoot. He said he would take this issue to the provost and let me know what they decide. A few days later he called me and said it was okay to take my laboratory on loan to FIT; however, if any scientist in the future wanted to have parts of my laboratory, I would be obligated to give it to him or her. I did not like that last part, but I had no other choice but to agree. Incidentally, this last clause came back to haunt me later on. I signed this agreement, which had a clause that the agreement needed to be renewed yearly and that UF had the ultimate say in the renewal. Imagine a university doing these things to its own brainchild; it was very sad. So this chapter of my life was finally closed for the time being.

I received an offer letter from the vice president of FIT, and he also asked me to visit Melbourne again to meet with the president of FIT, Dr. Lynn Weaver. I did visit the president, and he welcomed me with open arms and graciously asked me if there was anything he could do for me. I said I had been about to apply for promotion from associate to full professorship at UF. However, this whole turmoil had delayed me from doing it, so now I wanted to apply for full professorship at FIT. Dr. Lynn Weaver told me there was no need for that. With my scientific reputation, publications, and resume, he said I was more than qualified for the promotion. He promoted me to full professor immediately, and I was gratified with that.

FIT and the vice president increased my salary to $65,000 from the $57,000 that I was making at UF, which often happens when you change universities. However, this salary was given to me on hard money and not on good old soft money! The first snag with this move came when I received the contract to be signed. The contract clearly said the position was for a year and a half. I was alarmed because that wasn't what we'd been told. I immediately called the vice president and asked him about it. He said that was just a formality because we were not in a department and were not tenured. He told me not to worry about anything and assured me that what we agreed upon still held. For a moment I thought that what Jerry was cautioning me about was right ... on the money!

Now that all the paperwork was done on the laboratory and our salaries, I turned my attention to the move, which had its own complications. FIT paid for the move of the laboratory, and I had to rent a house in Palm Bay, which was a city adjacent to Melbourne. Since I was leaving in February 1989 to Melbourne, my wife said we should not take our son, Michael, out of school. She also was taking education courses at UF to further her career in library science, and she didn't want to lose that. So the plan was for me to rent a house in Palm Bay till the end of May, and then my family would join me in early June.

So I did that and left on weekends to spend time with my family in Gainesville. It so happened that my brother Lutfi (the biochemist) came from Australia to visit me and stayed with me in the rented house in Palm Bay. We had great times.

The lab was successfully moved to FIT, and they gave me a real large room and did the plumbing to cool the laser. When I first negotiated my move to FIT with Dr. Rafert, he asked me to apply to be director of SRI. I said I would, but I never did since to me that was an administrative chore. Vice President Allen Mense hired Dr. Marshall Kaplan as director of the SRI. Kaplan was an aerospace engineer and an educator. He also wrote a very good textbook on space engineering. I began to worry about acquiring research grants to continue what I had been doing at SAL. The hard money did not work well for me. They simply gave me a sense of security that I didn't need!

Unfortunately, I was asked to attend meetings at the SRI director's office, and he opened three centers inside the Space Research Institute. A secretary was hired and other personnel. These things worried me because all I could see was an administrative infrastructure that would cost money and not bring grants. I was also busy looking for a house. I bought one in Melbourne, and my family moved with me in early June. I still live in that house today.

I began to feel that this was a different mode of research operation for me, since now I was on my own. I was working without having a research-only organization like SAL. I felt as if I had to write proposals to support three other PhDs who were not used to writing proposals on their own and acquiring funding. Even though we were officially on hard money, we still needed to bring in grants since we were 100 percent on research. The remaining members of SRI were basically administrators, and they were not going to write proposals and get funds. Also only Tom Rusk was in my field of research. Katoot and Torre were young PhDs in the field of cosmology. Neither of them had written a proposal to get funding to do research in cosmology.

I began to feel the effects of the mistake I'd made in bringing them with me to FIT. At one point the vice president for research asked me why I have to have them with me. I told him it was sheer loyalty. They had no place to go, so I felt obligated to take them with me. Loyalty is a good thing, but it can put you in a lot of trouble, as has happened to so many politicians, for example.

The Idea of Building "Spacecraft Florida"

After the space shuttle *Challenger* disaster in 1984, NASA established the Astronauts Memorial Foundation. It was housed in the Space Coast and later at the Kennedy Space Center (KSC), not KFC (Kentucky Fried Chicken). A lot of people I meet confuse the two! The funding for this organization came from the proceeds of selling car license tags that commemorated the *Challenger* disaster. The Astronauts Memorial Foundation needed to do something with the money. They came up with the idea of asking the Florida universities to build a spacecraft and call it *Spacecraft Florida*. It was supposed to be a miniature satellite with one or two probing instruments. Bruce Rafert, the one who invited us to come down to FIT, became very interested in this idea. So we started talking about building *Spacecraft Florida*, and he asked me to prepare notes on what scientific instruments we could fly on this spacecraft. He contacted Dr. Edward J. Weiler at NASA, who was the head of space missions at Goddard Space Flight Center, and set the date for traveling and giving a presentation.

I worked hard on the notes and then gave them to Bruce to present. The presentation didn't go well, and NASA did not show any interest in funding a project like that. Actually they did not believe that SRI was ready to take on a mission like that, certainly not with the type of staff we had, most of whom had no experience in space missions. Now I began to worry that we were not going to have research funds to justify the existence of SRI.

Center for Geo-space Environmental Research

At the same time, Kaplan asked me to form a center inside SRI that dealt with space debris, which was a growing problem for NASA at the time, and become the director of it. I agreed simply because it didn't seem to me that being director of a scientific center was administrative job. I formed the center and called it the Center for Geo-space Environmental Research. I sent an announcement to the Department of Physics and Space Science, and the Mechanical and Aerospace Department at FIT asking any interested professors to join the center. It took a while, but I had about three professors and one MS student of mine that joined the center. Speaking of graduate students, FIT did not follow through with their promise to give stipends to my three PhD students. They called me many times asking whether they could come to Melbourne, but I had to tell them there weren't any stipends. They were broken hearted, and so was I.

Our media specialist at SRI sent the news of forming this center to newspapers, which caught the attention of the Boulder, Colorado, space environment laboratory, which was an arm of the National Oceanic and Atmospheric Administration (NOAA). They called me and asked me if my center was a duplication of theirs. I explained to their director, Dr. Ernest Hildner, that I was interested in space debris studies and interplanetary dust, and he said then there was no problem. This contact made me establish a relationship with that center for a few years.

The Florida Space Symposium

Another idea started floating around after the failure of the *Spacecraft Florida* project. The new idea came from the director of SRI, Dr. Marshall Kaplan. He said that a space symposium at FIT would foster collaborations on research between SRI and others. SRI designed and printed pamphlets that were distributed at universities and other research institutions all over the United States. This cost a considerable amount of money. Kaplan asked me to form sessions for the space symposium and suggest chairs for these sessions. He specifically asked me if I could invite Jerry Weinberg to head a session. The vice president, Kaplan, and Rafert had the idea that they snatched me out of Jerry's organization and that Jerry was not happy with that. Some of this was true, but when I called Jerry and asked him to chair one of the sessions, he agreed.

I invited Dr. Murray Dryer from the space environment laboratory at Boulder, Colorado, to make a presentation on the space environment. I also invited an air force scientific officer who funded research on space debris to the session that I chaired. Kaplan invited Dr. Bob Forward, a well-known physicist, to give the final discourse of the symposium on the status of the much-sought-after unified field theory of the universe.

All in all, the symposium went well, but it did not generate any promises of funding or collaborations or anything of that nature. It gave SRI some publicity but nothing at all that would secure its future. It did give us a good feeling to see so many scientists flocking down to Melbourne for the symposium, but perhaps that was due to the fact that we were so close to Disney World, EPCOT Center, Universal Studios, MGM, and so on!

Renewing Our Contracts

A year and a half had almost passed since we'd started working at FIT. I'd begun to wonder nervously about when the renewal of the contracts would be coming. By August 1990, I got in the mail the contract that I had been waiting for. It was one of the biggest shocks in my life. The contract, which was already signed by the vice president for research, said basically that due to lack of funds, I should seek employment at other universities. It said that I was welcome to stay at FIT, but if I did so, I would be put on soft money, i.e., I would have to provide my own salary from research grants. Well, guess what: Jerry's predictions came true. Hurray for Jerry. The contracts for the other PhDs that came with me said the same thing. It was a sad day. My colleagues asked me what we were going to do, and I said I didn't know. Right now I was shell shocked. I went home early that day and told my wife (who was not working at the time so she could take care of our son) what had happened, and she was shocked too.

Embry-Riddle Aeronautical University

The next day I started thinking about the Embry-Riddle Aeronautical University at Daytona Beach. The dean there had just invited me to give a talk about my research a few days before the contract fiasco. So I thought I would capitalize on this chance and seek employment there. My associate Torre told me that he had contacts at Utah State University's cosmology group and that he may get a chance to go there. Tom Rusk told me that he would work with his old friend Bruce Rafert and stay at FIT. Katoot, on the other hand, had no place to go, and he pleaded with me to take him to Embry-Riddle with me. I said I would (another mistake).

I used the opportunity of giving my colloquium at Embry-Riddle to negotiate a deal with the dean. I asked him to pay 75 percent of my and Katoot's salaries, and we would supply the rest from research grants. He agreed to this deal and said he had to approve it with the president. He called me later and said the president had approved it. and scheduled a meeting between him, the president and Katoot and myself. Katoot and I went to a meeting with the dean and the president, and I gave a presentation about our research and what we intended to. Then the most bizarre thing happened afterward. As we shook hands with the president and went back to the dean's office, the dean said, "This is wonderful agreement. You get 25 percent of your salary guaranteed by the university, and you bring the rest from research grants." I was shocked again, and I told him right then thanks but no thanks. This was not what we had talked about, and I was really surprised. I immediately left feeling angry at this weird way of dealing. I told my wife everything when I got home. She was not surprised because she didn't count on anything until it was 100 percent guaranteed. She liked FDIC for the banks, and she knew there was no FDIC for soft money!

Katoot accepted the new deal and went to Embry-Riddle. I stayed at FIT going to my office and making contacts with NSF since I had a proposal for two years being evaluated that would cover about one third of my salary for each of two years. My wife said, "Don't worry. We have credit cards; we can live for a while." Great!

Chapter 13

A New Era for Me

O ne morning I got into my office and got a surprise phone call from Dr. Mense, the vice president of FIT, saying that he wanted to see me. We met, and he told me that he could get me an in-house grant for $36,000 from funds that FIT got annually from the Florida Solar Energy Center (FSEC). He said this would carry me until I got an answer on my NSF proposal. All I needed to do was to write a short proposal about research to see if my particles could keep the heat out of the roofs of houses. This was an idea that I'd started when I was at UF. We theorized that if our sand particles could reflect laser light, then they should do the same thing with solar light. This meant they would save energy by reflecting heat from the roofs of houses, something that FSEC would be interested in. I thanked him for this opportunity and went and did the proposal. It was funded immediately, and I started working on it.

Since the grant was only $36,000, I could not do it properly. Ideally, I would have had two houses, one with regular roof shingles and another with shingles coated with pure silica sand particles. Since I didn't have the funds for that, I instead bought two large sheds from Home Depot. I asked a graduate student to put them together on FIT land that was not being used at the time. I decided to mix the particles with polyurethane as adhesive and spray (with a good pump) the roof of one of the sheds. We then insulated the walls of both sheds and installed air thermometers in both of them.

I instructed my graduate student to read the temperatures each day at the same time and other days at different times. The temperatures of the two sheds varied between 20°F to 15°F and sometimes 10°F, depending on the weather. The coated shed was lower in temperature. I presented these results in a meeting at FSEC, and they were impressed. I don't know why, but no follow-up took place to further investigate. Maybe they did not have the necessary funds for a proper experiment, which would cost much more than the $36,000 they'd given me through FIT. Also they may have been reluctant to get into the roofing business. Certainly my results were encouraging, so I really don't know why they did not pursue this idea further.

NSF Comes through for Me

As soon as my grant from FSEC ended, I heard from the NSF that my proposal was funded. The funding amount was $57,865, and the proposal was titled "Dynamics of Plasma–Dust Interactions in the F-Corona and Interplanetary Shock Waves." This funding came from the NSF Solar Terrestrial Program. I thought, *Yeah, I am back in the saddle!*

The Formation of the Spaceport Florida Authority (SFA)

The Florida legislators decided to establish the Spaceport Florida Authority. It was the nation's first and was designed to promote private-sector launches from Cape Canaveral Air Force Station, which is adjacent to KSC. In November 1989, I went to the public meeting to vote on a new executive director of the established authority and voted for Edward O'Connor. Ed won, and I was pleased because I thought he was the best candidate.

In 1989, SFA was modeled after airport and seaport authorities. SFA was broadly empowered to develop, finance, and operate spaceports statewide. The underutilized launch facilities at the Cape Canaveral Air Force Station were identified as the initial operational site for the authority.

The Spaceport Florida Authority had some significant successes during the 1990s, developing hundreds of millions of dollars in infrastructure for commercial, military, and NASA programs. In accordance with its charter from the state, the authority also developed several successful space-education and economic-development programs. The first launch they had was for my total-solar-eclipse rocket launch in Mexico.

Around 2000, after the departure of its first executive director, Ed O'Connor, the Spaceport Florida Authority was renamed the Florida Space Authority (FSA), and its priorities changed from spaceport operations to statewide space-related economic development. Two spin-off entities were also formed at that time: the Florida Space Research Institute (FSRI) and the Florida Aerospace Finance Corporation (FAFC). FSRI and FAFC were not successful, and after FSA shifted its focus away from being a transportation authority, the agency was ill equipped to make strong progress on its economic-development priorities. A state commission in 2006 recommended dissolving FSA, FSRI, and FAFC and creating a new agency called Space Florida.

The Technological Research and Development Authority (TRDA)

I spoke about the formation of the Astronauts Memorial Foundation earlier from the proceeds of car license tags. The legislators in Tallahassee, Florida, formed another authority, also from the proceeds of car license tags, and they called it the Technological Research and Development Authority (TRDA). The purpose of this authority was to promote economic development and technology in Brevard County, where Cape Canaveral and KSC are located. The legislators appointed Frank Kinney as executive director. Kinney chose prominent figures from Brevard County, e.g., heads of corporations, to be members of the board.

Kinney, at the time, had an office at FIT close to my office, and

I used to say hi to him whenever I came across him, not knowing that one day I'd be asking him for funding. It was expected that the Spaceport Florida Authority would somehow team up with TRDA, and somehow I was the missing link. I was not thinking of these two organizations at all for getting funds, since I was used to applying for funds from federal agencies. However, I got a phone call from Jim Ralph, who introduced himself as the director of launch operations at the Spaceport Florida Authority. He asked me if I could use the unguided Super Loki sounding rocket for some kind of experiment. I said I would think about it and get back to him later.

At the time, my interest was in the region near the sun and whether or not there were temporary dust rings around the sun. I'd read a research paper by Peterson (1967) about his infrared observations during the November 12, 1966 total solar eclipse of the corona and found a peak emission that perhaps suggested the existence of a dust ring at four solar radii from the surface of the sun. Also MacQueen (1968) made scans from a stratospheric balloon-flown coronograph (a device that blocks the solar disk in order to observe the corona), on January 9, 1967, and found brightness enhancements at 3.4 and 4.1 solar radii. Others found similar things. These reports got my interest, and so I started thinking about how I could use the Super Loki rocket to observe the sun's corona during a total solar eclipse.

I immediately called a friend astronomer at the space environment laboratory at Boulder, Colorado, who knew about rocket capabilities. I explained to him what I wanted to do during a total solar eclipse. My friend told me that the Super Loki rocket was a ballistic shot and wasn't guided but if I launched it toward the sun and had an observational instrument that could look at a wide field of view, then I could do it. I asked him how wide the field of view needed to be, and he said something like forty degrees so I wouldn't miss the sun and its corona. Incidentally, I checked and found out that on July

11, 1991, there would be a long-duration total solar eclipse of little more than six minutes to be seen in Mexico. I had a big up ↑ thrill-of-research moment.

I called Jim Ralph and told him of my intentions, and he was jubilant. He said it was magnificent; the first Spaceport Florida Authority launch would be in Mexico, a foreign country. I also told him that we had a heavenly deadline that couldn't be broken: July 11, 1991, at high noon in the state of Nayarit, Mexico! We had to design, construct, test, calibrate, and mount a new small telescope by then. We started March 15, 1991, so we had close to four months, a tight schedule. We couldn't tell the moon to stop moving for a while and delay the eclipse because we weren't ready!

Me explaining the payload for the eclipse experiment. From left to right: Frank Kinney, executive director of TRDA; Jim Ralph, launch operations director at SFA; Edward O'Connor, executive director of SFA; Nebil Misconi.

I asked Jim Ralph where the funds were going to be coming from, and he said TRDA because we have collaborations with them. I quickly wrote a proposal and submitted it to the executive director of TRDA, Frank Kinney. Frank asked me to attend a meeting and give a presentation on the experiment to the TRDA board. The board had some questions for me that I answered well, but I was a little worried because there was stiff competition with other proposals. At the end of the meeting, I was awarded over $120,000 to do the observations. The vice president for research at FIT started laughing when I told him about the funding. He said, "Well, today you made over $120,000. What are you going to bring in tomorrow?" It was really a joyful moment for me and gave me a feeling of redemption. I was put on soft money, and I proved to myself that I could do it on my own. It was also a definite up ↑ thrill-of-research moment.

The Race to Get Ready for the Total Solar Eclipse

As the principal investigator of the experiment, I started a tight mission to complete this work, and I used all the help I could get from the experts I knew. I told everyone that we were going to build two instruments and fly the best-performing one. The remaining one would be just a backup, and the decision of which to fly would be mine. I called the two payloads A and B. While only one of them would fly to observe the total solar eclipse, the remaining payload could eventually fly, just for a different purpose. At the time I had no idea what that could be.

A professor of mechanical engineering at UF did the design of the instrument. Dr. Frank Giovane, a former colleague of mine at SAL, designed the baffle system, a system of spiraling edges in front of the lens of the telescope. The purpose of the baffle system was to reject the off-axis light from falling on the lens. The baffle system had to be painted black just like in regular cameras. However, this black paint couldn't be ordinary paint from the store. It had to be space worthy; it had to be able to withstand the harsh space environment, like the hard vacuum and the severe low temperatures. Regular paint would flake off, and the outgassing due to the hard vacuum could cover the lens with paint. So I had to get a special paint made by a university in Illinois. They usually did work with NASA, and they were recommended to me. The amazing thing was that the small can of paint cost me $450. When I asked them why the price was so high, they said, "How many cans do you think we sell a year, ha-ha!"

Frank Giovane suggested I call the instrument SEEC (solar eclipse extended corona), pronounced cleverly as *seek*. Several other experts in instrumentation did their part, among them Dr. Gunther Eichhorn, who was a former colleague at SAL. I asked him to be the manager of the experiment, since he was an excellent all-around instrumentalist. He was working at the University of Arizona and had to fly every now and then to Melbourne.

However, the star of this effort was the engineer Jack MacKisson who had worked with us at SAL. The big challenge was that we needed to put a small telescope inside a cylinder that was only two inches in diameter and thirty-two inches long. The cylinder would house the telescope, the digital and analog boards, a transmitting system, and the batteries for power. It would have been impossible without Jack MacKisson. Jack used the advent of microelectronics at the time to reach unprecedented miniaturization.

Jack used silicon photodiodes to detect the brightness and decided to put in fourteen of them. They were distributed in circular fashion around the center of the tube. It was a terribly difficult task to place the silicone photodiodes inside that small tube. Some engineers told me that it was impossible. Jack used a special microscope to look through the tube and guide him as he placed them one at a time.

We had to alter the existing design of the Super Loki payload case. We eliminated the need for a parachute since we were not going to recover the payload; this gave us more space in the payload for our instrument.

The Huge G-Forces on the Rocket Payload

The other problem we had to face was that we needed to release the payload out of its housing, the dart tube. The instrument had to shear the metal screws that kept the heavy nose cone in place for flight stability. The nose cone then would tumble out of the way of the telescope. To release the payload from the dart tube, we put a timed explosive underneath the payload inside the dart. The explosive would deliver about 120 g's to the payload. This would be huge jolt to the payload that would definitely destroy all the instrumentations inside unless we found a way to prevent that.

We came up with the perfect solution to this problem: we needed to fill the payload with epoxy resin mixture that would harden quickly and cement every piece in the payload so nothing could move at all. There was one problem, though. The mixture of epoxy and resin could not get hot before hardening; if it did, it could heat up the instrument to the degree of destroying it. Luckily we had a very good materials department at FIT, and one graduate student took it upon himself to do the epoxy resin mixture. He made sure that it would harden at a safe temperature; I believe it was about 60°F.

The dart tube also had an ablation material on its outside surface that by evaporating would protect the instrument from the intense friction heat with the atmosphere, sort of similar to what they do in the Apollo, Gemini, and Mercury capsules. The rocket and the payload were supposed to make approximately five rotations per second during the flight for stability reasons, and this spin rate created the intense friction heat.

However, before we hardened the payload, we ran into some problems. Some of the silicon photodiodes were failing the test after they'd been put in. So we did not have fourteen silicon photodiodes in each payload; we had eight in one and nine in the other. Those eight and nine photodiodes stayed stable throughout and into the launch. I asked for a test observation of the star Vega with our instrument, and I was very happy that the light from Vega was satisfactory and showed the same profile done with other established telescopes.

Make no mistake: I knew that it was unlikely that we'd detect enhancements around the sun that could suggest the existence of temporary dust rings around the sun. The field of view was too large at forty degrees in diameter, but we had to do that because our rocket was a ballistic shot and not guided. I did not have the funding or the time to do an experiment on a guided rocket during a somewhat rare *total* solar eclipse. Also the geography of where the eclipse would take place was a logistical problem too. It would have been better to observe the sun's corona in the infrared part of the spectrum, but that was a whole different instrument that would have been more complicated to build in such a short time. Anyhow, I was happy to be able to take the chance.

I was also asked how I would take the data while the payload was spinning at approximately five rotations per second. I said that the electronics could gather the data much faster than five rotations per second, so this posed no problem. There would be some jitter, but this also didn't pose a problem for the same reason.

After potting the insides of the payload, nothing could move inside. The lens and filter were protected by an aluminum lip that was connected to the aluminum tube with very strong screws (see diagram of the instrument in appendix B). So now the time had come to test the payload for shock at 120 g's. The problem I had was that I didn't have money in the grant to do tests with big corporations. I heard that Dr. Lynn Weaver, the president of FIT, had friends in the DBA Corporation in Melbourne, so I called him and asked him if he could arrange such a test. He said he would. I told the president that this was the first space hardware that FIT was going to launch into space.

DBA arranged for a test using a slip table to simulate linear 120 g's force of impact and about 4 g's of random motion in the lateral direction. DBA engineers conducted the test while I was there in the theater with head sets on for protection against the loud sound. After the test was conducted, we hooked payload A to the Hewlett-Packard spectrum analyzer to see if everything was working fine, and indeed it was. This was an up ↑ thrill-of-research moment and a great relief.

We conducted a similar test at the Harris Corporation in Palm Bay for payload B. To my great relief, the result was similar to the test at DBA. Both tests at both corporations were free of charge, and I sent them letters of thanks.

Contacting the Autonomous University of Mexico City

Before I made any preparation for the rocket launch, I contacted the astronomy department at the Autonomous University of Mexico City. I had many conversations with the chair of the department, the late Professor Alfonso Serrano. Alfonso was a very likable person, and we had a good professional relationship, even though by that time we hadn't met face-to-face. We talked over the phone and many times used Dove Fax with my Mac computer. Faxing using a computer was hardly popular at this time. I used faxing to send him drawings that had info on the design of the instrument. Alfonso told me that I had the full support of the entire department and the Mexican equivalent of the NSF organization in Mexico City. He said that whatever I needed, they would gladly provide. Alfonso was in the field of galaxies, black holes, neutron stars, and so on, but he showed great interest in the total solar eclipse and could not wait to witness it.

Alfonso invited me to visit with him in preparation for the event. He also took it upon himself to get all the necessary permissions from the Interior Department of Mexico and had Betty Cruz, of the Mexican Interior Department, be the representative of that department for this operation. She had the responsibility of coordinating between the Mexican Navy and Air Force to clear the area on the day of the launch as well as the day before.

Alfonso told me this would be the first rocket launch that would climb to fifty miles above Earth in the history of Mexico. I was pleased to hear that.

SFA had contracted the Orbital Sciences Corporation to do the launch of the two rockets. The first rocket would be launched on the day before the eclipse to study the wind pattern and do a dry run. The second rocket would be used for the main event. The two rockets from the Orbital Sciences Corp. warehouse in Arizona were to be driven to Nogales on the US–Mexico border. The two rockets would end up in Tepik, the capital of Nayarit, Mexico. Betty Cruz did the coordination by bringing the Federales to escort the two rockets from the border of Mexico to Tepik. Later on, the Mexican television stations carried the news of the trip of the rockets as it took place.

In preparation for launching a rocket on the eclipse day, Jim Ralph (launch operation director of SFA) and I made two trips to Mexico. The first trip was to meet with Alfonso and Betty Cruz to go over the rocket trajectory, other aspects of the flight, and our needs. We talked about the eventual splashdown of the payload into the Pacific Ocean some twenty miles from the shore of Nayarit. They asked us if we needed any navy recovery of the payload. We did not, because we would be receiving the data from the payload via a US Air Force portable communications dish. SFA talked to the 45th Air Force Wing at Patrick Air Force Base at Cape Canaveral and acquired this portable dish on loan. We also discussed building a temporary launchpad for the rocket and decided to do that in the next trip. The hospitality of the Mexican officials was just unbelievable.

Betty Cruz also told us that there could be a security issue at the launchpad and that she would ask the army to send personnel to secure the area. The launchpad was going to be in a farming area, so many farmers would likely converge on the area, prompting the need for security check. She said once the word got out about the rocket launch, they would gather like flies to witness it. She also told us that the governor of Nayarit, Celso Humberto Delgado Ramírez, was a fan of eclipses and was very willing to give us complete support for our mission. She told us that we could bring as many people necessary for the operation and that the governor would accommodate them in the best hotel in the capitol city, Tepik, at no charge. I was so happy to hear these things that it definitely made me have a giant up ↑ thrill-of-research moment.

Selection of a Launchpad in Nayarit, Mexico

During our first trip to Mexico Cruz told us that we would meet some farmers who had land about ten miles from the Pacific shore. She suggested I ask them to donate part of their land to build the launchpad. She also assured us that one of them would volunteer for sure. So Jim Ralph and I went out to Mexico to iron out more details and select a place to construct a launchpad. Orbital Sciences Corporation told us that all they needed for a launchpad was a thick concrete pad, eight feet by eight feet. This requirement was the easiest one to expect for sure. Cruz and other officials took us in their military vehicles to an area about twenty miles from the Pacific Ocean. We met several of the farming community owners, and I gave a brief speech about what we wanted to do, which was translated to Spanish as I spoke. One farm owner asked how many acres we needed. I started laughing and said perhaps one or two acres with no trees on them. He then invited us to his house for a meal and offered to donate the acres we needed.

We were delighted and had a nice day with the farm owner and his family, and we thanked him very much. He gave us stakes to put for the area we select and Ms. Cruz and Dr. Serrano asked me to select the particular area I like. I did so and they said that they would pour the concrete for the launch pad. I was told much later after the launch that the governor of Nayarit made the spot of the Launchpad to be a small museum; I can't confirm that for sure because I never went there after the launch.

Problems with the Patched Antenna

The antenna and the transmitter of the Super Loki rocket payload were not suitable for the data to be acquired. So we need to do something else appropriate for the kind of data we need to get. I knew a graduate student at FIT Mr. Lee Caraway who was an expert in antennas. He suggested to me that we do a patched antenna at the bottom of the payload, a thin cylindrical patch approximately two inches in diameter. Luckily, a professor at FIT had ordered a new Hewlett-Packard spectrum analyzer for over $100,000. This wonderful instrument was a lifesaver for tuning our antenna. FIT was in no way like NASA or, for that matter, the private corporations that had every kind of equipment available.

I didn't know much about antennae, but I learned quite a bit from Caraway on how to tune an antenna and how delicate it could be. If a tiny portion of the patched antenna changed, the frequency would change dramatically. I had to spend many evenings late at work to check from time to time what the antenna was doing. To my big surprise, Carraway tinkered with the antenna slightly and showed me how quickly the frequency changed. Carraway succeeded in stabilizing the frequency at 1680 MHz for payload A. For payload B he had a lot of trouble centering it on the same frequency for reasons not known to me. This caused me to delay my departure to Mexico, while I sent the rest of the crew (four people) ahead of me. I recall staying up until midnight for at least three nights as I watched Caraway tinker until he finally stabilized it at the same frequency.

I was packed and ready for my flight to Mexico, and as soon as the frequency stabilized in the second payload, I rushed to the airport and flew to Nayarit. About twenty-nine people were waiting for me at the hotel in Tepik. Among them were the director of SFA, Ed O'Connor; Jim Ralph; engineers; and press personnel at SFA. I had the press person at FIT, Gwendolyn De'Court; my crew; the experiment manager, Dr. Eichhorn; and engineer Ramzi Nassar.

On the Mexican side there was Dr. Serrano, Betty Cruz, and many other Mexican Navy, Army, and security personnel. There were also a few American tourists in the area who had heard that there would be a rocket launch for the eclipse and had come to the hotel to get some info. The Mexican Army asked me if I wanted to allow the American tourists to attend the launch, and I said yes, so they were bussed with all of us to the site.

Calibrating the Backup Payload the Day Before the Eclipse

Because of the problems we encountered in tuning the antenna on the backup payload, we had no time to calibrate the backup instrument. Now for this instrument to be a true backup it had to be calibrated to be viable for launch. In my flight to Mexico, I carried the payload, a thirty-three-inch cylinder, by hand and had the calibration equipment in the luggage area of the plane. Dr. Eichhorn was waiting at the site of the launch for me to bring the instrument and the calibration equipment so he could perform the calibration. Talk about cutting it close! The calibration had to be done on the afternoon before launch day.

To get out of this mess, I called Jim Ralph before I left for Mexico to tell him that I was coming and needed to calibrate the instrument. He then called the governor of Nayarit and told him about the problem. The governor said no problem and offered his private plane. When I arrived at the Puerto Vallarta Airport, the governor's pilot was waiting for me with the private plane. When the pilot saw the calibration equipment, he realized that one of the seats on the plane had to be taken out in order to fit the equipment. In a few minutes he had mechanics take out a seat of the plane and fit the equipment. I was flabbergasted!

The pilot flew me to the launch site. The trip lasted about half hour, and I felt like a big celebrity. I asked myself, *Is this really happening?* I was also afraid, though, because it was only my second time on a small airplane, the first being the time I flew to Green Bank, West Virginia. The pilot noticed that and said, "Señor, there is nothing to worry about; this is a very safe plane." His words calmed my fears, and I told him gracias.

Explosion of the First Rocket

As soon as I arrived at the launch site, Dr. Eichhorn was waiting and ready to do the calibration. However, he first asked me if I'd heard what had happened today. I said no, and he pointed to some pieces of metal along the launchpad. He told me they were the remains of the first rocket that had been launched in a dry run to test the wind pattern. This ominous news was certainly a down ↓ thrill–of–research moment for me. I asked what happened, and he said as soon as the rocket launched, it exploded above the launchpad. People had to hurry to get out of the way.

I worked on the calibration with Dr. Eichhorn, and we finished it in time to go back to the hotel. I spoke to the manager of the launch operation for the Orbital Sciences Corporation about why the rocket exploded. He said these things happened sometimes, and he didn't know why! That evening everyone bombarded me with questions about why the rocket exploded and what was going to happen tomorrow with the second rocket. I told them I really didn't know but hoped things would work out tomorrow.

Questions to Be Answered before the Launch

We had three big banners at the launchpad, one for the Spaceport Florida Authority, one for the Autonomous University of Mexico City, and the third for the Florida Institute of Technology. The night before the launch I stayed up late wondering what was going to happen the next day and whether or not this huge effort by so many people was going to fail. Another worry arose when one of the engineers came to me and said that he had heard that they had discovered a crack in one of the fins of the rocket and were going to fill it with liquid aluminum locally. I still don't know whether that report was true or not. At this point, I had three major questions:

1. At what angle from the base of the pad should the rocket be launched?
2. At what altitude from the ground should the fuse be activated for the small explosive to detonate so the payload will shear the nose cone screws and go out in space?
3. Which payload should we launch, A or B?

I had done some calculations concerning these first two questions, but I had to finalize them that night. So I did some more calculations and more thinking about what I wanted to do and decided that the launch angle should be eighty-three degrees from the surface of the pad. This angle was well within the range of the Viper rocket, which Orbital Sciences Corporation had recommended to us. The Viper rocket was a slightly more powerful rocket than the Super Loki rocket. I also decided that the altitude at which the explosive would be detonated would be 223,000 feet, where I believed that the atmosphere would be too thin to affect the flight of the payload. I relayed these two choices to the director of launch operations of Orbital Sciences Corporation.

In any case, I woke up in the morning and thought that this would be a good day, a sort of jolt of optimism. I had not seen a total solar eclipse before in my life. I had seen partial solar eclipses and annular solar eclipses (where the apparent size of the moon is smaller than that of the sun) but not total. I was pretty nervous and could feel the weight of the responsibility I had on the outcome of that day. I had involved a lot of people and kept after them all the time, so we could meet this heavenly deadline. However, I was also excited about viewing the total solar eclipse, believe it or not.

The total solar eclipse was supposed to start a few minutes after noon. A military bus took us all to the launch site, and we arrived at approximately ten o'clock. I asked the director of launch how things were going, and he said it was great: the weather was great, and there was minimal wind. The sky was clear, and the sun was out. Birds were flying, and everything looked perfect, like the calm before a storm. I realized why Cruz wanted to have so many soldiers surrounding the launch site; I saw many farmers heading toward us, but the soldiers kept them in check. I told the people that the sun would be blocked, and the sky would go dark. The birds would try to hide, and the stars would come out for a little more than six minutes. I told them not to worry: the sun would come back!

I was told that I could decide which payload to launch no later than thirty minutes before the launch. So I kept both payloads operating and checked with the computer on all the functions too see which one was doing better. In fact both payloads were doing well, so I decided to go with payload A.

As the big event approached, everybody was getting excited, especially Dr. Alfonso Serrano. He, like me, had not seen a total solar eclipse before. As the time approached, the rocket was situated in the upright position and readied for launch. The anticipation on everybody's face is not easy to portray with words. Almost all the attendees shook my hand and wished me great luck. I responded that I really needed it.

The governor of Nayarit was in his helicopter hovering quite a distance from the launchpad. Finally the moment came, and the moon started chipping away at the disc of the sun. The birds started flying or fleeing, sort of anticipating something to happen. The horses at the nearby farms were feeling uneasy and moving around a lot, especially when we approached totality. Dr. Serrano lay on his back in the dirt and shook his legs and arms, laughing so loud and saying, "I have not seen anything like this!" It was a wonderful feeling to see him do that.

I was looking at my special watch given to me by Orbital Sciences Corporation's director of launch, while he waited for my hand signal to launch the rocket. The flight of the rocket took about two minutes to reach apogee, or the highest point of its climb. So I had to arrange the launch time so that the payload would come out when the totality set in. I gave the hand signal, and the Viper rocket roared. A big cloud of fumes ensued, and the rocket disappeared quickly from our sight. Gunther Eichhorn was inside the launch van and at the controls of the Motorola VME-10 advanced computer bus, which I'd paid $10,000 from my grants to get. He was ready to receive the data and quite excited. He was wearing a T-shirt that said "We did at the South Pole and now in Mexico." His reference to the South Pole was when he went there to observe the 1987 supernova, which I mentioned earlier.

The moment of truth was upon us, and I could see the engineers moving the air force dish to receive the signals in a sort of frantic way. Jim Ralph said to me, "Look … look! You are getting the data." I was not so sure, so I walked to the engineers operating the dish. They gave me the bad news that we were getting no data whatsoever. This confirmed my worst fear. I thought there should be at least some signal coming from the payload, perhaps not data but at least the beacon signal that was built in to let us know that the transmitter was working.

Chapter 14

The First Rocket Launch in Mexico's History

Rocket Failure

Can a rocket failure make someone cry? Yes. I walked onto the launchpad and cried like a baby. Dr. Gunther Eichhorn, the manager of the experiment, approached me and put his arm around my shoulder. He said, "I share your grief. This was a long journey, and many people put a lot of time and effort into this." I couldn't help but think of the people involved in NASA's major space missions and how they must feel when something goes wrong; perhaps it was much bigger and more lasting than my feelings. The Mexican officials at the launch gathered around me and said they'd arranged for a big celebration. They said they were going to take everybody to an island and cook fish for dinner and drink a lot of Pacífico beer!

A few hours later, I recovered fairly quickly, especially after having couple of Pacífico beers. The Mexican hosts were gracious and hospitable and tried to make me feel far away from what had happened that day.

Ed O'Connor, the director of SFA, told me not to worry. He said they were going to have many launches in the future and I would be leading the way of course. All these statements made me feel better. Gwendolyn De'Court, FIT's publicist, had arranged for a phone hookup to the launch area with the newspaper *Florida Today*. I made a brief statement, saying that my heart was broken for the failure of getting any data on the sun's corona. It was published the next day with my photo holding the instrument.

If there was anything that could take away from the sinking feeling I had that day, it was the Mexican hospitality with the dinner, the boat ride, and the island tour. However, another major factor was the few bottles of Pacífico beer, which definitely can help in a situation like this. Jim Ralph, the director of launch operation at SFA, said that I was suffering from launch trauma, and to a certain extent he was right.

The Search for the Rocket Payload

The following day we conducted one news conference with the Mexican media. They asked many questions, and they were after me to say what went wrong and whether I wanted to blame anybody. I told them that the advent of microelectronics was the key that we relied on to do this experiment. As far as who was to blame, I really couldn't say, because I didn't have any facts in front of me. That evening Dr. Serrano and I did a TV interview on one of the Mexican channels, which in a way was hilarious because of the language problem. The questions were given to us first in Spanish and then translated into English for me. Dr. Serrano answered in Spanish, and then his answers were translated into English so that I could understand. Similarly, my answers were in English and then were translated to Spanish. But through it all we came out fine, believe it or not!

Betty Cruz asked the military to search for the rocket and the payload. The Mexican Army walked in files for about five miles in a fan like formation away from the launchpad looking for any pieces of the rocket or payload. The Mexican Navy also searched the waters looking for floating objects. I was told that neither the army or the navy found anything.

Until this day I still cannot believe that a rocket and its payload can disappear like that without a trace. However, over the next two days the search continued and extended, but they still came out with nothing. It may be noteworthy that Orbital Sciences Corporation was also involved in the search. I examined the videotape of the launch, and I could see that the rocket began to veer a little bit to the right before it disappeared in the video due to some clouds. I honestly don't know what this means though.

I heard many rumors that Orbital Sciences Corporation knew what had happened but did not want to tell us. Their official story was that the launch was successful but the payload failed, which is not out of the realm of being true. But since we couldn't find a piece of anything, I remain skeptical about the outcome and what really went wrong. Certainly, the fact that the rocket the day before exploded on the launchpad did not help matters at all. Added to this was the rumor that one of the fins of the rocket that was launched on the day of the eclipse had a crack that they filled with liquid aluminum locally. The fact there was no beacon signal from the instrument was puzzling too.

Jim Ralph went to Arizona to meet with the personnel of Orbital Sciences Corporation and talked to them about what had happened in Mexico. He told me that they took him to a hangar where he saw pieces of the first rocket that had exploded. He also said they had an adjacent hanger. He asked to go there to look for pieces from the second rocket, but they said no, that there was nothing there. Jim was skeptical and thought that they were covering something up. In any case all of these speculations didn't help me much; the fact remained that I didn't get any data, no matter how good or bad it would have been, from the total solar eclipse. I stayed after the launch as a guest of the governor of Nayarit at a Puerto Vallarta resort for three days. That was a timely perk to get me over my sorrow. I sent my thanks to the governor through the resort personnel.

Going Back to the United States

I flew back to Houston, Texas, and walked through airport security carrying payload B, the aluminum cylinder thirty-three inches long and two inches in diameter. The security officers never asked me what I was carrying! Jim Ralph bet me they would never let me pass through in Houston carrying payload B because it looked like a pipe bomb! I couldn't believe I won the bet and that they didn't question me about what I was carrying, but those were the days before 9/11. Nonetheless it was still astonishing!

A year after the scientific adventure in Mexico, Jim Ralph called me and said he wanted me to make a dummy payload because the Mexicans wanted to put it in their newly constructed space museum. I had a small amount of money left in the grant, and I asked the machine shop in FIT to make one and send it to Mexico City. I made another trip to Mexico City but did not have the time to confirm the existence of the payload in the space museum. I have no reason to doubt its existence, and I hope to go there sometime and see if it's there.

A Dinner in My Honor by SFA and TRDA

I was surprised when Jim Ralph called me and said they were having a dinner at the Holiday Inn in my honor for what I accomplished in Mexico. He said I would be sitting at a table with Congressman Jim Bacchus and the directors of SFA and TRDA. Most of the employees in SFA and the board members of TRDA that funded the rocket experiment attended the dinner. The director of SFA, Ed O'Connor, and the executive director of TRDA made speeches about the rocket mission in Mexico and my accomplishments. They also said that this was just the beginning and that if I wanted to, I would be doing more rocket experiments in the near future with their support. This was a really nice gesture, and it made me feel better about what I'd done, even though it wasn't successful in the end.

Chasing Total Solar Eclipses

The failure to get any data in Mexico made me more eager to try it again, and at times it became an obsession with me, I'm afraid! The next total solar eclipse would be viewable from the Atlantic Ocean, so I contacted the Naval Research Office of the US Navy. I asked them if they would be interested in launching a Super Loki rocket from one of their ships in the Atlantic Ocean during a total solar eclipse. They said they would look into it and get back to me. A few days later I got a call from them saying that they were interested but the costs were enormous. They said it cost about $300,000 every day for the ship to sail into the area of the eclipse totality in the Atlantic Ocean. This fact of course dampened my hopes completely. I was mostly pursuing this because I still had payload B ready to go, and I had been charging the batteries on it weekly.

I looked for other possibilities of total solar eclipses, on land, but nothing was close in time, and I had to give up the idea completely. Little did I know that payload B would make another flight several years later but for another reason.

Inviting a Mexican Delegation to FIT to Discuss Collaborations

After the rocket experiment in 1991, Dr. Alfonso Serrano developed a great interest in building SEEC class instruments like the one we flew in Mexico. He asked me to send him all the blueprints of how to build the instrument, and I did. He asked his optics team at the department of astronomy to study these blueprints and improve on them. I also asked my friend Dr. Frank Giovanni to visit him in Mexico City and meet with his optics team. I paid for Dr. Frank Giovanni's travel expenses with an NSF-funded travel grant that I had. I told Jim Ralph at SFA that I intended to invite Dr. Serrano and others to visit FIT and talk about doing future collaborations with Mexico. Jim immediately said that SFA would pay for their travel expenses and their stay in Melbourne, Florida. Dr. Serrano had financed almost all of our stay and meals and so on in Mexico, so Jim was returning the hospitality. Dr. Serrano, Betty Cruz (representing the Mexican Interior Department), and a female student of Dr. Serrano's flew to Melbourne for the visit. (See the photo from that meeting.)

Representatives from UCF

The engineering department at UCF heard about this meeting at FIT. Dr. Jerry Ventre of the UCF engineering department contacted me and said he wanted to attend the meeting with the dean of UCF's college of engineering, Dr. Gary Whitehouse, who later became the provost of UCF. When Ventre, a space scientist, joined UCF, he brought with him a major research grant of perhaps $2.5 million. Ventre and Whitehouse were both present at the meeting, and after several presentations by the Mexican guests, the SFA director, and me, we started discussing collaborations. The fact that representatives from UCF attended the meeting made me feel very good, meaning that several institutions were interested in what I was doing. The only thing that came out of this meeting was that the Mexicans, FIT, and I agreed to continue collaborations. Dr. Jerry Ventre expressed his admiration of my work and the instrument that I came up with to observe the solar corona. Jerry Ventre's praise played a major role later on in my moving out of FIT and joining UCF.

The Mexican delegation at FIT meeting. Bottom row from left to right: Betty Cruz, Alfonso Serrano, Nebil Misconi, Jim Ralph, and a Mexican student. Upper row from left to right: Jerry Ventre, Ramzi Nassar, Pavo Sepri, Robert Sullivan, Gary Whitehouse, and Edward O'Conner.

A few months later, Dr. Serrano invited me to visit the Autonomous University of Mexico City. This university was the biggest in the world and had 250,000 students at that time. It occupied many city blocks. He also welcomed other officials from FIT to come with me to establish formal agreements on collaborations. So I asked the Dean of FIT's College of Engineering, Dr. Robert Sullivan, to go, and he agreed. Bob Krieger, chairman of the board of TRDA and the owner of Orbit Publishing Company, expressed his interest in going with us. He said he would pay his own way, and I welcomed the idea. This time I decided to take my wife, Irene, and my son, Michael, on the trip for I wanted them to see a neighboring country.

Dr. Serrano was the ultimate host, and we held meetings with the dean of the College of Engineering of the Autonomous University of Mexico City. Both sides expressed their willingness to collaborate on future space missions. However, there were no concrete resolutions made or specific commitments, to my surprise; I expected to see more done in these meetings. Dr. Sullivan, the dean at FIT, told me that he would convey these exchanges with the Mexicans to the president of FIT and see if he could get some funds to do experiments with the Mexicans.

After we returned to Melbourne, Dr. Serrano contacted me and said he would send a Mexican student to visit with me, as he was getting him involved in space research with us. The student gave me a Mexican purchase order for $4,500 to purchase the latest PC computer in the US market at the time. He said we could use this computer for designs of instruments and other calculations for mutual benefits. So I bought a Dynamic Micro 486 computer with 50 MHz clock speed, which was state of the art at the time. I started using that computer, and when Dr. Serrano told me he needed it, I would ship it to him.

Unfortunately, future collaborations never materialized with Dr. Serrano for in 1992 he became the director of the Institute for Astrophysics, Optics, and Electronics. Perhaps this appointment gave him new responsibilities away from space science. Later on he spearheaded the Large Millimeter Telescope constructed in Mexico. Alfonso was a well-known astronomer and astrophysicist in Mexico and abroad and controversial at times. I remember him telling me that he did not get along well with Conacyt, the equivalent of NSF in Mexico. Our contact with him began to fade away, and although I continued talking to him over the phone, I never saw him again. Unfortunately he passed away in 2011 from pancreatic cancer. I developed a good working relationship with Dr. Serrano, and I have fond memories of it. One of these memories that sticks out in my mind is when he gave me a large, strangely shaped bottle of Mexican vodka that had a warm inside. He told me we would drink this bottle of vodka together on the border between the United States and Mexico. We never had the chance to do it, but I always remember that.

The Governor of Nayarit Visits Florida

The Spaceport Florida Authority continued to further the relationship with Mexico that I started with my solar-eclipse launch. However, this time I was left out of the loop for reasons that I do not understand still to this day. They took Governor Celso Humberto Delgado Ramírez and his entourage to the Florida Panhandle and invited Florida Governor Bob Martinez to be with the Mexican governor. SFA wanted to establish a launchpad in the Florida Panhandle for Super Loki rockets and perhaps other bigger solid-fuel rockets. The area they selected was in Cape San Blas. I read all this in the Florida newspapers, but I never knew any details as SFA had stopped contacting me. If I remember correctly, they did launch a couple of rockets from Cape San Blas, but I am not sure of the details or the outcomes.

Payload B from the eclipse experiment stayed in my office for many years, and I continued to recharge its rechargeable batteries in hopes to fly it someday!

Chapter 15

Adventures in doing
Research with High Returns

Answering the Call from Dr. Donald Brownlee

I was in touch with Dr. Donald Brownlee, who was the chief scientist of NASA's *Stardust* space probe, which collected cometary dust and returned to Earth. Dr. Brownlee was one of two reviewers (I don't know the identity of the second one) who looked at a contributed paper that I wrote on the spin of cosmic dust. The paper was published in the *Journal of Geophysical Research*. In that paper I had a section on previous observations that found accumulations of dust at certain distances from the sun, which I referred to as perhaps temporary dust rings around the sun. Dr. Brownlee then suggested I explain why there would be dust rings around the sun theoretically.

While I was thinking about Dr. Brownlee's suggestion, it so happened that I got a master's degree student at FIT to advise, Laura E. Pettera. So I made the theoretical paper for explaining the possible dust rings her thesis project. My theory was that as the protons from the sun impacted the dust particles, they slowed them down, what I called *ion-drag*. Since the magnitude of the ion–drag (or proton–drag) differed with the size of the dust particles, a bunching up of particles of similar size created a sort of density wave that looked like a dust ring.

I gave Laura the computer program that I was using and asked her to modify it to do the calculations on this project. She ran the calculations on the computer, and we reviewed them together.

However, suddenly Laura left to Arizona without informing me about her plans and before she finished her degree. I still don't know what prompted her to do that. I wrote the paper and submitted it for publication to *Planetary and Space Science Journal* and put her name as a second author on the paper. I never heard from Laura and could not send her a copy of the paper, since I had no address for her. I sent a copy to Dr. Brownlee and thanked him for making the suggestion that resulted in an interesting paper.

The Gas-Grain Simulation Facility (GGSF) Proposed for the International Space Station

As my enthusiasm for observing total solar eclipses faded away, I began to go back to my original research in the spin of interplanetary dust particles. I read an announcement from NASA that they were going to build a facility that would fly on the International Space Station (ISS). They called this facility the Gas–Grain Simulation Facility (GGSF). This facility would do experiments to study the interaction between dust particles or grains and photons, and the plasma in space, i.e. protons, electrons, and some heavy nuclei. I realized that this was a golden opportunity for me to study the spin of particles from space. I immediately called Dr. Judith Huntington, who was NASA's person for this facility. After a few phone calls I managed to explain to her exactly what I wanted to do, and she was supportive of my ideas. A couple of weeks later, Judith called me and said NASA was going to have a conference on the GGSF facility at the Desert Research Institute in Las Vegas. *My God, They Couldn't Have Selected a Better Place Than That!*

Judith also asked me if I wanted to be a chairperson for one of the sessions of the meeting that dealt with spectroscopy. I immediately agreed and said it was an honor. Between fifty to sixty scientists from all over the United States and Europe attended the conference. Before attending the conference, I sent Judith a summary of the experiment that I intended to do using the proposed GGSF facility on the ISS. I then received in the mail a booklet on the conference, and to my delight my experiment was on the "strawman" payload of the GGSF, meaning my experiment was among those initially picked to be on the payload of the facility. It was a great start for having your experiment approved by the NASA-appointed Science Working Group (SWG) for that facility. There is an SWG for every space mission.

The organizers of the meeting arranged for exhibit places in the hallways of the large building. I took this opportunity and brought my videotapes of laser particle levitations that I did in Gainesville. I couldn't display the laser particle levitations from the Goddard Space Flight Center because they were photographed in 8 mm Kodak film, which was a type of photography that was no longer used. The levitation videotapes attracted many curious scientists who were attending the meeting, and they asked me many questions about it.

Offer to Become Director of the Desert Research Institute

The meeting lasted a whole week, five days of meetings filled with presentations *and a weekend for gambling!* During the week I noticed an ad displayed in the institute for getting a new director. Later some of the people who worked at the Desert Research Institute talked to me about the possibility of me becoming the new director of the institute. I normally never said no to any proposition like that before giving it some thought. This one didn't take long, though. The next day I told them I didn't have any intention of doing that, because I was happy doing what I was doing. Can you imagine my dedication to research on soft money? Here I was being offered a secure job on hard money, and I turned it down. I felt as if maybe I should see a psychiatrist!

I simply enjoyed my research very much and was strongly dedicated to it. Plus I was optimistic about the GGSF facility. If

I could get my experiment on the GGSF facility, I would have continuous funding for at least ten to fifteen years and a team of scientists, engineers, and graduate students to keep me busy perhaps close to retirement age. Research on soft money was most difficult when I was trying to string along series of grants of the order of $50,000 or $100,000 and needed several of them to pay my salary.

I met Dr. Fogelman, a high up in the administration of the GGSF. He saw the videos of my laser particle levitation and encouraged me to submit an introductory proposal to his office of the order of $350,000. I was delighted to hear that. I was riding so high during this trip to Las Vegas because I thought that the GGSF was going to enable me to do the research I'd been dreaming of for a long time, along with financial stability. On the final day of the conference, each chairperson gave his concluding remarks about his session. I was happy to see that Dr. Mayo Greenberg (my former teacher) was in the audience, and we chatted after the meeting adjourned. Mayo had some colleagues with him and wanted to go gambling in the casinos with me. However, in the commotion after the meeting adjourned I lost where they were, so I had to go alone to gamble.

Scientists Gambling in Las Vegas

I'm sure some of the scientists sneaked out in the evenings and gambled in the casinos. No one can blame them really; they are human after all! I had too much to do during the week being a chairperson, so I saved the casinos for the weekend. I am also sure that some of the scientists did not gamble at all because they thought it was silly or were too involved in their research. With gambling you should call it quits if you win. If you don't, you'll likely lose your winnings and perhaps start losing your own money as well. That was exactly what happened to me that night. I won a modest $150, and because I needed to stay up to catch a flight at five o'clock in the morning, I continued playing. I lost my winnings and lost another $100. However, as gamblers often say, I had fun doing that.

A Great Setback, Delivered to Us by NASA

I went back to Melbourne and got busy writing the proposal that Dr. Fogleman had suggested. At the same time everyone who had an experiment on the strwman payload received three volumes from the TRW Corporation, which was supposed to build the GGSF facility, asking us to review their plans to see if they satisfied each scientist's facility requirements. I worked hard to review these volumes and make recommendations for necessary changes. The chief engineer of the GGSF facility sent me a letter thanking me for all the suggestions I made. Judith told me that she was impressed by my suggestions and that few of the scientists who attended the meeting did any of that. Maybe they knew something that I didn't!

In any case, by the time I finished the proposal and mailed it to Dr. Fogelman's office, horrible news came down the pike: NASA had canceled the GGSF facility for financial reasons. NASA said that the cost of building the centrifuge for the ISS was becoming too big, and the centrifuge was an essential component of the American part of the ISS. I talked to Dr. Judith Huntington about this terrible news and suggested that I write a generic letter to all the user scientists of the GGSF asking them to write letters to NASA asking for the reinstatement of this facility. She thought that was a great idea and may put pressure on NASA. So I wrote a generic letter and mailed it to approximately fifty to sixty scientists. I got some responses from them and copies of their letters to NASA, but I was disappointed that not all of them responded. Perhaps they knew it would fall on deaf ears.

Then more surprising news came: NASA asked the European Space Agency to build the GGSF facility. They also asked us to team up with European astronomers to use the facility. I got several e-mails from NASA's Ames Research Center, encouraging me to collaborate with the Europeans to do my experiment. This to me was a nonstarter because it would be difficult to coordinate with the Europeans and build my experiment and fly it on their GGSF. When I was at SAL, we had some bad experiences collaborating with European scientists and not just because we had trouble communicating with them. It was hard to do our own experiments with other scientists who sometimes had different ideas about how to go about doing it. There was also the question as to who should take the lead. That was the nature of the beast!

I did not contact anybody concerning the GGSF in Europe, and on top of that my proposal was denied funding because it was only useful to NASA if I teamed up with the Europeans. I had good relationships with the European astronomers in my field; however, that didn't make it practical to team up with them on an experiment like this one. These developments ended an exciting chapter in my research career that would have been phenomenal.

Going to the Moon!

This adventure was probably the most exciting prospect in my entire career. I met Dr. David Webb, who had a PhD in political science, in a meeting to elect Ed O'Connor director of SFA. We both voted for him. If I may digress here, I really get angry when I hear the words *political science*. How can politics be a science? In my opinion that is really an insult to science. But this has no reflection on David Webb; David was a great gentleman, and his specialty was space policy. At one time he was a professor at the University of Central Florida, and he and Dr. Joan Johnson Freeze (also in space policy) established an institute for space policy at UCF. David Webb contacted me about a proposed mission to the moon called the Lunar Prospector mission. We decided to discuss it over lunch in Melbourne.

David told me about Gregg Maryniak, who was president of a large movement to continue going to the moon. David said a lot of these people were Trekkies and *Star Wars* fans. He also said that they had contacted some of the moon scientists who were idle from the discontinued Apollo program and looking for things to do. The Maryniak group contacted Dr. Alan Binder, who was from the Lunar Research Institute and had been principal investigator on the Viking mission to Mars. Binder had directed the construction of a gamma-ray detector to search for buried water on the moon's poles. The detector was supposed to fly on one of the canceled Apollo missions, so now Binder had a good instrument but no way to the moon.

David said they were looking for a university that would adopt this project and put out some money that would be matched by the Gregg Maryniak organization. They would collect donations from all the members of the movement to match whatever the university put in.

David also told me that if I wanted to, I could head this mission. I thanked David for this tip and promised him that I would get back to him after I gave it some thought. I talked to Dr. Marshall Kaplan, who was the director of the Space Research Institute (SRI) at FIT, and asked that our conversation be confidential. He asked me if he could talk to the vice president of research, Dr. Alan Mense, and I said yes. I then thought about what was in it for me to do this major mission. The answer came to me a day later: if I could piggyback a small satellite on top of the Lunar Prospector probe, then I could observe the sun through multiple total solar eclipses with the Earth's favorable alignment. I remembered hearing one of the Apollo astronauts talk about seeing these eclipses while the mission was orbiting the moon. I got so excited that I slept very little that night.

I called David and told him that I was very much willing to do what he suggested. David was surprised at my determination. I explained the observations I could do with solar eclipses, and then he understood my excitement. I organized two major meetings at FIT with the scientists and engineers from Houston, Texas, headed by Dr. Alan Binder. The first meeting was to acquaint ourselves with this new team. I was surprised to see that Dr. James French[3], a well-

---

[3] Dr. James French co-authored a book "Space Vehicle Design" wit Dr. Michael Griffin who became NASA Administrator few years ago. I taught this book several times while I was at UCF.

known aerospace engineer in the Apollo days, and the Lockheed Martin Skunk Works rocket-propulsion team came to the meeting. Marshal Kaplan, an aerospace engineer, was very impressed to see Jim French in the meeting.

I told Alan Binder's team my intention of flying another mini-satellite piggybacked on the probe to observe the eclipses, and he said he had no problem with that whatsoever. We decided to have another meeting where we would structure the leadership and responsibilities of each person on this mission. Another important issue to discuss was how to go about financing the mission. I thought it was time to involve Jerry Weinberg. I talked to Jerry over the phone, and he was shocked to hear about what I was planning to do. I still remember him saying, "Are you sure you want to be the director of this mission? I don't question your qualifications, but do you know what kind of life you would be leading?" He said I'd be getting about fifty faxes a day and would hardly see my wife and son! I said this was a chance in a century, and he agreed. Jerry happily attended the second meeting.

The second meeting took place at a convention center at the Hilton Hotel in Melbourne. At least twenty to thirty people attended. I had prepared charts showing the organization for the mission.

I put myself as the director of the mission and explained the building of the satellite that would piggyback on the prospector instrument. I also said that FIT was ready to deposit $150,000 in the bank to be matched by donations from Gregg Maryniak's group. Dr. Alan Binder questioned why FIT had the directorship of the mission. Marshal Kaplan immediately said that FIT was putting out the gold! I asked Alan why he was so concerned about who was the director and responsible for the success of the mission. I told him I had the backing of the university, and he sort of nodded in agreement.

I sensed in the second meeting that the commitment to this mission was sort of wavering. The killing statement came from Gregg Maryniak toward the end of the meeting. He said, "You can have this mission all to yourself, and we will support you." We adjourned with the idea to meet again in the near future. Jerry told me at the end of the meeting that he had doubts about this mission, and he said FIT's contribution of $150,000 was nothing. I agreed with him and said nobody had consulted me about the amount they were going to offer. I then met with Dr. Alan Mense, the vice president for research at FIT, and told him that this mission, if it took place, would put FIT on the map nationwide. Mense agreed but said the university was not ready to take on a mission like this. FIT didn't have the capital or the infrastructure to handle something this magnanimous. He was right, and my great dream dissipated, sad to say.

There were no more meetings after that, and I told Dr. Alan Binder over the phone that I didn't think we could go through with this mission. In 1995, NASA chose the Lunar Prospector to be the first peer-reviewed, competitively selected mission in its new low-cost Discovery Program of Lunar and Planetary Missions. Alan Binder became the manager and mission director of all phases of the $65 million mission. The probe was launched to the moon on January 6, 1998, and conducted a nineteen-month orbital mapping mission of the moon. Dr. Binder was also the principal investigator and manager of the $4.4 million Lunar Prospector data–analysis program. I heard later that FIT in all its facets was a $65 million operation. When I heard all this, I told myself that sometimes you could reach for the gold and not get it. This was a profound and the greatest down ↓ thrill-of research-moment for me.

Chapter 16

Meeting Nobel Prizewinner Professor Hewish

Constructing the Interplanetary Scintillation Array (IPS) to Warn of Solar Storms

D
r. Ernest Hildner, the director of the space environment laboratory at Boulder, Colorado, invited me to give a talk and stay a couple of days to discuss research collaborations. This was my first trip to Colorado, and it was an interesting one. I was amazed by the thin air in Boulder, which I noticed as I walked the streets. The thing that blew my mind was the fascinating view when I ate lunch in the cafeteria. On one side there was a humongous supercomputer inside of a glass-enclosed area, and on the other side were mountains. Words cannot describe the feeling I got when I saw these two things.

In any case I gave my talk the next day. About twenty scientists attended, and the talk, "Plasma-Dust Interactions Near the Sun," was received pretty well and generated interest among the scientists, whose specialties were in the area of solar terrestrial interaction and the space environment as a whole. When I was a graduate student, I remember I read several articles on *interplanetary scintillation* (IPS) and how it could be used to forecast the onset of solar storms heading toward Earth. IPS takes place when strong radio sources in the universe send out their radio signals and they scintillate during the passage of plasma (free electrons, protons, and heavy nuclei in a rarefied gas or very low number density) from a solar flare interacting with those signals. We can define IPS as the random variations of apparent intensity of a radio source caused by the diffraction of the wave front as it propagates through the random variations in refractive index in the turbulent interplanetary medium (IPM). Hewish, Scott, and Willis (1964) were the first to recognize this.

Ernest Hildner Looking for a Research Saint!

Dr. Ernest Hildner wanted me to see how they were analyzing the data that they got from an IPS array located near the large Jodrell Bank radio telescope in the United Kingdom. I realized that the data was very noisy and that it would be difficult to get any meaningful data. I also realized that perhaps Jodrell Bank was too high in latitude and was affected by the northern lights. I told Ernie that I believed if we constructed an IPS array at lower latitudes like in Florida or in the Bahamas, then things would be different. Ernie said they'd been frustrated with this data and he'd been waiting for a dedicated researcher, a "researcher saint" in his words, like me to take the lead in getting this forecast to work. Ernie opened a new area of research for me to work on.

The onset of geomagnetic activity and ionospheric disturbances more often than not leads to the disruption of global radio and television traffic for military as well as commercial applications. They cause severe damage to electrical power equipment and telephones. In space, the propagating IPM disturbances and the resulting geomagnetic activity can perturb spacecraft orbits (drag radiation). Humans in space (and even airplanes travelers) are subjected to higher levels of radiation during such events. In short, geomagnetic storms disrupt communications, cause electric blackouts and damage to electrical power equipment, degrade satellite orbits and pointing of the satellite in space, disturb space-borne surveillance, decrease radio navigation's system accuracies, and so on.

Dr. Hildner told me that in order to forecast a solar storm, we had to rely on Earth-orbiting satellites, which could only give us a warning of one hour, which was not enough for power companies to send their people to protect transformers and prevent blackouts. A satellite like that, in those days, cost $200 million, whereas a permanent IPS array (a system of many antennas placed in rows on the ground and tuned specifically for this purpose) would cost perhaps $1 million to construct.

An IPS array could monitor some 1,200 radio sources. So basically there was no comparison between the costs of an IPS array versus a satellite. Also an IPS array could give a warning of more than six hours versus only one hour for the satellite. This is because an IPS array can detect a solar storm somewhat close to the sun, and it takes time for the storm to travel to Earth. Normally a solar-flare-associated storm will take roughly about sixty-nine hours to propagate from the sun to Earth.

The only major drawback of forecasting using an IPS array is that it cannot tell the direction of the interplanetary magnetic field, meaning + (up) or − (down). One of these directions does not harm the power companies' equipment; the other does. This means that the power company personnel would be going out to protect the transformers not knowing whether it was needed or not. At the time we had no solution to this problem. Still because of the small expense of building an IPS array and its longevity compared to satellites, it was still a good idea.

I went back to Melbourne, thinking, *Here I go again, branching into a whole new field, constructing a radio array.* A few days later, Ernie called me and said that he'd heard there was an island in the Bahamas purely dedicated for research, Lee Stocking Island. He said it may be a good candidate for an IPS array. He also asked me to write a brief proposal so that he could give me a grant of $20,000 to do some traveling. I went to work and wrote a short proposal, and indeed he sent me the $20,000 grant. I started thinking about how I could utilize this money in the best way possible. My colleague Dr. Michael Thursby at FIT was fascinated with the whole idea of building an IPS radio array observatory. Mike was an electrical engineer specializing in antennae among other things, and he was a perfect fit for my project.

At my invitation, Dr. Hildner and my good friends Dr. Murray Dryer and Dr. Yeh, all members of SEL, visited FIT for three days to talk about collaborations. The first evening I invited them to my house. They met my wife and my son, and we had a nice evening. After the visit, Dr. Hildner said he would give me complete support for building an IPS array in every way, except funding it, because they were not a funding agency. So once again I was writing proposals to funding agencies.

Michael Thursby's Meeting with Professor A. Hewish, a Nobel Prize Winner

With my grant money from Dr. Hildner, I decided to send Michael Thursby to England to Jodrell Bank to meet with radio astronomer Professor A. Hewish. Hewish had been the first to recognize the phenomenon of interplanetary scintillation in his radio survey of the sky (Hewish, Scott, and Willis 1964). Hewish won the Nobel Prize in Physics in 1974 (together with fellow radio astronomer Martin Ryle). He won it for his work on the development of radio aperture synthesis and its role in the discovery of pulsars. Hewish and Duffett-Smith had constructed an IPS array, and he was sharing his data with the space environment laboratory in Boulder. I asked Thursby to make sure that he talked to Duffett-Smith, who ran the array, to get all the details on how that array was constructed since we may do some improvements. Thursby had lengthy discussions with Hewish and even more with Duffett-Smith. Thursby told me that he was going to use YAG antennae since they were better suited. He also suggested other improvements on what they had at Jodrell Bank.

An IPS Array in the Bahamas

If we were going to build an IPS array, it needed to be the proper size to gather the maximum amount of information. For many reasons that are beyond the scope of this book, Thursby and I decided to propose building a 33,800 square- meter array that would have 4,096 antenna elements on a piece of land to be determined later. The labor would be intensive, which made it a perfect project for students to be involved in building and learning. Incidentally, this wasn't going to be the first IPS array to be built in Florida (as we envisioned first before considering the Bahamas). Professor Tom Carr from the UF astronomy department at Gainesville, Florida, built a radio array and was the first to discover that there were weak radio waves coming from Jupiter.

Lee Stocking Island was privately owned and leased to the Perry Institute for Marine Science (PIMS), a nonprofit organization based in Florida since 1970. PIMS operated a tropical marine laboratory located on LSI in the central Bahamas. I liked this island because its unique, remote location offered excellent opportunities for scientific research and education programs. It was in a marine environment that had been minimally impacted by humans. I told Michael Thursby to contact them and ask if we could establish an IPS array on the island. The answer we got was a definite yes.

Using my $20,000 grant, I made arrangements for Michael Thursby and me to travel to Lee Stocking Island to choose a site for our IPS observatory. There were hardly any people there, only researchers and graduate students. Michael and I searched the island thoroughly and picked the spot to place the IPS array. While we were there, I swam at one of the beaches; the water was so clear I could see the fish. The swim was really wonderful.

Michael and I decided that the best approach to this was to propose for a test array instead of the full array. This way the funding request would be lot less, and chances are good that we could get more funding after we showed successes with the test array. I thought the best place to request the funding was from the NSF Solar Terrestrial Program, which had funded me earlier in 1990 as I mentioned previously. Our first proposal was declined because they don't fund experimental research, only theoretical. They suggested that I submit a proposal to a different division in NSF called Upper Atmospheric Facilities. Usually, this program funded the construction of observatories. I was also told unofficially that I was not really into the Solar Terrestrial Program's areas of research! This was one of the turf battles in research; they circled the wagons once an outsider came in to get funding from their program.

Scientists who did research on dust particles, like me, had a similar problem with NASA. There was a saying that "The dust research proposals fall through the cracks of NASA." Ernest Hildner (SEL Director) had warned me earlier that I might have problems getting funding from an area that was not in my own turf. This was sort of strange to me because my PhD thesis was titled "Solar Flare Effects on the Zodiacal Light." Hildner told me it wasn't the solar flare but the dust that was giving me a problem. Basically the scientists proposing to the Solar Terrestrial Program were physicists and did not have traditional training in astronomy. My good friend Dr. Murray Dryer, whose friendship I still cherish to this day, told me the same thing as Dr. Hildner about turf battles. Murray offered to help in the next proposal and to go over it thoroughly and make comments. As a result, I went on a mission to study everything there was that the scientists in the Solar Terrestrial field, that the NSF program was funding had published, so I went on a reading spree before writing the new proposal.

When I finally finished the proposal, it was the biggest and most complete proposal I'd ever written. Michael and I ruled out the idea of building the IPS array on Lee Stocking Island because of the logistics and costs of sending people there back and forth to build the array. Ernie Hildner said it would be helpful if I could guarantee that FIT would supply the land for the array. I contacted the president of FIT, and he wrote a strong letter guaranteeing that FIT would supply the land. I included the letter at the beginning of the proposal. The total cost of the budget was close to $200,000.

I submitted the proposal, and after few months I got a letter that declined funding. This was shocking news to me because I'd spent at least six months working on that proposal. So this was another down ↓ thrill-of-research moment. On top of that the reviewers' comments were astonishing to me. Almost all of the reviewers said that the proposal was too long. Some reviewers said that the letter from the president of FIT wasn't strong enough, so they didn't know if he was really committed to giving the land, which amazed me. You'd think after all this that I would quit, but no.

Another Connection with Mexico

While I was writing the previous proposal for the array, I referenced Mexican scientist Dr. Silvia Bravo, who was well respected in that field. Silvia had published many papers regarding solar-terrestrial activities. I contacted her and asked if she was interested in building an IPS radio array in Mexico. She said she had always wanted to do that but didn't have the people or the technology. So on the visit to Mexico when I took my family and the dean of the College of Engineering at FIT, we visited Sylvia at her office at the Autonomous University of Mexico.

Lee Caraway, the graduate student who worked on the patched antenna in the rocket experiment, was with us. He gave a very good presentation to Sylvia about how he would go about building the array. Lee was a graduate student of Dr. Michael Thursby. Sylvia said we had to choose a site for the radio array and told us about a piece of land outside Mexico City on a mountain. I told her that we could send Lee Caraway to work on this with her, and whenever Dr. Thursby or I was needed, we would travel down.

Sylvia got the funding from Mexico to build the IPS radio array, and she and Lee selected a piece of land. The people at the space environment laboratory in Colorado were happy when I told them about the collaboration with Silvia Bravo. Sylvia wrote to me complaining about the morale of the Mexican workers on the building of the array. She offered to pay for Michael Thursby and I to travel out to help. She also offered to pay per diem for meals, but she had no money in the grant to pay for our time spent in Mexico. I told her that neither Dr. Thursby, who was on hard money, or I could leave our jobs to work in Mexico with no salary. I told Sylvia I wished I could help, but these were the realities.

Lee Caraway came back from Mexico after two months, and he complained about having to leave his family for so long. I didn't have any communications with Sylvia after that. Unfortunately, Sylvia Bravo died before the project was finished. They dedicated the array to her. The executive summary from the official website of the array describes the following about the project, as of the year 2001:

> We report the construction of a 64x64 wavelength dipole antenna element, occupying an area of 10,000 m² (70 x 140 m) to carry out interplanetary scintillation (IPS) observations. This will be a dedicated (24 hours) radio array for IPS observations of nearly 1000 of well-known radio sources in the sky, which is being built in the state of Michoacan (350 km north-west from Mexico City, 19° 48' and 01° 41'). This array will be part of a global warning network of solar activity associated storms, ionospheric disturbances, and other solar wind studies. The Mexican IPS array will have very similar characteristics to the array in Cambridge, but with some significant advantages such as better electronic components, higher operation frequency (140 MHz) and its location at lower geographic latitudes. The project consists of two phases. In the first phase we built a prototype radio array near Mexico City, which contained all the basic elements of the final array but covering a smaller area. In the second phase we are building the final array in Michoacan and we expect to finish and initiate the first IPS observations by the end of

this year with assistance of technicians from the NCRA in India.

I had mixed emotions reading this. The Mexicans did what we wanted them to do to the letter, but we were not involved at all. It was really sad for me to be shut out of funding to do a project like this and then see other countries doing it. Sylvia did what we had suggested, building a test array first and then a final array. The final array was built later at a different location. I'm glad to see that my good friend Dr. Murray Dryer is now on the board of the International IPS Global Network. As much as I hate to say this, if it weren't for my contact with Dr. Sylvia Bravo and my suggestions, this project would not have seen the light.

Chapter 17
Getting Involved in Military Research

Laser Body Armor

Following my attempts to protect satellites from military laser beams, I found out that there was a threat of CO_2 lasers on military soldiers in war theaters. The US Natick Army R&D Center in Natick, Massachusetts, solicited proposals for the construction of laser body armor for soldiers to protect them from shoulder-carried CO_2 lasers. This solicitation caught my attention because I was interested in defending against heat. In my earlier studies of material science I found out that salt would reflect radiation at infrared wavelengths but absorb radiation in the visible part of the spectrum. I found a CO_2 laser at FIT from a professor who was not using it anymore. Now that I had a 20-watt power CO_2 laser, I crushed commercial salt into tiny, micron-size particles. I set up the laser on my optical table and passed it through a prism to a zinc selenium (ZnSe) slide. I also mounted my low-infrared energy detector 10^{-9} watts (this number tells how low an infrared energy it can detect) and directed it through a thin layer of micron-size salt particles on the slide. The CO_2 laser was pulsed to avoid damage to the detector in one hundred cycles starting at 200 MW to 20 watts.

Using my other grants I bought some protective eye goggles. The beam from a CO_2 laser is invisible to the human eye and is in the infrared spectrum centered at 9.4 and 10.6 μm wavelength. A CO_2

gas laser could range in power, peaking at a gigawatts continuous wave (CW) laser that could obliterate satellites in orbit. I wrote a proposal to Natick, and it was approved for funding. That was an up ↑ thrill-of-research moment.

The CO_2 lasers that were a threat to soldiers were those of modest power that were light enough for a soldier to carry on his or her shoulder. This was why the Natick R&D Center wanted to develop a flexible body armor to protect the soldiers. Natick also wanted the body armor to be resistant to the heat from explosions of tactical nuclear warheads. Natick assigned two scientists on their staff to work with us. They agreed to come down to Florida to my laboratory, so I could show them one convincing experiment.

I wanted to show them what happened when I *didn't* have the salt particles on the slide and the laser was pointed at a piece of paper: as soon as the CO_2 laser was fired, the piece of paper in my hand ignited, and I had to throw it away before I burned my hand. The next step was to put the layer of particles on the slide. I fired the laser at 20-watt continuous power and then put my hand on top of the slide. The visitors from Natick yelled at me not to. I kept my hand over the slide, and the layer didn't even get hot at all. They were worried and said to be careful, but I assured them I had done it several times before. They were completely convinced that the layer of particles rejected the heat and completely reflected it away from the target, which in this case was my hand.

Now that I had proven the principal, the hard part was how to apply this layer of particles on a flexible suit that soldiers could wear it all the time. They mailed me some pieces of soldiers' uniforms to experiment with. I attached the layer with polyurethane as adhesive. I sent them some samples to zap with CO_2 lasers. They told me that the armor held up well. At their request, I then traveled to Natick to discuss the issue of how to apply these layers on the suits. I asked them if we could have a double layer of suits then sew adjacent pockets with particles inside them. They said it may be possible, but they were worried about the weight of the suit and the ease of walking and running. I left Natick with no good resolution.

A week passed, and they called and asked me to write a final report to distribute to many of the army centers since this research was still unclassified. This would give them a chance to get some new ideas on how to apply my methodology to the suits. I agreed and wrote a final report that was published and distributed all over the army's centers of research.

Doing Research on the M1 Abrams Tank

I found a solicitation for proposals in the *Business Daily* (I recommend this as a resource for all researchers on soft money—check the *Business Daily* daily!) for ways to defeat laser ranging for tanks. Bells immediately started ringing in my brain. Laser ranging is a methodology used to determine the distance to any object, including the moon, accurately. I knew that I could suppress a laser beam hitting a target for ranging using my layer of micron-size particles. i.e. the particles will diffuse its signature to the degree where there is no reflection back from the beam to detect by the enemy thus defeating laser ranging. I was surprised that this solicitation was not classified because laser ranging played a major role for the United States against the Soviet-made tanks during Operation Desert Storm.

This would be a big deal for the automotive tank command: they would be able to prevent the enemy from finding the position of US tanks while being able to find the position of enemy tanks via laser ranging. I immediately responded to the solicitation with a proposal to the automotive tank command at Warren, Michigan. They responded immediately saying this proposal did not fit the solicitation; however, they would issue a special solicitation for which my proposal would be a better fit. As soon as the new solicitation came out, I revised my proposal and resubmitting. My proposal promised to deliver a coated sheet of steel four feet by four feet to simulate the outer skin of the tank and deliver it inside two months.

My graduate student and I worked hard on the test article, and this time I included both the pure silica particles and the salt particles. I included both particles because I did not have classified clearance, so I had no knowledge of what kind of lasers they were using. I had some guesses, but that wasn't good enough.

Two months passed, and we delivered the test article on time, again using polyurethane as an adhesive. The polyurethane did not have enough time to cure completely, so the scent was amazing, as I was told later by one of the army personnel. A few days later I got a fax from the tank automotive command detailing the itinerary of my visit there to do a test. The test site was at the Grayling proving grounds in Michigan, which was basically a big forest with dirt roads.

I stayed at the Holiday Inn in Grayling, and the next morning army personnel came and took me to the test site in an armored vehicle, which gave me a strange feeling as a civilian. They were very nice, cracking jokes and making conversation. They asked me if I had ever been inside an Abram M1 tank. My answer of course was no, and they said I was going to get the chance today. Because I am only 5′6″ tall, they had to lift me to put me inside the tank, which was very funny. We all laughed at that. For the first time I saw the telescopic instruments inside the tank. They made me operate it, and I was immensely impressed.

To me this was one of these moments in my life that I would never forget. I saw the target article, which was about a mile from the tank through the telescope inside the tank. They got me out of the tank, and they said that was as far as I could go since I did not have classified clearance. I was surprised that I was not going to see the test and know the results, but you can't argue with the military! I asked them if I could have a photo with the tank, and they said sure. See photo.

The army personnel took me back to the hotel. They told me that they were going to do the tests and that I'd hear about the results when I was back to FIT. I jokingly asked them if they really knew what they were doing, and they laughed very hard and told me not to worry! It was then noontime. I had time on my hands, so I went sightseeing to the Mackinac Bridge and then drove back to Detroit for my flight back. I waited for about two weeks and then called the tank automotive command about the results of the tests. They told me that the tests were positive at first, but as the tank came close to the test article, they became negative. I said this was great because laser ranging was important at far distances, and I told them I could make some improvements to remove the negative result at close distances.

The leader of the testing group and me in front of the M1 Abrams Tank

To my great surprise they said no. They were going to classify this whole test. I asked if they would give me classified clearance so I could continue the research. They said no because giving me classified clearance would cost them about $35,000, and they didn't have that kind of money.

This turn of events was shocking to me. I tried to convince them that I needed the classified clearance so that at least I could write the final report for the grant, but they insisted they couldn't. They stopped returning my phone calls, and I lost contact with them. A year later, I got a phone call from Atlanta, Georgia, from one of the army offices asking for my final report on the grant. I told them I couldn't write the final report because I didn't know the details of the final results, e.g., at what distance did the result switch from positive to negative? Furthermore no other details of the tests were given to me. The Atlanta office asked me to write some sort of a final report, but then they stopped pressuring me. I haven't heard from them since then.

In any case, I still feel that this experience was pretty exciting. I never thought that in my entire life I would be doing research like that and carrying out a test like that. I did send a copy of the itinerary of the test conducted at the Grayling proving grounds to the president of FIT for his info but never got any response from him.

My Final Year at FIT

In 1995, Frank Kinney, executive director of the Technological Research and Development Authority (TRDA), contacted me and asked if I wanted to fly payload B from the eclipse experiment. Frank wanted to fly it because his organization had already paid for its construction. As I mentioned earlier, I had been recharging the batteries inside that payload at regular intervals to keep it flight ready. I was very interested in flying it. There weren't any *total* solar eclipses coming up at that time, though, so I had to come up with some other research to fly the rocket payload. This was by no means easy. I was used to designing instruments to fit an experiment, but now I had to design an experiment to fit the instrument because I couldn't change the structure of the instrument since it was already cemented in epoxy-resin!

After considerable thought, I decided I wanted to study the extinction by the Earth's atmosphere of stars and other objects. Extinction means that part of the light from stars, galaxies, and so on, that get absorbed or scattered as it passes through the atmosphere to the ground-based observatories. Going a step further with this idea, I wanted to monitor the pollution in the Earth's atmosphere. A major part of extinction is the result of pollution, man–made or not, like aerosol, dust, soot, and so on, particles in the atmosphere.

A New Method to Study Extinction in the Atmosphere

I developed a new methodology that is explained in my most recent scientific paper (Misconi, 2011) and the broad new methodology that I proposed applied to any similar condition. For example it could be used at Mars to study dust storms at nighttime. Basically, the new method was accomplished by observing the bright stars above the atmosphere (from space) and from the ground with a similar instrument. This way I could deduce the difference in the brightness between the two readings (space versus ground). So my methodology would work if we observed several bright stars from the ground with payload B and then observed the same stars from space using a Super Loki rocket and payload B. This way I'd have two readings with one instrument.

I wrote a proposal explaining all the above to TRDA. The proposal also included an educational part that involved the Aerospace Academy students at Cocoa High School, a magnet school selected and funded by the National Science Foundation (NSF). I involved Dr. Barry Grossman from FIT, who supervised the students from the Aerospace Academy in building a miniature transmitter and other electrical circuit boards. This training of the students took place at Brevard Community College on one of their campuses in Palm Bay, Florida (next to Melbourne). So the proposal had two parts: the rocket flight of payload B and the involvement of the students from Cocoa High School.

Unexpectedly, two conflicts developed concerning my proposal. The first conflict was between TRDA and the Spaceport Florida Authority (SFA). Because of what happened to payload A in Mexico, TRDA decided to launch the Super Loki rocket from NASA Wallops Flight Facility instead of in Florida by SFA. The second conflict was between TRDA and FIT, which I didn't know much about. The only thing I knew was that FIT did not like that TRDA was paying only 5 percent overhead to FIT and any other university for that matter.

Frank Kinney and I flew to Wallops and met with the officials there to make all the necessary arrangements for the launch of payload B. It was a pleasant trip with Frank, and I had a really good time meeting several of the specialists there.

While these two conflicts were going on, I got a surprise phone call from Dr. Jerry Ventre from the University of Central Florida. Ventre asked me what I was doing at FIT and suggested I move to his university, UCF! He told me to think about it and let him know because he could arrange for a meeting between me and the chair of the mechanical and aerospace department at UCF, Dr. David Nicholson.

I talked to my wife, Irene, and my son, Michael, and then made the decision to meet with the chair at UCF. Ventre arranged for the meeting, and I went to Orlando and met with David, who told me that they needed to get into space research because of their proximity to Kennedy Space Center. He said if I joined UCF, we would become the only game in town for space research, referring to the idea that I would be launching a rocket from Wallops. I told David that I would think about it and get back to him soon. This move was a major crossroads for me because if I accepted, I would be working on hard money and not soft money! My family loved this idea!

I visited David again and told him that I'd made my decision to move to UCF, and he offered me a $76,000 salary (a raise of $10,000 from what I was making). They would also pay the expenses to move my laser laboratory and my office. Incidentally, to the reader, $76,000 salary may not seem like a lot; however, living in Florida, it was a very generous amount. There is no state tax in Florida and only 6 percent sales tax. Plus property tax is low, and the cost of living is lower than other states, such as New York or California. In actuality, $76,000 may be equivalent to $100,000 or more in other states.

I announced my pending move to FIT's administration, and they promised to help me in the move, which was good to hear. I got in touch with the director of research at UF, Bill Walsh, and he negotiated with the vice president for research at FIT, Dr. Noonan. The end result was that for just $8,000 from my NSF grant at the time, I was allowed to move my laboratory up to UCF and the lab belonged to me. This was a very good deal, since my laser laboratory cost $250,000 to assemble over the years.

Moving to UCF

By December 1995 the laboratory and my office were moved to UCF's engineering college at Orlando. Unexpected problems appeared, and I ended up joining the department of engineering technology instead of the department of mechanical and aerospace, as I had been promised. However, the department of mechanical and aerospace administered my third year of my NSF grant ($45,000). They also administered the rocket launch from Wallops Flight Facility. I spent the first spring semester at UCF teaching the course Space Systems Concepts for juniors and seniors. It was my first test for teaching undergraduate courses, and I did very well, judging by the students' high ratings. I also picked up two senior students to work with me on my NSF grant and on the rocket experiment.

Chapter 18

Rocket Launching at NASA Wallops and Education Programs

M y next goal was the Launch of Payload B at NASA Wallops Flight Facility. This was a good public relations experiment that paid dividends with UCF. It was again the *first hardware ever flown* by UCF into space. I was in touch on an almost-daily basis with Frank Schmiddlin, the expert on Super Loki rocket launches at NASA, to make arrangements for this launch. Also I was in touch with the Aerospace Academy at Cocoa High School to arrange for selecting students to travel with me to witness the launch. Their teacher Gil Burlew, who was selected later as the best teacher in Florida, chose the students and got them ready for the trip. NASA was very interested in getting high school students excited about space. I also was in touch frequently with Keith Kohler, the public relations director at Wallops, to inform him about the students we were going to bring with us and other related matters. Keith's public relations team was getting ready to broadcast interviews with the students nationally on the NASA TV Select Channel.

The selected high school students included a diverse mix of girls and boys and white, black, and Hispanic students. To save on costs, we took buses from the high school and a female chaperone for the female students. Burlew was responsible for all the students, about fifteen of them. The two senior students that I chose from

UCF to help me with the rocket experiment drove separately to Wallops. The two students, Bob Davis and George Rausch, were responsible for acquiring the data using a computer that we took with us.

It took two days on the bus to go from Cocoa to Wallops in Chesapeake Bay. We spent a night in a hotel, which was a lot of fun for me because I had the chance to talk to the students. Payload B was with me at all times, and I guarded it as if my life depended on it.

At Wallops, I had several meetings with the launch staff and Schmiddlin. I also found out from the team that NASA was thinking of closing Wallops Flight Facility for financial reasons. Wallops had a lot of NASA planes and also solid-fuel rocket launches. They told me that this launch with the students coming here was beneficial and brought good publicity for the NASA facility. I was happy to hear that and wished them good luck in the future. This idea was clearly shelved, and NASA Wallops now is very active and carrying out rocket launches.

I met with Wallops engineers, and we used their HP spectrum analyzer to test payload B. The huge radar dishes at Wallops were prepared to follow the frequency of the payload. All in all, it was so much easier to launch from Wallops than from Mexico, for obvious reasons. Mexico was not prepared for rocket launches at the time, though they made an impressive effort to support the launch.

A Serious Problem with Launching the Payload

When we designed the two payloads, we put in a simple switch that turned the payload on and off, located inside a reachable hole in the rocket's payload casing, a really simple idea. However, as I was talking to the engineers at Wallops, they told me that we were not allowed to turn the payload on while it was inside the payload casing. It needed to be in the off position as soon as we put it inside the payload casing on the launch ramp. NASA had established this safety precaution previously because a Super Loki rocket had once launched unexpectedly and prematurely because it got a radio signal from somewhere, risking the lives of those who were near it.

The Super Loki rocket is a solid-fuel rocket. It is launched when a radio signal turns on a heating element embedded inside the powder fuel of the rocket, causing it to ignite. Our payload, when turned on, would send radio data on the health of the instrument, and there was a small possibility that these signals could ignite the rocket and launch it prematurely, potentially harming the personnel at the launchpad.

In the previous accident, the rocket had been directed toward the ocean at the time when it launched prematurely. Luckily there were no boats or ships at the time. This NASA restriction meant that we had to turn on our payload while it was in flight so as not to endanger the launch personnel. This was definitely a low ↓ thrill-of-research moment for me. I panicked a bit, as I had only a day before the launch and this could negate the launch and all the efforts that had been done so far. In my panicky mode I turned to the engineers and asked for their help.

After several hours, one of the engineers, God bless him, came up with a unique idea. He suggested we put a ring around the on–off switch and extend a chain from the ring to the launcher structure. This way, the force generated during the launch of the rocket would cause the ring to move the switch into the on position. There was a risk of perhaps 20 percent (in their estimate) that it may slide and not turn the payload on, but it was worth taking because it was the only solution the engineer could think of. I said, "Let's do it."

I knew that we couldn't design an on–off circuit and insert it into the cemented payload. Also we would need to design a radio receiver to turn the payload on while in flight. It was simply impossible to do, given the time constraint we had. The two engineers assigned to us worked very hard to design the solution and test it manually. They told me they thought it had a good chance of success, *with some prayer.* If it didn't work, the payload would remain dead, and as terrible that was, I still thought it was worth the chance.

After my prayers and my two UCF students' prayers the launch time came, and they put us in bunkers behind the launchpad. I was connected by phone to the data-acquisition team, which was a few buildings away from where we were.

The launch took place on time, and I was very happy to see that the payload was on and communicating with the computer we had, giving what we call *dark current data*. However, two minutes later when the payload was out in space, the person in charge of the data reception said, "I am sorry; your digital circuit board inside the payload quit working." Another big low ↓↓ thrill-of-research moment hit me.

The telemetry engineer went on to say that the payload took data for about two seconds, and after that all they could receive was the beacon signal from the instrument. The beacon's signal continued for more than twenty minutes until the payload splashed into the Atlantic Ocean and the payload went silent. While the payload was inside its casing it could not see any brightness and therefore was just transmitting the dark current data. As the instrument came out of the casing, about fifty miles above ground, the data started changing, and the brightness numbers went up for a short amount of time before it quit working. Although it was an unsuccessful result, it was far better than what we got in Mexico for the following reasons:

1. We proved that the instrument could come out and shear the screws of the nosecone and be free in space.
2. The beacon signal successfully came on after the unfortunate failure of the digital board in transmitting the data.
3. The beacon signal stayed on for the estimated duration of the free fall of the instrument till the splashdown in the ocean.
4. The communications engineers followed the path of the payload as close as possible, before the splashdown in the ocean.

"I Shall Return"

Following these developments, I immediately went to the data-acquisition department. As soon as I arrived, a woman from the launch team greeted me with a rose. This was a very nice gesture. At this moment I recalled General Douglas MacArthur's famous saying "I shall return." I then said, "I shall return to Wallops." They applauded me and said they looked forward to that.

They briefed me on what had happened, and they gave me a big reel of magnetic tape and a printout that showed the data for a couple of seconds and then the beacon signal all the way to the splashdown in the Atlantic Ocean some twenty to thirty miles from shore. The telemetry engineers told me that they followed the payload all the way as near as possible to splashdown and that then the beacon went silent

I should point out here that payload B was about five years old and was embedded in epoxy-resin. Who knows what aging did to that mixture surrounding the circuit boards. This is just a thought; it could have been something else. Well, for three days, the NASA TV channel had the high school students' interviews and my interview on repeatedly, which gave us some publicity for UCF. The videos of the launch and the interviews were shown to the dean of the college of engineering, Dr. Martin Weinelista, and he was very pleased. I tried to make sense out of the data for these two seconds but to no avail. I then wrote a final report to TRDA stating what happened.

The first course that I taught at UCF, Space Systems Concepts, took a lot of preparation on my part. It had diverse subjects, such as orbital mechanics and space environment, which I knew well already; however, there were other subjects that I hadn't studied before, like rocket propulsion, space-vehicle attitude determination and control, atmospheric reentry, thermal control, spacecraft power, and spacecraft telecommunications. It was pretty interesting to study these topics. I learned a lot, and then I had to teach what I'd learned!

My appointment to the department of engineering technology

was a six-year tenure-track appointment. Though I'd done research for more than twenty years on soft money, this had no effect on tenure in the academic world. By that time I had published more than twenty refereed national and international journal publications. The fact that I'd already had the status of full professor didn't mean anything either! However, the big bonanza was that I was on hard money for six years, believe it or not, which gave my family a great relief. After the six years I had to apply for tenure, which was kind of strange because I would be sixty years old. Normally people go for tenure in their late twenties or early thirties.

A Chance to Become Director of the Florida Space Institute

I can't believe how many times Florida astronomers and space scientists have tried to establish a space institute or center. Jerry Weinberg had the Space Astronomy Laboratory (SAL), which he had wanted to enlarge into the Florida Space Science Institute. That idea failed because Jerry did not get the $2.5 million from the Florida space committee headed by Jeb Bush. Instead the committee gave the money to FIT to form the Space Research Institute (SRI). SRI lasted for about three years, failed, and was closed. UCF had a Center for Space Education, headed by Dr. Jerry Ventre, but he moved to the Florida Solar Energy Center (FSEC). The UCF administration decided to solicit proposals for a new director of the space-education center and at the same time form a Florida space institute. Another attempt, please?

Two astronomers and a mathematician proposed to form this institute: Dr. Himberto Cambins from UF, mathematics professor Ron Phillips, and myself. A selection committee was formed to interview the candidates. The committee interviewed me and were very impressed by my proposal, as the dean told me later. The dean of the College of Engineering took me to lunch that day and told me that the job was mine and that I should go and familiarize myself with the suite for the space-education center and meet the secretary there. He told me all I needed was the provost's approval. I had an interview with the provost, Dr. Gary Whitehouse. The interview went well, and I thought that I had gotten the job.

This was in July, and I didn't feel like driving often to Orlando to follow up. I thought it was best to wait for a letter from the provost, and then I could start working. By the end of the month the dean called me. I went to see him, and he gave me a letter from the provost. The provost said that while he was impressed with my ideas and proposal, he felt that it was best to have Dr. Ron Phillips be the director of the Florida Space Institute, since he had been working at UCF for many years and was more suited for this administrative job. I was shocked. I was disappointed because all month I had been generating a lot of ideas on how to make this institute succeed. Anyway, it wasn't meant to be.

The world of academia was strange to me, very different from what I was used to. Nonetheless, in the years that followed, I started teaching a myriad of courses in the engineering technology, mechanical and aerospace, and physics departments. I also got a joint appointment with the physics and aerospace departments. There was no astronomy department at UCF because the state of Florida had decided to consolidate astronomy only at one state university, the flagship University of Florida at Gainesville.

In the first year that I joined UCF the University of Florida donated a telescope (I believe it had a twenty-six-inch lens) to us. UCF also hired astronomer Dr. Nadine Barlow as director of the Robinson Observatory that housed the telescope. I was not aware of these developments until I received an invitation for the dedication ceremony of the observatory, believe it or not! I met Dr. Barlow at the dedication ceremony and wished her luck in her new assignment.

UCF was allowed to teach introductory astronomy to freshman students from any department. I was then asked to teach introductory astronomy to the honors college students and did that numerous times. In the following years the physics department was allowed to establish an undergraduate astronomy major. This was how I ended up teaching astronomy courses, such as Planetary Astrophysics and Introduction to Astrophysics.

I had to teach three courses per semester and occasionally four. The courses I taught, I had *never* taken in my life. I taught courses like Statics and Dynamics, Energy Systems, Space Technology, Computer Applications, Quality Control, Senior Design, Fluid Mechanics, and so on. It was great to be an astrophysicist because I could teach practically anything (not quite) with no trouble. The chair of the engineering technology department, Dr. Richard Denning, asked me one time if there was any course at UCF that I couldn't teach. I laughed and said yes, music. He laughed too. I told him that I could teach as long as I was one chapter ahead of the students in the textbook. Often I had no idea what the next chapters were about.

UCF's Long-Distance Learning Program

UCF is a commuter university, and at the time I joined, it had about twenty-two thousand students. When I retired a few years ago, it had about fifty-eight thousand students. I also heard that UCF is the largest university in the United States in terms of the number of students. However, as of the last five years the University of Arizona pulled ahead of UCF. One would think that UCF's dormitories would be huge, but they're actually very small, since it's a commuter university. UCF was one of the few universities that pioneered long-distance learning.

In the mid-1990s and early 2000s, all lectures were taped, and the students could access these VHS tapes at many sites in Orlando, Cocoa, Melbourne, Palm Bay, Tampa Bay, Miami, and even in North Carolina and Minnesota. The VHS tapes were sometimes mailed to students, and they could view the lectures in their homes or in a special center for viewing. It was a remarkable system.

Some of the professors didn't like the system, simply because they couldn't retract anything or erase any mistakes in their lectures since they were taped. I loved this system because I had ample experience from my TV appearances in Baghdad, and I considered it as if I was on television. I even started my lectures by saying, "This is the Dr. Misconi show; it is the infusion of entertainment and enlightenment!" I borrowed that from the Glenn Beck radio show, which I enjoyed listening to when I drove to Orlando. I infused a lot of humor in my lectures, and the students loved that style. My ratings with the students went through the roof, as Bill O'Reilly would say about his popular show.

The other thing that I liked about long-distance learning was that at times it cut down my driving from Melbourne. For example, I had my office moved from the Cocoa campus to the Astronauts Memorial Foundation building in the visitor center at the Kennedy Space Center (KSC). So I recorded my lecture at KSC, and the students could view it in Orlando and everywhere else, and that meant less driving for me. As you may expect in later years the system was changed to making DVDs and not VHS tapes.

There were of course also disadvantages to the system, as with anything. For example, there was no face-to-face contact with the students, and I had to answer their questions via e-mail or phone, which had many disadvantages. This system of long-distance learning also required that the tests be done in test centers at the student location. UCF established quite a few test centers all over Florida. The tests then were mailed back to me for grading. The tests were proctored by employees I didn't even know!

Having Two Offices

In universities, office space comes at a premium. When I moved to UCF, they gave me an office at the UCF Cocoa campus. I was happy with that because then I had to drive only about twenty-two miles from my house in Melbourne. I had already made the decision not to sell my house in Melbourne and move to Orlando because I thought that would be a major disruption for my son, Michael, and his education. Also my wife's job as a librarian was in Satellite Beach, which is across the Indialantic River Bridge from Melbourne. If we moved to Orlando, she would have to quit her job. However, once I joined the engineering technology department, which at the time was at the research park on the Orlando campus, they gave me an office there too. So now I had two offices, one in Orlando and the other in Cocoa ... wow! I maintained two offices at UCF until I retired. What a lucky guy!

Doing Research While in Academia

Did I stop doing research while at UCF? No ... not on your life! Once a researcher, always a researcher—it was in my blood! After the rocket experiment at NASA Wallops, Dr. Larry Chew and I wrote a five-year proposal to TRDA for carrying out a space education for high school students and to do some rocket and balloon experiments. I told Frank Kinney, TRDA's executive director, that I did not want to be the principal investigator of this grant and would rather be coprincipal investigator. I didn't want to be involved fully in a space-education program, because I wanted to do some more hard-core research.

I also was very busy with my third-year NSF research with the two graduate students from UCF. In that research, I enlarged the computer code that follows particles orbiting the sun to include particles in eccentric orbits. We ran the code on the computer several times, and the results were terrible. The numbers coming out made no sense whatsoever. I asked the students to keep checking every statement of the code but to no avail. Finally, I woke up on a Friday morning, and I thought, *Oh my goodness, we forgot to put a quadrant check for the trigonometric terms in the equations.* My students immediately put in a subroutine for a quadrant check, and the numbers started to make sense. This was a great thrill-of-research moment for me. I analyzed the data and wrote a research paper that was published in the *Planetary and Space Science Journal.*

Suggesting Proton-Particle Levitation in Hard Vacuum

I stated earlier that dust particles could spin due to photons interacting with the particles' surface irregularities. In my research papers I called this the *Paddack effect* in recognition that Dr. Stephen Paddack was the first one to suggest and investigate this effect. Following my suggestion, now it is recognized as the Paddack effect throughout the literature. I also derived an equation, using the random-walk principal, to measure Particles spin due to proton impacts as they orbit the sun. This is basically a statistical mechanism but nonetheless shows how the particles can spin very fast.

One day I asked myself why I couldn't levitate a particle using protons, instead of photons from a focused laser beam. This way the levitated particle didn't have to be spherical in shape; it could be irregularly shaped, mimicking interplanetary dust particles. I did calculations to show what number density of protons was needed to levitate a particle inside a hard vacuum chamber.

I found that it was indeed possible to do this using what is called a *theta pinch*, which basically is similar to a proton gun. I immediately wrote a paper and submitted it to the *Laser and Particle Beams* journal. It was accepted and published (Misconi 1996); my hope is that someday some researcher will do this and levitate particles using protons. If this experiment is carried out successfully, then one could shine a laser beam and focus it on the particle from the side and spin the particle, basically simulating the Paddack effect. This would be killing two birds with one stone: studying the Paddack effect and the Misconi effect at the same time.

Trying to Launch Again at NASA Wallops

I contacted Frank Schmiddlin at NASA Wallops Flight Facility and told him that I was returning to Wallops as I'd promised! I also told him that I intended to fly another payload using a Super Loki rocket, and he was delighted.

Red Sprites and Blue Jets

I explained to Frank Schmiddlin that I wanted to put a TV camera in the payload and put it up into a lightning storm in the atmosphere and photograph *red sprites* and *blue jets*. Astronauts had reported these sightings on the space shuttle, shooting magnificently above the cloud cover. This project had one logistical problem: I had to go to NASA Wallops and wait for a lightning storm so I could chase it with the rocket!

This would also prove my concept that this rocket could be used to do photometry or photography. I became the adviser for the American Society of Engineering Technology (ASET) and began training the students in designing the payload of the rocket. NASA Wallops sent me two dart tubes (payload casings) free of charge, and that got the students excited. Wallops assigned David Moltedo to be the point of contact at the facility. Using a grant of $12,000 from a proposal that I wrote to UCF's student government, we purchased two Sony miniature cameras that were state of the art at the time. The cameras would fit inside the two-inch-wide tubes easily. Since the data would be video streamed, we contracted a company to construct a video transmitter at 1.8 GHz. This was the frequency recommended by the telemetry team at NASA Wallops. We also purchased space-worthy rechargeable batteries to supply power for the instrument.

The students made many tests for this instrument through the hallways of the building and out to the parking lot and beyond. We always got videos from the sites, which proved to us that the instruments worked at least in the short range. This new instrument design was by far easier than the SEEC instrument that I'd help build for the eclipse, especially since Sony made the cameras and another company built the transmitter, which meant I didn't have to worry about either of those. It was time to cement the instrument with epoxy resin so it could withstand the 120 g's. This was a milestone since it would be difficult to change anything in the instrument after cementing it. The students found a company that did epoxy resin cementing. All in all the students and I worked together on and off for about a year and a half, and I started making plans for going to NASA Wallops and doing tests with the instrument. While I was making these arrangements, I received unexpected news from Moltedo.

Changing the Reception Frequency

NASA Wallops informed us that their new frequency was peaked at 3.0 MHz and that we had to retune our transmitter to this frequency. This meant that we had to break into the payload that was cemented with epoxy resin and also ask the company that built the transmitter to adjust it to the new frequency. Below is a sample of my communications with NASA Wallops through e-mail:

Hi Professor Misconi, well it seems we have a definite problem now; we launched the thunderstorm rocket on Monday, July 17th into a thunder storm over a 100 miles out. They were looking for a storm way out in the gulf stream, and I think it would have been too far out for you guys to get a piece of. We only set up 9 times on this rocket and they were looking for the same storm a 100 miles out. It seems the storms came from the south, went out to sea and these were the types we set up for. I don't recall any coming from the west, and passing over us. So I guess we will have to see what else we can do. The sounding rocket office suggests you still bring your payload up to Wallops for preliminary checks, and maybe you can talk to us at the same time and try to get some support from Public affairs and the sounding rocket office. Sorry about the delay and I sure hope we canstill do this thing,

Dave

09/07/2000

Hi yes, no news is good news, we are working out a launch window now, and trying to get your rockets into a window which doesn't conflict with our schedule. We have a viper lllA on schedule for the 15th, plus some other small rockets so we are considering that time frame. I'oll let you know when I get it more definite and try to give you as much of a heads up as possible. I am also working on the OSD and need some additional info soon. Be talking, Dave

07/25/2000 at 06/15 AM

Hello Professor Misconi, sorry I took so long to get back, was trying to get up to speed in this frequency think before we cause you to make a costly mistake. A couple of more answers from you and we should be in agreement. The transmitter frequency of 2279 MHz should work fine as we agreed upon earlier. What is the output voltage of your camera? How are you going to deviate the carrier frequency to 3 MHz peak? Are you going to be able to tell from the blockhouse that your payload is working? See you later, Dave A. David Moltedo

Hi Prof. Misconi, wow, what are you doing up on the computer after midnight? Anyway, sounds good to me. Just give me enough time to schedule other folks in to this so we can get things rolling. I will schedule your time here and take care of badges, etc. I will need names, time and length of visit, etc. as soon as you know. Thanks, Dave

Helllo David: As I told you on my recent phone message to you that both transmitters frequencies are being changed to the 2279 MHz frequency that your telemetry folks requested. We carved the potting on the first payload and made it accessible to the company's engineer. We expect to have them back in a week's time hopefully. I would like if we can arrange for a trip for couple of students to go up to Wallops and check the transmitter's reception by your telemetry people. I will notify you when the transmitters are fixed and received by us, so then we can talk about the trip. The 3 MHz peak, we were told by the companies engineers are deviated automatically by the transmitters. I have already answered the other questions in your message of August 2nd. Let's hope there is still time to pull this off. I am counting on that especially since the media here are still asking us when the launch is going to take place not to mention the people at the University. Look forward to hear from you.

Prof. Misconi

The Disappearing Payload

After we changed the frequency to the new requirements (peak at 3.0 MHz), we needed to also change the antenna to transmit at this frequency. The student president of ASET, who was also the head of the student team working on the instrument, told me that he knew a company in Chicago that could tune the antenna to the new frequency or replace it with a new antenna. He was visiting his father in Chicago, so he wanted to take the instrument with him to have it fixed. I said sure since I had complete trust in him. Plus he had contributed more than any other student to building this instrument.

What happened after that was really bizarre, the strangest thing that I ever encountered in my entire professional career. The student and the payload completely disappeared. The student didn't respond to any of my numerous e-mails to him. I asked the other students to watch for him on campus, but nobody saw him. A few months later I told Dave at Wallops what had happened. Dave was shocked and said he had never heard anything like this before. I told him I shared the same feeling and that should the payload show up, I would be in touch with him. We never communicated after that. Eventually the local TV stations in Central Florida that were waiting to show details of the rocket launch and the results gave up asking me when the launch was going to take place. There is no question in my mind that this was a down ↓ thrill–of–research moment.

Chapter 19

My Interactions with: the Media, Brazilian Scientist, and Buzz Aldrin

Appearing on Local TV Stations

I had several TV appearances on local stations in Gainesville and Orlando. In Gainesville I was asked to comment on a woman finding a small rock meteorite in her backyard after she heard a loud sound. In Orlando I appeared several times on the local news to explain the student projects that we were doing, including the remodeling of the space shuttle for tourism and the rocket experiment at NASA Wallops Flight Facility. After I returned from the rocket launch in Mexico, one of the Daughters of the American Revolution invited me for a TV interview on a local station in Melbourne. The half-hour interview was all about the rocket launch for the total solar eclipse in Mexico.

My Separation

In February 1999, my wife, Irene, decided it was best to get a separation, and she moved to Satellite Beach. My son, Michael, was in his junior year at the University of Florida in the College of Journalism and Communications. He took the news of the separation as well as could be expected. His friends took him to a bar and got him drunk, and I thanked them for that necessary step!

Time to Apply for Tenure

Living alone in a four-bedroom house was not easy for me. I had to make an adjustment, and I got used to it fairly quickly. The year was 2001, a new millennia and for me a time to solidify my hard money status at UCF. I'd forgotten a bit what it was like working on soft money. I didn't have to work so hard to get grants, and I got to feel like a government employee! That is really funny to me! I was sixty-one years old, and it was difficult to get a big space-mission grant from NASA because of my age. These space missions take years (ten or more) to accomplish, so my age was an issue. In any case, I spent the whole summer of 2001 assembling a huge tenure-application package. Dr. Ron Eaglin, the chair of my department, told me that he had never felt a heavier folder than mine. Well, obviously I had done so much by then that the folder would be heavy.

I assembled many support letters from well-known scientists that I knew. I've included the letter from Dr. Donald Brownlee in appendix A. Dr. Brownlee was the director of NASA's Stardust space mission that went to comet Wild 2 and returned cometary particles to Earth for the first time. He also was the first to collect interplanetary dust from the Earth's stratosphere, using retrofitted U2 planes given to NASA by the US military. These particles are at the Johnson Space Center at Houston, Texas, and are known as the Brownlee particles.

My Suggestion to Hit a Comet or Asteroid with a Small Rocket

I also cherish very much the letter of support that I received from my classmate Dr. Seung Soo Hong, former chair of the astronomy department at Seoul National University. Seung Soo wrote, "I still remember in one of those brain storming sessions he suggested to fire a 'big gun' from a satellite to a nearby asteroid and to observe the scattered light of the Sun and man-made source by the dust excavated from the asteroid surface. The SAL team couldn't materialize the idea then. But to think back, this was a brilliant idea, with which one can characterize the nature of ligorith particles for a reasonable price." A copy of the full letter can be found in appendix A.

NASA implemented the same idea I suggested in that meeting in the Lunar Prospector mission and with other comets. Wouldn't it have been fun if I had patented that idea then!

The Tenure Vote

The tenure evaluation process went smoothly, and the end result was thirteen votes yes and zero no from my department, the college of engineering committee, and the university at large committee. I also applied for the teaching award, which I received, resulting in a $5,000 raise. It was a very good year, as Frank Sinatra says.

My Son's Movie

My son, Michael, graduated from the University of Florida in 2001 and decided to make a twenty-minute movie that summer to show at film festivals. I received so many phone calls from women in Orlando and other places in Florida wanting to be part of his movie. Michael called his short movie "The Treaty." He assembled the cast of actors and actresses and set out to film the movie in Gainesville. I was amazed at his capability of running this operation. He even got the city of Gainesville to block a street for him and got the police department to control the situation. To make a long story short, he showed this movie at several festivals in Melbourne and Fort Lauderdale and at other places. His movie was not selected for the important one, the Sundance Festival, which disappointed him somewhat. Nonetheless with a few other people he formed his own company, Blue Juice Films. Michael now owns his own company called Digital Zoetrope for making TV commercials, and he's been very successful. He is waiting for a chance to produce a big-time movie.

Establishing a Space-Science
Technology Program for a BS Degree

In the early years of teaching at UCF, I started teaching a course called Space Systems Technology, and it was a successful one with the students. This prompted the chair of the department to suggest I establish a program that would give a BS degree in space–science technology. So I started the tedious work of approving a program through a university, which I wouldn't wish on anybody. Drs. Richard Estes and A. Rahrooh helped me prepare all the documents needed for the new program. Pretty soon, I had nearly thirty students enrolled, better than some astronomy student numbers! A lot of the students were enthusiastic and wanted to learn as much as they could, and in two years we had graduates. Some of them ended up working at KSC with the space shuttle solid rocket boosters and others in testing batteries for the shuttle and other main launch rockets.

While I was teaching these numerous space courses, I established a relationship with KSC where I could bring students with me to tour the launchpads and other facilities. We stood underneath the space shuttles, and one time they allowed me to climb the ladder and look inside the *Endeavor* space shuttle, which was an awesome moment in my life. Another time we took the same space elevator that took the Apollo astronauts to the moon, another great moment for an immigrant!

When we toured the large Vehicle Assembly Building, I was surprised to hear the workers at the solid rocket boosters of the shuttle say, "HI, Dr. Misconi." This was definitely an up ↑ thrill-of-*teaching* moment. Another instant worth mentioning was when I took the students to stand below the huge Titan rocket just below the bells of the engines and told them that this rocket would be launched in just two days. We also saw the huge and deep concrete construction below the launchpads where millions of gallons of water would be sprayed to cool the launchpad and prevent a sound shockwave from destroying the vehicle into tiny pieces! All these activities were definitely great fun.

Collaboration with Brazilian Scientists

I was contacted by a professor from Brazil, who said they wanted to build an IPS array in Brazil as we had done in Mexico. He wanted to visit Florida and meet with me along with two other scientists. He also said that they already had a piece of land picked out for the array in Brazil. I said that was wonderful since Brazil had ideal latitude near the Earth's equator and away from the magnetic activities near the poles. I welcomed him to come to Florida, and he gave me a date for their visit. Although I was at UCF at the time, I decided to have the first meeting at FIT since Dr. Michael Thursby had been involved in the Mexican project and was the expert on constructing the array. After the first meeting at FIT we would then take them to UCF. I told the dean and the chair of my department, and they said, "The Brazilians are coming."

We had the first meeting and talked about all the logistics of doing the array in Brazil. They wanted Michael Thursby's and my help to build this array, and we agreed to be part of the team. One of the visitors showed me a manuscript of a paper he wanted to publish about the IPS array. He asked me if I could go over it and make some corrections and suggestions, and I said sure. At the end of the meeting they asked if we could take them to the Best Buy store in Melbourne! That surprised me, but then I guess scientists can be tourists too. We took them to Best Buy, and they bought some cameras and other things. They also told me that they couldn't go to UCF, because they didn't have any time, since they had to go to Colorado to meet with scientists at the space environment laboratory at Boulder.

That was the last time I saw them or heard from them. I faxed the paper that they asked me to go over with my corrections and suggestions but did not get any response! I searched the Internet for any IPS array in Brazil and didn't find anything. I did find a radio observatory that they had built or are still building, to study the sun and galaxies but it had nothing to do with IPS. This was how this collaboration ended unfortunately.

Redesigning the Space Shuttle Fleet for Tourism

I was a senior design course instructor numerous times. One of those times, I suggested to four senior students an ambitious project. There was a lot of talk about retiring the space shuttle fleet, and I thought that would be a waste. I thought that NASA could convert it into a tourism fleet and make money, which would pay for research that NASA was doing. The students surprised me with what a good job they did on the project.

One of the students worked on the economic side of the project and suggested a novel idea: a national lottery program to select travelers. People could enter into the lottery by buying a one–dollar ticket. Through rigorous calculations and some assumptions, he determined that this lottery program could give NASA a $20 million profit over the flight cost, which was around $400 million. The remaining students designed seating for twenty tourists and many other modifications to convert the space shuttle to be a tourism vehicle. They then submitted to me a final report, which was pretty impressive.

A reporter from the *Orlando Sentinel* contacted me after he heard about the project and told me that he'd like to do an article about it and take photos of the students and me {the article was published on April 28, 2001}. I sent a copy of the final report on the project to NASA's education liaison at KSC, and he acknowledged receiving it. I then called the editor of the national newspaper *Space News*, based in Washington, DC. I told him about the project and also told him that I would be sending a letter to the editor about this project. He welcomed the idea and said that he looked forward to receiving it.

He published my letter and changed the title to "Ticket to Ride." Below is a copy of that article:

RY

"Space News" Weekly Newspaper
Vol. 12 No. 20   May 21, 2001
Page 14

SPACE SHOTS

"There is a decreasing interest of governments in the launcher sector. Commercial successes can be seen as a good reason for governments to discontinue investment, to the detriment of the original motivation — strategic access to space. ... The role of governments needs to be expanded."

— **Jean-Jacques Dordain, director of launchers, European Space Agency,** in May 17 remarks in Paris during the "World Summit on the Space Transportation Business."

LETTERS

A Ticket To Ride

Responding to a challenge put forth by Professor Nebil Misconi, at the University of Central Florida, our team of four engineering technology seniors devised a conceptual design for modifying the space shuttle for commercial use.

With design being our major area of concentration, we presented a proposal to modify an existing shuttle's payload bay area to carry space tourists. The project report may be the first of its kind, and hopefully will serve as a starting point for a debate about the commercialization of space.

The design, if implemented, could possibly solve two problems for NASA. First, the concept would provide alternative missions for the aging space shuttle fleet after the completion of the international space station.

Second, the revenue-generating idea proposed by the report, although far-fetched, could infuse much needed profit into the budget-strapped space agency. The following is a synopsis of our report:

The space shuttle program has been a shining example of United States leadership in space for two decades. With the demise of the X-33, this workhorse will continue to deliver cargo into orbit for years to come. With the budget shortcomings and the completion of the international space station, however, the role and mission of the shuttle fleet is undefined.

This team's proposal would re-design the space shuttle to carry passengers into low-Earth orbit, dock with the international space station and bring them safely back to Earth.

It will not be an easy task, but it is not overly complex either. The payload bay of one space shuttle could be modified by fabricating and installing a secondary substructure that would be attached to the existing frames and stringers.

Inside this structure, seats would exist to carry up to 18 passengers into orbit. The structure would also have a galley, two personal hygiene stations, sleeping quarters, and exercise stations.

Once in orbit, the passengers would have a variety of options to keep them entertained. There would be tours of the space station, as well as experiments that could be performed on the shuttle. Passenger selection would be achieved through the use of a national lottery. The profit realized by the use of this method is estimated (by our model calculations) at over $20 million per seat.

Although proven to be an effective space travel vehicle, the space shuttle has no defined role established beyond the completion of the space station.

By redesigning the one shuttle to carry passengers, NASA could re-stimulate interest in space and at the same time collect much needed revenue that could revitalize other space programs.

Bill Bailey
Matt Ducsay
Michelle Kiaaina
Matt Scalise
University of Central Florida
Orlando, Fla.

ITORIAL OFFICES: Moscow   Tel Aviv
shington   Simon Saradzhyan   Barbara Opall-Rome

The day the article appeared in *Space News*, something simply awesome happened at noon! While I was talking to the office assistant of the department, the famous astronaut *Buzz Aldrin*, the second man to walk on the moon, was leaving a long message on my machine. I went back to my office to see if there were any messages from the students and listened to a message from Buzz Aldrin saying that he enjoyed reading the article in *Space News* and that he was very much for space tourism. He said we needed to talk about this as soon as possible, and he left a phone number for me to reach him.

My Conversations with Moon Astronaut Buzz Aldrin

The most prominent events in my life are probably my two conversations with Dr. Buzz Aldrin. I ran back to the department and to the office assistant. She looked at me and asked, "What is wrong with you? Your face is red, and it looks like you got hit by a train." I said that I had. The chair of the department came out of his office and asked me what was going on. I told him the story, and he was really surprised and said that was something to remember, something historic. I then went back to my office and called Buzz Aldrin back. I explained the project to him and what we did with the students. I couldn't believe that this was happening. It was like I was daydreaming. I knew that Buzz Aldrin got his PhD from MIT in physics, so I had to be careful with what I said to him.

Buzz said he was interested in the project and wanted to know more about it. I was delighted that he was interested, and I offered to send him a copy of the final report. He asked me to please do that. The chair of the department asked me if I wanted him to tell the dean of the college of engineering about it, and I said sure. I taped Buzz's message to me so I could save it. I thought, *You don't come from humble beginnings in Baghdad and then speak to the second man who landed on the moon; it is almost impossible to expect something like that to happen!*

I told the dean that I asked Buzz about him visiting UCF, but Buzz said that UCF couldn't afford him. The dean asked me if I'd asked him how much it would cost. I hadn't, because I felt it was not appropriate. The dean showed strong interest in Buzz Aldrin visiting UCF and wanted me to probe this idea with him. I told the dean that if he wanted me to do that, it had to be my show or no go. I knew that there were elements at UCF who would try to steal the show for themselves to advance their own agendas. The dean said that he would think about it, but he never got back to me after that.

I had two very enjoyable phone conversations with Buzz Aldrin, and we talked about many issues, including the idea of going back to the moon. He also suggested new orbital mechanics maneuvers to do that, which I found fascinating. I took recordings of these conversations because I felt they were historic to me. I made some attempts to meet with him, but they never materialized because of his heavy schedule.

The following is a sample of my e-mails with Buzz Aldrin:

From: Nebil Misconi
To: starbuzz1@aol.com
Subject: Fwd: Space News "Ticket To Ride" Letter

Dear Dr. Buzz Aldrin:
I am forwarding the message from Darren Buck from the United Space Alliance Corp. I enjoyed tremendousely chatting with you over the phone. I will keep in tounch. Thanks,
Dr. Nebil Misconi

Chapter 20

Final Observations

Proposing to Study the
Atmosphere of Mars

A collaboration program was formed between the University of Florida and the University of Central Florida about doing space experiments jointly, through NASA. I wrote a proposal to study the column density of dust in the Martian atmosphere during nighttime. The recent Mars missions by NASA had studied the dust and aerosols in the Martian atmosphere during the day by observing spectral lines from the sun as seen from Mars. The dust in the Martian atmosphere is important to study because Mars has frequent dust storms that could contaminate equipment on the surface of Mars and even hamper visibility to a critical degree. However, these dust storms and their severity had not been studied at night, and without this study, future Martian astronauts would not know when to cover and protect their equipment from dust, especially if a sandstorm started at night.

To solve this problem, I proposed a similar methodology that I developed before to study pollution in the Earth's atmosphere. I suggested using the star tracker for navigation on every Mars mission for studying the extinction in the Martian atmosphere during the night. I suggested flying the star tracker on the space shuttle (the fleet was not retired at that time) to observe a few select bright stars in the sky from space. The same star tracker on the mission to Mars could then observe the same bright stars from the surface of Mars. This way we would have two readings: one above the Martian atmosphere and the other from below the atmosphere. Using computer models the astronauts then could determine the severity of the dust storm during nighttime.

After a month or two, I got a letter from the provost, saying that the proposal funding $150,000 had been declined. No reasons were given. This outcome really disappointed me simply because there were no scientific reviews to reject the proposal. However, I did not dwell on this outcome because I was within three to four years of my retirement, and if this proposal had been funded, it would have lasted for many years. Instead I published a paper after I retired that explained this whole idea (Misconi 2011).

Chairing Committees for Tenure Evaluation and Other Awards

When I joined UCF, they put me on the research committee of the college of engineering. This committee basically awarded $7,000 in seed money for writing proposals to get grants. I participated in selecting those faculty members who should get that money. After a few years my department asked me to represent it on the teaching-award committee and the research-award committee. After a few more years I was asked to be chair of these committees. This was sort of fun to do when my head was not on the block, although it took a lot of work to read every candidate's resume and assess his or her accomplishments.

After I got my tenure, I became a member of the tenure-awarding committee and ended up chairing it. Similarly I also became a member of the promotion committee, which determined promotions from assistant to associate to full professor. These two committees were agonizing at times because if we denied an associate professor tenure, he or she had to leave the university. So in a way, we really affected people's lives, which was pretty hard to do. There were quite a few people who ended up having to leave the university.

Meeting the Love of My Life

Let's get to a happier subject. As I previously mentioned, in February 1999 my wife, Irene, and I separated. In October 2003 we formally got divorced. In the ensuing years, I occasionally went to bars and met some women, but I never met anyone that I thought could be my companion for the rest of my life. My son, Michael, continued to live with me after he graduated, and he had several girlfriends over the span of four years. By 2003, he had met the love of his life, Juliet, and in 2005 they were making plans to move into an apartment together.

At the beginning of 2005, I saw a TV commercial about the dating service e-Harmony, and I decided to try it. I talked to few women who had been matched to me by e-Harmony, and then I started talking on the phone with Mary from Michigan. We started having lengthy conversations in February 2005 and continued until I met her in Florida in May.

Mary was a widower whose husband had died of lung cancer. She was a professor of dental hygiene and also the dean at the Oakland Community College in Michigan. Mary was then retired, but I was still at UCF. When we met for the first time in Florida, we quickly realized that we were well matched. We met on May 9, 2005, a day that we will both remember as long as we live.

Mary and I are still together, and she is my sunshine. We have not gotten married because we like our relationship the way it is, and at our age getting married is not important in our view. I could write a whole book on our relationship, and maybe I will. Mary is the love of my life, and I feel very lucky to have found her. Many thanks to e-Harmony for getting us together (this not a commercial for e-Harmony)!

My ex-wife, Irene, and I

Mary and I

Mary in Key West

My son, Michael; his wife, Juliet; and their daughter,
my only grandchild (so far), Madelyn

The Possibility of the Earth Colliding
with an Asteroid or Comet

This idea of an asteroid or comet hitting the Earth possessed me for a while, and I wanted to do something about it. I thought that perhaps the best way to prevent this from happening was to use an existing technology that could potentially destroy an asteroid or a comet before it hit Earth and did tremendous damage. It is an accepted theory that the dinosaurs disappeared because of an asteroid hitting the Earth at the Yucatán Peninsula in Mexico some sixty-five million years ago. The impact of that asteroid created a huge crater that still exists today. The probability of such a catastrophe is about one in every one hundred million years, so we are may be overdue for one! An asteroid, a few kilometers in size, could destroy all the species on Earth.

The way the dinosaurs disappeared is that the dust that was generated from the huge blast engulfed the Earth in darkness, hiding the sun. The sun was invisible for approximately two years until the dust settled down on the ground. As a result of the sun's disappearance, most of the plants and trees and an estimated 85 percent of all species on Earth died. So the dinosaurs had no more food to eat and went extinct. This scenario is also called a *nuclear winter*, in reference to the damage that can take place after a nuclear exchange on a large scale.

The possibility of an asteroid or comet hitting Earth is a serious threat to the future of humankind and our planet that NASA and other concerned government agencies should take seriously. Comets can show up from nowhere in a matter of four months, and if a comet is by any chance on a collision course with Earth, then we better have a solid plan to avoid such a catastrophe. For example, in 1973, Luboš Kohoutek discovered a comet about four months before it crossed the Earth's orbit and turned around the sun. Its orbit was never a danger to Earth, but it's an example of how quickly comets can appear. If a comet suddenly appeared just four months before it was set to collide with Earth, then we would have only four months to work out a solution. This is a very short time, so we should have a plan in place ahead of time to protect humanity and our beautiful planet.

Similarly we don't know where all the asteroids are in their orbits and how many of them cross the Earth's orbit. NASA and observatories on Earth have made some progress in finding the asteroids and determining their orbits, but it's never enough. All it takes is for one asteroid to slip through the detection system, and a catastrophe will take place. For comets it's a whole different ball game. A huge number of comets are sitting either at the Kuiper belt or farther away in the Oort cloud at the edge of the solar system. At the Kuiper belt all it takes is a small perturbation by Jupiter, and a comet will be hurling down toward the sun. If it happens that the comet is on a collision course with Earth, then disaster will ensue. The possibility of a comet colliding with Earth is not that high, but let's not forget that the Earth has been bombarded by many comets throughout its long history (approximately four and a half billion years).

Using the Weapons That Can Destroy the Earth to Save It: Going beyond Edward Teller's Suggestion

To my thinking there is nothing more important than making the Earth safe from such cataclysmic events and keeping the human race going. It took a lot of pains and sacrifices and agonies to get where we are today on Earth. With all that in mind, I started asking myself if weapons of mass destruction could save the Earth from such a disaster. That was exactly what the famous physicist Edward Teller, the father of the hydrogen bomb, thought of doing in the 1980s. The problem with using hydrogen bombs or nuclear bombs to destroy an asteroid is that the space surrounding the asteroid is in a hard vacuum, and therefore we cannot generate kinetic heat shockwaves as we can on Earth. The Earth's atmosphere allows us to generate these devastating shockwaves. The radiation that comes out from these weapons would not destroy the asteroid. The radiation can kill human beings and all living things but not rocks or metallic bodies.

The scientific community dismissed Edward Teller's suggestion for these reasons. However, nuclear weapons can be very effective in destroying an asteroid, if they can be embedded inside it, like how in in the movie *Armageddon* they sought oil drillers to detonate the bomb inside. If the nuclear weapon detonated on the surface, it would only create a crater and that's about all. It would also deliver strong momentum to the asteroid.

Considering all this, I thought that using the Robust Nuclear Earth Penetrator (RNEP) to penetrate the asteroid and blow it up may be a viable solution. The US military was researching and developing the RNEP to use against underground caves in which terrorists could hide. That was before the capture and the killing of Osama bin Laden. However, even long before the capture of Osama, Congress cut the funding for the program. Congress worried about the radiation from detonating nuclear bombs inside these caves underground. They worried about a lot of collateral damage and killing innocent civilians in the process.

I'd heard on the news that these bunker busters could really penetrate pretty deep inside hard concrete ground using conventional weapons. So it seemed to me that if they developed and manufactured the RNEP, it would be a good candidate to destroy asteroids. I suggested to my students in the senior design course that they study this idea, and they researched the Internet to find information on how strong the blast would be and did some calculations on what the depth inside the asteroid was needed to be successful. I thought that even if the first penetration was not enough, another RNEP could be sent and targeted to hit where the first one went in order to increase the depth if necessary. I don't know if this level of targeting is possible, but if it isn't, then my suggestion would be to hit the asteroid somewhere else and detonate two warheads at the same time.

This may sound like science fiction, but let's face it: most ideas started out like science fiction and then became a reality. There is, however, another problem: many astronomers believe that destroying an asteroid will create smaller pieces that will eventually get to the Earth and do damage. My thinking is that if we are serious about this idea, we can do a trial experiment by destroying an asteroid with an orbit that is not dangerous to Earth at all. Then we can find out how big the fragments are and what kind of orbits they get into.

In any case I decided to send a letter to the editor of the prestigious magazine *Physics Today*, hoping that I'd get some feedback from the physicists and the astronomers about this suggested method. I waited two months and didn't hear anything from the editor. I decided to send an inquiry to him about the letter, and he sent me the reviewer's comments about my letter. The reviewer said there was nothing new in this idea, that it was the same idea that Edward Teller proposed in the 1980s. I was surprised at that because in the 1980s nobody had heard about Earth penetrators, especially the RNEP. As far as I know, they did not exist then. I believe that I have read somewhere that even though the RNEP program was scrapped, the United States has the capability to put it together and revive it very quickly.

Letter to *Space News*

After the four students researching this project submitted a final report to me, I wrote a letter to the editor of *Space News* explaining my ideas and the students' report. The editor made one change: retitling the letter as "A Good Use for NEP." The actual letter follows here:

June 24, 2002
Issue

www.spacenews.com

LETTERS

A Good Use for NEP

Considering the danger that large Earth-crossing asteroids or comets pose to human civilization and our planet, I ask the question: can the "Nuclear Earth Penetrator" (NEP) destroy such objects?

The NEP was designed by the U.S. military for possible use in destroying deep caves in Afghanistan as part of the war on terrorism. Descriptions of these weapons suggest that they have the capability to burrow deep inside rocky terrain and could explode a nuclear weapon to destroy caves.

Very little is known to academics about this weapon's capabilities. However, it seems that it could be modified to operate in the space environment and be useful for demolishing a threatening asteroid or a comet that suddenly appears on a collision course with Earth.

We are overdue for a collision similar to the one that presumably destroyed the dinosaurs some 65 million years ago. Comet Hale-Bopp in 1997 was likely 100 times more massive than the object that wiped out the dinosaurs. And Hale-Bopp was discovered only months before it slipped by Earth. Should a comet appear again with such a short notice, we need to be ready to intercept and destroy it before it collides with Earth. Saving civilization and life on Earth is, to say the least, of utmost priority.

I have asked a group of students under my supervision at the University of Central Florida's Material Mechanical and Aerospace Department to study this idea. This study is exploratory, and if encouraging results materialize, then I intend to seek a financially supported investigation. Funding, to further this study, could come from the U.S. Space Command and NASA centers.

Obviously, we need to know more about the capabilities of the NEP. Such information, however, is classified. Some encouraging information has surfaced through the news media. For example, there can be penetration of more than 100 feet before detonation of a conventional device. We realize that there are many questions to be answered. Should multiple warheads be used? Must several NEPs be used at the same time? At what velocity should the NEP be propelled to strike the asteroid or comet to be effective?

I cannot, in this letter include all the questions that need answers. My purpose is to focus attention on this idea and get perhaps a larger study initiated. I have always believed that weapons of mass destruction can and should, when appropriate, be used to benefit mankind.

NEBIL Y. MISCONI
Orlando, Fla.

■ Readers are encouraged to express their views in letters to the editor. Letters may be edited. Please include name, address and telephone number. Unsigned letters will not be published, but names will be withheld upon request. Send letters to 6883 Commercial Dr., Springfield, VA 22159, or to jgillis@hq.space.com. Letters to the editor, opinion and editorial columns may be published or distributed in print, electronic or other forms.

I expected to get strong reactions from the space community and perhaps even strong criticism for my ideas. I hoped the letter would start a dialogue, good or bad. But none of that happened for reasons I still don't know; I checked *Space News* every week to see if there were any responses, to no avail. I had expected that such dialogue could affect the minds of the politicians and maybe they would reinstate the RNEP program for this purpose. The world should have every solution at its disposal in the case of a threat like an asteroid collision.

My *Florida Today* Article

I did not give up on this idea completely, and I wrote an article in the *Florida Today* newspaper, which is issued in Brevard County, home of the Kennedy Space Center. I wrote the article in the hope that it would attract the attention of NASA at KSC. I wanted the article to appear in a section called "Guest Columnist." The editor made changes to the article to make it easier to understand for the newspaper readers. He also suggested to change the title of the article to something that would attract the attention of the readers' of his newspaper. He made the title "A Really Big Bang: Nuclear Weapon Could Target Earth-Bound Asteroid." The following is a copy of that article:

● FLORIDA TODAY

COLUMNISTS

A really big bang

Nuclear weapon could target Earth-bound asteroid

Nebil Misconi

Guest Columnist

It is well known the U.S. military has wanted to develop a weapon called the Robust Nuclear Earth Penetrator, or RNEP.

This weapon could be used as a war instrument to destroy underground hideout caves and hardened nuclear weapons development facilities of foreign countries that are deemed dangerous to U.S. national security.

I would like to suggest that if this weapon were developed, it could be used to destroy asteroids or comets that are discovered to be on a collision course with planet Earth.

Such an encounter will be cataclysmic.

Many scientists believe that an asteroid may have destroyed the dinosaurs and 85 percent of all living species 65 million years ago. More importantly, astronomers believe that our planet is overdue for a similar cataclysmic encounter.

As an astronomer at the University of Central Florida, I have been studying this issue for several years and think the RNEP should be developed, followed by an investigation of its feasibility to destroy an asteroid or comet heading straight for Earth.

That's the only way we could know if it could meet the threat.

Especially since the time available to deal with a suddenly-appearing comet would be just a few months.

The idea would be to detonate a thermo-nuclear weapon or a series of nuclear weapons deep inside an asteroid or a comet nucleus.

The enormous blast would reduce the target into small pieces of rocks, diverted far away from their original Earth-crossing orbital path, and so no longer be a threat to Earth.

However, little is known and published in the public domain about the RNEP because the project is classified, leaving many questions to be asked and answered.

For example:

■ How deep could the RNEP penetrate the surface of an asteroid before detonation?

■ Would multiple hits be necessary for this process to be effective?

■ Would all the fragments be diverted from a collision course with Earth?

■ What is the proper speed of collision of the RNEP with the target to be effective?

It would be impossible to answer some of these questions without a test, which is why one would be needed.

The basic technology to accomplish this exists at the present, and to my knowledge Congress had given funding for the development of the device.

However, the funding was terminated in October 2005. I think it should be restored—not to use RNEP for military purposes, but for the purpose of having a weapon to attack killer asteroids and comets.

To me, it's highly exciting to think the very weapons that are developed to destroy the world could now be used to save it. ■

Misconi is an astronomer and professor at the University of Central Florida's College of Engineering in Orlando.

Again, I got no response from anyone about the article and nothing from NASA at KSC. It seemed to me as if I was talking about a politically incorrect topic. Maybe I was—who knows?

My Lectures

Every chance I had in my lectures, I tried to tell the students about my research experiences and especially the ever-changing improvements in the computer industry from the old days.

Newton's vs. Einstein's Famous Equations

On many occasions in my lectures, I mentioned to the students that I would love to study which equation had a more profound impact on physics: Newton's second law or Einstein's famous equation E = m c². Newton's famous second law is

$$F = m a \tag{3}$$

That is, the force (F) is equal to the mass (m) of the body times the body's acceleration (a). In my graduate student days we used to say that you could do galaxy dynamics by simply using Newton's second law. You can also do dynamics using Newton's law as long as the speed is much smaller than the speed of light.

Einstein's famous equation is

$$E = m c^2 \tag{4}$$

That is, energy (E) is equal to the mass (m) times the square of the speed of light (c). This law is more popular than Newton's second law in our times. I think it would be interesting to study which equation advanced physics more. It could spark a robust discussion among people who study physics. This may not be a valid argument to present, but it's something that I feel interesting to explore for the history of physics.

Students' Phobia about Physics and Math

This is a phenomenon that I'd noticed since I came to UCF and got involved in teaching. A lot of my students asked me not to go too deep into physics or math. When I asked them why, they said it was too difficult and they didn't like it. This was a big change from the days when I was graduate student in the 1970s. We were very competitive and so indulged in physics and math. During my teaching years, I had some good physics students that left the physics department and joined the school of business. When I asked them why, they said business had more money and physics was too difficult! I'm not the only one talking about this, but I thought I would throw my two cents in! This phenomenon can have severe repercussions if it is not turned around. So far we still have the edge in Nobel Prizes in science, but I wonder how long that is going to last.

My Mother's Passing

In October 2011 my mother Columba (which is Latin for dove) passed away at ninety-two, and with that I had lost both of my parents. My mother was an amazing woman as she managed to raise six boys and one girl and rarely complained about it. She gave my father all the conveniences of pursuing his research into Arabic literature and Islamic history. She supported all his efforts in publishing his books and was an ideal wife to him and mother to us God rest her soul.

Final Reflections

I feel so fortunate to have had the opportunity to immigrate to America which gave me the freedom and career I was dreaming of. I understand why so many people wish to live here. I had many friends and acquaintances' in the Middle East that daydreamed about the liberty afforded them in America as well as the American way of life and American ideals and principles. I hope that in the near future the US will fix its immigration policies so that immigrants, like myself, can come legally and pursue their dreams.

Research in America is supported by the fact that we have the liberty to explore many ideas in various ways. I was able to do a significant portion of my work on soft money and do it in my own style. Solar activity has been a significant part of my research of the cosmos.

Due to my observations of the interaction of solar activity with the earth (as well as other planets) I have been skeptical regarding a current suggestion that global warming is caused solely by the increase in CO_2 emissions. I do not see many of the global warming scientists paying attention to solar activity and its known cycles. For example, "The Maunder Minimum" of sunspots number observed during the period between 1645 to 1715 (Eddy J. A., 1976). During one 30-year period within the Maunder Minimum there were much lower than 50 sunspots observed whereas the modern day number is over 50 spots, (J.E. Beckman and T.J. Mahoney, 1998). This caused a mini ice age that killed thousands in Europe and North America and other climate change such as draught. This ice age was correlated to a lack of sunspots on the sun. We do not know what happens when the sun is very active with a lot of sunspots; does it quantitatively warm up the Earth's atmosphere and surface? Steve Goreham has discussed the role of the sun in climate change in his book "Climatisim" (2010), Chapter 5.

The predictions about how much sea levels will rise vary widely. Some scientists say sea levels will have risen in feet and others say inches one hundred years from now. Which one is it? Do we know exactly how much the oceans on Earth absorb the extra CO_2? How does this compare to emissions from volcanic activities? If we have answers to these questions, then how accurate are those answers, or do we know for sure?

The other point I like to make here is that all the catastrophic effects of global warming is predicted to happen and culminate for one hundred years from now. The question then is, are we going to have combustion engines running on gasoline for the next one hundred years? Judging from the tremendous advances that were made in our era, it's possible that we could have electric and perhaps even fusion cars a hundred years from now. This latter may be far out, but who knows. Since 1970 I have been hearing that fusion reactors to generate electricity will be a reality in the next twenty years, and then in the next thirty years, and it has not happened yet. In fact we are still pretty far from that goal, but breakthroughs can happen that will speed it up considerably.

My final observation on this topic is that the research on global warming must include the variations in solar activities, after all the sun is the source of heating the Earth to begin with.

How the Two Potential Problems Compare

The danger of a catastrophe from an asteroid or a comet colliding with our planet has been documented and seen to happen, unlike the danger from global warming. Just look at the crater in the Yucatan Peninsula and the one in Arizona. The asteroid or comet or a large meteorite that hit Siberia in 1908 at Tunguska was a large <u>explosion</u> which occurred near the <u>Podkamennaya Tunguska River</u> on June 30, 1908. The explosion occurred at an altitude of 3–6 mile. It is classified as an <u>impact</u> even though the asteroid or comet is believed to have burst in the air rather than hit the surface. Different studies have yielded widely varying estimates of the impacting object's size, on the order of 200 ft to 620 ft. It is the largest impact event on Earth in <u>recorded history</u>.

To give an example, there are prominent scars on Jupiter from the impact of the comet Shoemaker–Levy 9. These scars were more easily visible than the Great Red Spot and persisted for many months.

Global warming, however, is not a demonstrated catastrophe with the exception that the global temperature has increased by 0.7° C, though there has been no increase since 1998 (S. Goreham, 2010). Also some sheets of ice in the North Pole are melting, though none are in the South Pole. Finally, what's the point of restricting carbon emissions in the United States while the rest of the world does not show the same intent? I strongly believe that the threat from an asteroid or a comet hitting the Earth is inevitable. We should be researching every plan that has been suggested (including mine) on how to divert or destroy an object that can destroy mankind and other living forms from our planet. Surveying the skies for these objects is not enough unless we have a plan on how to protect our planet from them.

In Conclusion

I've always felt that I had an interesting career and that I would not exchange it for any other. I am fortunate to have had a career in astronomy and space science, and I would not trade it for any other field. Forgive me for being so adamant about it.

My life appears in my memory like a movie. I am so thankful for having opportunities that enabled me to excel in a meaningful way. I accomplished my goals pretty much. Most people work on the ground, but I worked in the sky, the overhead hemisphere. I think of my life as a long series of ups and downs with the dialogues in different languages. I spoke English in the United States and occasionally in Istanbul and Baghdad, Arabic in Baghdad, and Turkish in Istanbul. I wrote some poetry in all three languages. I had friends from many different cultures, including Iraqis, Turks, and Americans. I also studied in schools in Iraq, Turkey, and the United States.

Let's get serious here; I would love to see students rise up to the challenges of science today. There is no better example than Professor Stephen Hawking. Can anyone believe what he's accomplished with the disease he has to endure? He could have easily given up and done nothing. Hawking is a living legend for all students to see and take notice.

I believe that the thrill of research is better than any drug that anybody can manufacture. It is better than alcohol, marijuana, and all the other recreational drugs. The greatest high in my opinion is the one you get from proving your research predictions to be correct. Do you think that Newton, Einstein, Hawking, Feynman, Fermi, Teller, Oppenheimer, Dicke, Whipple, and many others would have traded what they were getting from their theories for alcohol or marijuana highs? I completely and confidently bet they would not have.

Finally, I hope this book will inspire some students to reach for the stars.

References

Beckman, John E. and Mahoney Terence J. (1998). "The Maunder Minumum and Climate Change: Have Historical Records Aided Current Research", Proceedings of a conference held in Puerto de la Cruz, Tenerife, Spain, April 21-24, pages 212-217.

Eddy, John, A. (1976). " The Maunder Minimum" Science, Vol. 192, No. 4254, 1189-1202.

Goreham, Steve. (2010). "Climatism." ISBN 978-0-9824996-3-4, New Lenox Books.

Hewish, A., P. F. Scott, and D. Willis. 1964. "Interplanetary Scintillation of Small Diameter Radio Sources." *Nature* 203 (September 19): 1214–17.

MacQueen, R. M. (1968)y. "Infrared observations of the outer solar corona" *Astrophysical Journal* 154: 1059.

Misconi, N. Y. 1996. "A New Technique for Levitating Solid Particles Using a Proton Beam." *Laser and Particle Beams* 14 (3): 501–10.

Misconi, N. Y. 2004. "Numerical Simulations of Rotational Bursting of F-Coronal Dust in Eccentric Orbits Due to Coronal Mass Ejections." *Planetary and Space Science* 52: 833–38.

Misconi, N. Y. 2011. "Detecting the Light of the Night Sky in Mars." *Natural Science* 3: 285–90.

Paddack, S. J. 1969. "Rotational bursting of small celestial bodies: Effects of radiation pressure." *Journal of Geophysical Research* 74 (17): 4379.4381.

Peterson, A. W. 1967." Experimental Detection of thermal radiation from interplanetary dust." *Astrophysical Journal Letters* 148: L37.L39.

Wang, W. X., and N. Y. Misconi. 1999. "Quasi-Analytical Solutions for Apsidal Motion in the Three-Body Problem: Sun-Minor Planet-Jupiter." *Earth Planets and Space* 51 (11): 1181–94.

Recommendation Letters

Letter from Professor Donald Brownlee, director of the Stardust NASA mission to Comet Wild 2, in support of my tenure application at the University of Central Florida (UCF).

From: brownlee <brownlee@astro.washington.edu>
To: <reaglin@mail.ucf.edu>
Date: 9/22/2001 9:27PM
Subject: Nebil Misconi

Dr. Ronald Eaglin

I am writing to evaluate the scholarly credentials of Dr. Nebil Misconi in regard to his consideration for tenure at the University of Central Florida. I am familiar with Dr Misconi's publications and I have had several scientific contacts with him over the last decade.

I will comment mainly on his research papers but I would also like to mention that the information in his tenure promotion packet is impressive evidence that he is a very energetic and creative teacher as well as a researcher. His efforts with student projects is notable. Creating actual flight projects for students is really remarkable and this opportunity must be quite motivational for the upcoming generation of space scientists and engineers.

Dr. Misconi's research has covered a broad number of topics related to the distribution, dynamics and various effects of dust in the solar system. His contributions have been significant and they have remarkable breadth ranging from A.) a recent analytical solution (refreshing and rare in the age of numerical simulation) to an aspect of the 3-body problem to B.) physical levitation of solid particles with a proton beam. Most of his work over the past 25 years has focused on orbiting solar system dust particles but the implications of the work extend to a much wider range of problems in astrophysics. The nature, dynamics and evolution of circumstellar, interstellar and even intergalactic dust are now areas of acute interest to many types of astronomical investigations. As astronomy has expanded to cover all wavelengths, the effects of dust and the clues from its existence and properties have become evermore important. It is now known that most stars are surrounded by dust disks. The work that Dr. Misconi and others have done on the Sun's dust cloud is applicable to other stars and planetary systems. Full understanding of dust and its dynamics is absolutely critical for several future NASA missions. An outstanding example is the Terrestrial Planet Finder (TPF) mission, where knowledge of dust and its distribution and dynamics around stars is essential for designing the mission and ultimately for interpreting evidence for the presence of terrestrial planets around other stars. Some of the topics that Dr. Misconi has studied, the effects of planets, small scale structure, ring formation and near-star effects all are very important to TPF, a mission that will use very large interferometer telescopes in space to distinguish the infrared brightness of extra-solar terrestrial planets from the much larger signal from circumstellar dust. Dr. Misconi's work on variations in the symmetry plane and general causes any type of structure in zodiacal glow and emission are very important to TPF and similar missions.

Of Dr. Misconi' other work, I have been particularly fascinated by his studies of rotational bursting. His detailed investigations imply that grains close to stars should be spun to such high spin rates that they burst. This is a fascinating physical phenomenon any might play a major role in understanding how the heavy element abundances of stars may or may not be changed by accreted debris from comet clouds. It has been suggested by some, that surface compositions of some stars particularly some white dwarfs are enhanced in this manner. If grains burst near stars, they probably cannot be accreted.

One of Dr. Misconi's most significant publications was his 1979 Nature paper on streaming of interstellar grains into the solar system. The paper predicted that interstellar dust should stream into the solar system from the direction of, the then detectable, interstellar gas and it also described the interaction of the extrasolar particles with the solar wind and the IP magnetic field. The paper was timely and highly prophetic as the stream of interstellar dust was detected just a few years later by instruments on the Ulysses and Galileo spacecraft.

I believe that Nebil Misconi is an excellent, productive and accomplished space scientist. I certainly recommend him for promotion and I am confident that he would be promoted to tenure if he was at the University of Washington.

Sincerely,

Don Brownlee

Dept. of Astronomy
University of Washington
Seattle, WA 98195
(206) 543-8575
brownlee@astro.washington.edu
...

Letter from Dr. Seung Soo Hong, former chair of the astronomy department at Seoul National University at Seoul, South Korea, in support of my tenure application at the University of Central Florida (UCF).

ASTRONOMY PROGRAM, SEES, SEOUL NATIONAL UNIVERSITY
56-1 Shinrim-dong, Kwanak-ku, Seoul 151-742, KOREA

FAX: (02) 887-1435
PHONE: (02) 880-6626
E-MAIL: sshong@astroism.snu.ac.kr

September 17, 2001

University of Central Florida Tenure Committee
c/o Dr. Ron Eaglin, Chair
Department of Engineering Technology
University of Central Florida
Orlando, FL 32816-0021
U.S.A.

Dear Tenure Committee,

This is to support tenure application by Dr. Nebil Y. Misconi at University of Central Florida. It is my pleasure to share with you some of my experience I have had with him over the last three decades. Nebil and I did our graduate studies at the same university, State University of New York at Albany, at about the same time in early 1970s.

In school days he and I made a good contrast to each other. In doing homeworks, for example, I heavily relied on my analytical skills and tried to be rigorous in mathematical sense; while he sought for short-cuts to get approximate answers. Mine might be more complete than his, but mine was not so much cost effective as his. He always came up with workable solutions. He was an idea man, and still is.

Under the guidance of Prof. Jerry L. Weinberg, then Mr. Nebil Misconi analysed the ground based observations of the Zodiacal Light, which is the sunlight scattered by interplanetary dusts (IPDs). On the other hand, I constructed in my thesis a unified model of interstellar dust grains under Prof. J. Mayo Greenberg. Because of the connection I had with him via dust, I could fully appreciate what he was doing in his thesis. He traced the location of maximum ZL brightness along the entire 360° range of ecliptic longitude and showed that the symmetry plane, which is the plane of the maximum IPD density, doesn't coincide with the ecliptic plane. In fact he proved that the symmetry plane is not a single plane, but a warped surface. This was a big surprise to every one in the field at the time.

He correctly suggested that Jupiter and Venus are the two major gravity sources that would pull the IPDs toward their orbital planes and make the maximum density plane of the IPDs a warped surface. This suggestion was then a very bold one, because his data didn't have enough angular resolution to show the physical link. But he cleverly defined a contribution function, with which he was able to probe the geometrical relation between the region of maximum contribution to the ZL brightness and the orbital characteristics of the two planets. It was the practical utility of the contribution function that led him to make an important prediction. The idea was simple and coarse, but powerful enough to reveal the underlying link between the symmetry plane and the planetary orbits.

In mid 1980s I had an opportunity to work with Prof. J. L. Weinberg at the Space Astronomy Lab, to which Dr. N. Y. Misconi was also affiliated. It was there that I could witness another bold idea of his working. To understand the ZL phenomenon in general one has to have correct information on the scattering phase function of the IPDs, whose size ranges from 0.1 to 350 micrometers. Handling solid particles of IPD size was obviously a big headache; Dr. Misconi introduced laser levitation technique to his experiment and attacked the problem successfully. The experiment has provided valuable information on the scattering properties and the dynamics as well of small particles in interplanetary space. I still remember in one of those brain storming sessions he suggested to fire a "big gun" from a satellite to a nearby asteroid and to observe the scattered light of the Sun and man-made source by the dust excavated from the asteroid surface. The SAL team couldn't materialize the idea then. But to think back, this was a brilliant idea, with which one can characterize the nature of ligorith particles for a reasonable price.

Inspite of all the jokes he commands in every day life, he is a serious scientist who can muster clever and robust ideas. His mind is so practical that he always finds one of the easiest roads to practically obtainable solutions under given constratints. I know he has a great skill in diplomatic negotiations. His success stems from his fairness; he is no a greedy person. He will continue to be a productive scientist. I firmly believe he will be an important asset to your department.

Sincerely,

Seung Soo Hong

Scientific Journal Publications

Misconi, N. Y., and M. S. Hanner. 1975. "On the Possibility of Detecting Solar Flare Effects in the Zodiacal Light." *Planetary and Space Science* 23: 1329–35.

Misconi, N. Y. 1976. "Solar Flare Effects on the Zodiacal Light." *Astronomy and Astrophysics* 51: 357–65.

Misconi, N.Y. 1976. "On the Rotational Bursting of Interplanetary Dust Particles." *Geophysical Research Letters* 3: 357–65.

Misconi, N.Y. 1977. "On the Photometric Axis of the Zodiacal Light." *Astronomy and Astrophysics* 61: 497–504.

Misconi, N. Y., J. L. Weinberg, R. C. Hahn, and D E. Beeson. 1977. "Possible Effects of Mars on the Symmetry Plane of Interplanetary Dust." Paper presented at the 151st Meeting of the American Astronomical Society, Austin, Texas, January 9–11, 1978, *Bulletin of the AAS* 9 (2): 620.

Misconi, N. Y., and J. L. Weinberg. 1978. "Is Venus Concentrating Interplanetary Dust toward Its Orbital Plane?" *Science* 200 (4349): 1484–85.

Gustafson, B. Λ. S., and N. Y. Misconi. 1979. "Streaming of Interstellar Grains in the Solar System." *Nature* 282: 276–78.

Ratcliff, K. F., N. Y. Misconi, and S. Paddack. 1980. "Radiation Induced Rotation of Interplanetary Dust Particles: A Feasibility Study for a Space Experiment." In IAU Symposium No. 90, *Solid*

Particles in the Solar System, edited by I. Halliday and B. McIntosh, 391–94. Dordrecht, Netherlands: D. Reidel.

Misconi, N. Y. 1980. "The Symmetry Plane of the Zodiacal Cloud Near 1 A.U." In IAU Symposium No. 90, *Solid Particles in the Solar System*, edited by I. Halliday and B. McIntosh, 49–53. Dordrecht, Netherlands: D. Reidel.

———. 1981. "The Photometric Center of the Gegenschein." *Icarus* 47: 265–69.

Misconi, N. Y., and L. A. Whitlock. 1983. "A Model to Explain the 1973 Outbursts of Periodic Comet Tuttle-Giacobini-Kresak." Paper presented at the International Conference on Cometary Exploration, Budapest, Hungary.

Gustafson, B. A. S., and N. Y. Misconi. 1983. "Can Cometary Dust Perturbed by the Inner Planets Be an Explanation for the Observed Distribution of Interplanetary Dust?" *Cometary Exploration* 2: 121.

Hong, S. S., N. Y. Misconi, M. H. H. Van Dijk, J. L. Weinberg, and G. N. Toller. 1985. "A Search for Small Scale Structures in the Zodiacal Light." In *Properties and Interactions of Interplanetary Dust*, edited by R. H. Giese and Ph. L. Lamy, 33–37. Dordrecht, Netherlands: D. Reidel.

Misconi, N. Y., and E. T. Rusk. 1985. "The Gravitational Zones of Influence of the Planets Acting on Small Celestial Bodies." In *Properties and Interactions of Interplanetary Dust*, edited by R. H. Giese and Ph. L. Lamy, 377. Dordrecht, Netherlands: D. Reidel.

Misconi, N. Y., and J. L. Weinberg. 1985. "Ground-Based Observations of Near Ecliptic Zodiacal Light Brightness." In *Properties and Interactions of Interplanetary Dust*, edited by R. H. Giese and Ph. L. Lamy, 11–15. Dordrecht, Netherlands: D. Reidel.

Gustafson, B. A. S., N. Y. Misconi, and E. T. Rusk. 1985. "Could Artifacts of a Major Release of Dust from Comet Encke during Prehistoric Times Be Detected in the Present Zodiacal Light?"

Paper presented at international symposium Asteroids, Comets, Meteors II, Uppsala, Sweden, June 3–6.

Misconi, N. Y., E. T. Rusk. 1985. "The Size of the Gravitational Zone of Influence of a Planet Acting on the Orbital Elements of Small Celestial Bodies." *Planetary and Space Science* 33 (11): 1359–62.

Gustafson, B. A. S., and N. Y. Misconi. 1986. "Interplanetary Dust Dynamics I. Long-Term Gravitational Effects of the Inner Planets on Zodiacal Dust." *Icarus* 66: 280–87.

Gustafson, B. A. S., N. Y. Misconi, and E. T. Rusk. 1987. "Interplanetary Dust Dynamics II. Poynting-Robertson Drag and Planetary Perturbations." *Icarus* 72 (3): 568–81.

———. 1987. "Interplanetary Dust Dynamics III. Dust Released from P/Encke: Distribution with Respect to the Zodiacal Cloud." *Icarus* 72 (3): 582–92.

Misconi, N. Y., and E. T. Rusk. 1987. "Brightness Contribution of Zodiacal Dust along the Line of Sight in and out of the Ecliptic Plane and in the F-Corona." *Planetary and Space Science* 35 (12): 1571.

Rusk, E. T., N. Y. Misconi, and B. A. S. Gustafson. 1988. "Dynamical Effects of Jupiter, the Inner Planets and Poynting-Robertson Drag on the Lifetime of Interplanetary Dust." *Planetary and Space Science* 36 (7): 747–52.

Michaels, Donald J., et al. 1989. "'LASCO'—A Wide-Field White Light and Spectrometric Coronagraph for SOHO." In European Space Agency, *The SOHO Mission*, Scientific and Technical Aspects of the Instruments, 55–62.

Misconi, N. Y., E. T. Rusk, J. L. Weinberg, and Shousan Yu. 1990. "Small Scale Structure in the Brightness of the Zodiacal Light: Ground-Based Observations." *Planetary and Space Science* 38 (4): 517–27.

Misconi, N. Y., J. P. Oliver, K. F. Ratcliff, E. T. Rusk, and Wan-Xian Wang. 1990. "Light Scattering by Laser Levitated Particles." *Applied Optics* 29 (15): 2276–81.

Misconi, N. Y., E. T. Rusk, and J. L. Weinberg. 1990. "The Symmetry Surface of the Zodiacal Cloud outside the Earth's Orbit." *Planetary and Space Science* 38 (11): 1461–68.

Kwon, S. M., S. S. Hong, J. L. Weinberg, and N. Y. Misconi. 1991. "Fine Resolution Brightness Distribution of the Visible Zodiacal Light." In *Origin and Evolution of Interplanetary Dust*, edited by A. C. Levasseur-Regourd and H. Hasegawa, 183–86. Kluwer Academic Publishers.

Misconi, N. Y. 1993. "The Spin of Cosmic Dust: The Rotational Bursting of Circumsolar Dust in the F-Corona." *Journal of Geophysical Research* 98 (A11): 18951–61.

Misconi, N. Y., and Laura Pettera. 1995. "On the Possibility of Solar Dust Ring Formation Due to Increased Ion Drag from Coronal Mass Ejections on Circumsolar Dust." *Planetary and Space Science* 43 (7): 895–903.

Kahler, S. W., and N. Y. Misconi. 1995. "The Effect of Interplanetary Dust Grains on the Dynamics of CMEs." Paper presented at the SOHO Conference, Washington, DC.

Misconi, N. Y. 1996. "A New Technique for Levitating Solid Particles Using a Proton Beam." *Laser and Particle Beams* 14 (3): 501–10.

Wang, W. X., and N. Y. Misconi. 1999. "Quasi-Analytical Solutions for Apsidal Motion in the Three-Body Problem: Sun-Minor Planet-Jupiter." *Earth Planets and Space* 51 (11): 1181–94.

Misconi, N. Y. 2004. "Numerical Simulations of Rotational Bursting of F-Coronal Dust in Eccentric Orbits Due to Coronal Mass Ejections." *Planetary and Space Science* 52: 833–38.

Misconi, N.Y. 2011. "Detecting the Light of the Night Sky in Mars." *Natural Science* Vol. 3 No.4: 285–90.

Miscellaneous Articles and Photos

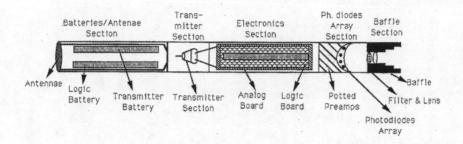

Sketch showing the SEEC instrument and its components

BUDGET (First Year)
(Sep 1, 1993- August 31, 1994)

1. DIRECT LABOR			$42,628
FIT Faculty	Title	Man Months	Amount
N.Y. Misconi (PI)	Research Professor Astronomer	3.5	20,128
D. E. Brownlee[1] (Co-I)	Astronomer	1.0	5,000
S. J. Paddack[2] (Co-I)	Chief, AMAO, GSFC		no cost
J.P. Oliver Co-I [3]	Associate Professor Astronomer	2.0	5,000
Electro-Optics Engineer[4]		2.0	5,000
Graduate Students			
2	EE	1/2 Academic Year	7,500

2. Fringe Benefits (23% of PI's DL)	4,629

3. EQUIPMENT	1,500
Miscellaneous Lab Supplies	1,500

4. TRAVEL	5,000
Commuting expense for Drs. Paddack, Brownlee, and Oliver	
2 Round trip Greenbelt, Maryland to Melbourne, FL	1,500
2 Round trip Seattle, WA to Melbourne, FL	1,500
5 Gainesville Fl. to Melbourne, FL	500
Meetings, 2 Trips 2 persons	1,500

5. Publications, photography, communications, supplies, etc.	4,100

6. Indirect Costs	17,982
41% of all items except capital equipment and students	

Total Cost $75,839

---

(1) University of Washington, Seattle, WA
(2) NASA, GSFC, Chief AMAO
(3) University of Florida, Gainesville, FL
(4) Florida Institute of Technology, Melbourne, FL

1. DIRECT LABOR $37,628

FIT Faculty	Title	Man Months	Amount
N.Y. Misconi (PI)	Research Professor Astronomer	3.85	22,128
D. E. Brownlee[1] (Co-I)	Astronomer	1.0	5,000
S. J. Paddack[2] (Co-I)	Chief, AMAO, GSFC		no cost
J.P. Oliver[3]Co-I	Associate Professor Astronomer	1.2	3,000

Graduate Students

2	EE	1/2 Academic Year	7,500

2. Fringe Benefits (23% of PI's DL)   5,089

3. EQUIPMENT   **1,500**

Miscellaneous Lab Supplies   1,500

4. TRAVEL   **5,000**

Commuting expense for Drs. Paddack, Brownlee, and Oliver
2 Round trip Greenbelt, Maryland to Melbourne, FL   1,500
2 Round trip Seattle, WA to Melbourne, FL   1,500
5 Gainesville Fl. to Melbourne, FL   500

Meetings, 2 Trips 2 persons   1,500

5. Publications, photography, communications, supplies, etc. **2,900**

6. Indirect Costs   **17,678**
        41% of all items except capital equipment and students

                                              Total Cost $69,796

---

(1) University of Washington, Seattle, WA
(2) NASA, GSFC, Chief, Advanced Mission Analysis Office (AMAO)
(3) University of Florida, Gainesville, FL

BUDGET (Third Year)
(Sep 1, 1995- August 31, 1996)

1. DIRECT LABOR $39,752

FIT Faculty	Title	Man Months	Amount
N.Y. Misconi (PI)	Research Professor Astronomer	3.0	17,252
D. E. Brownlee[1] (Co-I)	Astronomer	1.0	5,000
S. J. Paddack[2] (Co-I)	Chief, AMAO, GSFC		no cost
J.P. Oliver Co-I [3]	Associate Professor Astronomer	2.0	5,000
Electro-Optics Engineer[4]		2.0	5,000

Graduate Students

2	EE	1/2 Academic Year	7,500

2. Fringe Benefits (23% of PI's DL) **5,118**

3. EQUIPMENT **1,500**

Miscellaneous Lab Supplies 1,500

4. TRAVEL **5,000**

Commuting expense for Drs. Paddack, Brownlee, and Oliver
2 Round trip Greenbelt, Maryland to Melbourne, FL ... 1,500
2 Round trip Seattle, WA to Melbourne, FL ... 1,500
5 Gainesville Fl. to Melbourne, FL ... 500

Meetings, 2 Trips 2 persons ... 1,500

5. Publications, photography, communications, supplies, etc. **1,900**

6. Indirect Costs **18,151**
    41% of all items except capital equipment and students

	Total Cost	$71,421
	3 yrs. Total Costs	$217,056

(1) University of Washington, Seattle, WA
(2) NASA, GSFC, Chief, Advanced Mission Analysis Office (AMAO)
(3) University of Florida, Gainesville, FL
(4) Florida Institute of Technology, Melbourne, FL

Photo showing the sign pointing to the rocket launchpad. Also showing Ms. Gwendelyn De'Court the publicist at Florida Tech at the time.

Photo showing the Mexican soldiers guarding the rocket launchpad.

The Super Loki rocket launch structure at NASA's Wallops Flight Facility.

Similar photo as the above showing the NASA launch personnel.

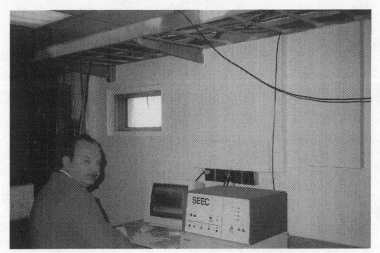

The author at the controls of the SEEC instrument.

The Super Loki rocket inside the launch helical tube.

The Super Loki rocket being transported for
launch at the NASA Wallops Facility.

The Misconi family: front row from left to right, Nebil
(the author), Amel, Lutfi, Naseer and Zuhair. Upper row.
Colomba, Nazar, and Yousif (Samir was not born yet).

*June 24, 2002
Issue*

LETTERS

A Good Use for NEP

‛Considering the danger that large Earth-crossing asteroids or comets pose to human civilization and our planet, I ask the question: can the "Nuclear Earth Penetrator" (NEP) destroy such objects?

The NEP was designed by the U.S. military for possible use in destroying deep caves in Afghanistan as part of the war on terrorism. Descriptions of these weapons suggest that they have the capability to burrow deep inside rocky terrain and could explode a nuclear weapon to destroy caves.

Very little is known to academics about this weapon's capabilities. However, it seems that it could be modified to operate in the space environment and be useful for demolishing a threatening asteroid or a comet that suddenly appears on a collision course with Earth.

We are overdue for a collision similar to the one that presumably destroyed the dinosaurs some 65 million years ago. Comet Hale-Bopp in 1997 was likely 100 times more massive than the object that wiped out the dinosaurs. And Hale-Bopp was discovered only months before it slipped by Earth. Should a comet appear again with such a short notice, we need to be ready to intercept and destroy it before it collides with Earth. Saving civilization and life on Earth is, to say the least, of utmost priority.

I have asked a group of students under my supervision at the University of Central Florida's Material Mechanical and Aerospace Department to study this idea. This study is exploratory, and if encouraging results materialize, then I intend to seek a financially supported investigation. Funding, to further this study, could come from the U.S. Space Command and NASA centers.

Obviously, we need to know more about the capabilities of the NEP. Such information, however, is classified. Some encouraging information has surfaced through the news media. For example, there can be penetration of more than 100 feet before detonation of a conventional device. We realize that there are many questions to be answered. Should multiple warheads be used? Must several NEPs be used at the same time? At what velocity should the NEP be propelled to strike the asteroid or comet to be effective?

I cannot, in this letter include all the questions that need answers. My purpose is to focus attention on this idea and get perhaps a larger study initiated. I have always believed that weapons of mass destruction can and should, when appropriate, be used to benefit mankind.

NEBIL Y. MISCONI
Orlando, Fla.

■ Readers are encouraged to express their views in letters to the editor. Letters may be edited. Please include name, address and telephone number. Unsigned letters will not be published, but names will be withheld upon request. Send letters to 6883 Commercial Dr., Springfield, VA 22159, or to jgillis@hq.space.com. Letters to the editor, opinion and editorial columns may be published or distributed in print, electronic or other forms.

The author with his son Michael.

Photo of the author.

Jerry Klein, UCF News Bureau

(407) 823-2730

Modify

A shuttle to carry passengers... a plan for a real space odyssey.

A PASSENGER VERSION OF THE SPACE SHUTTLE PROPOSED

April 18, 2001

A team of University of Central Florida engineering technology students has come up with a way to take paying passengers into space on the shuttle. They are even proposing a nationwide lottery for would-be astronauts who can't quite hack the estimated $9.4 million ticket price.

"This could actually be a money-maker for NASA," says professor Nebil Misconi, who taught the students' class.

"We propose a passenger module to go in the existing cargo bay," says student Mike Scalisa. " It would add 12 seats to the existing shuttle, for a total of 18 passengers and three crew."

Engineering Technology students (l-r) Bill Baily, Michelle Kiaaina, Matt Ducsay and Mike Scalisa have a money making idea for NASA.

Article in the UCF "News and Information" publication.

The module would have additional galley and bathroom facilities, sleeping quarters and an exercise area so the passengers could keep fit during their five-day trip.

While most seats would go to those able to pay their own way, student Matt Ducsay as done the math on a nationwide lottery for one ticket per trip,

"Given the average levels of participation in lotteries, we think a national lottery would generate about $21 million, enough to pay for the winner, and leave some extra for NASA."

The students have not talked to anyone at NASA about their plan, but they note the world's first paying passenger is due to visit the international space station on a Russian ship within a month.

-UCF-

Editors:

Nabil Misconi, 407 384-2156.

More News   Back to ⬡UCF

270

Students draw up tourists proposal

By Brad Buck
FLORIDA TODAY

If Dennis Tito can go up in space, why can't John Q. Public?

That's what a team of University of Central Florida students wanted to know.

So for their senior project in engineering technology, the group thought a lottery to select passengers might be just the ticket to get the average citizen in space. In the process, they think they've invented a cash cow for NASA.

The students estimated that to send a layman into space would cost $9.4 million, which Tito can afford, but most folks can't.

The students propose a module that would ride in the existing shuttle cargo bay. It would add 12 seats to the shuttle, for a total of 18 passengers and three crew members. The module would have additional galley and bathroom facilities, sleeping quarters and an exercise area so the passengers could keep fit during their five-day trip.

While most seats would go to those who can pay their own way, student Matt Ducsay has done the math on a nationwide lottery for one ticket per trip. Given the average levels of participation in lotteries, Ducsay estimates a national lottery would generate about $21 million, enough to pay for the winner to go into space free and leave some extra money for NASA.

"This could be a real money maker for NASA," said UCF professor Nebil Misconi, who taught the students' class.

The students have not talked to NASA about their plan.

Michelle Kinaina, a senior originally from Hawaii, said the project was about "how we could use the shuttle for commercial use, so that the common man can go into space."

Tito, a California businessman, paid $20 million to ride to the International Space Station with the Russians. The United States is not sharing any of his costs.

"We were trying to figure out how to get more passengers on the shuttle," Kinaina said. "We had to add to sleep quarters and a bathroom. We're proposing to gut out the payload section."

The students present their project, which they had to complete to graduate, today to the engineering faculty at UCF.

NASA spokesman Bruce Buckingham said Wednesday that having a tourist in space is a "pretty sensitive issue. We'd have to see the proposal first.

"Our preference would be that (Tito) not go at all," Buckingham said. "We're hopeful that space tourism would be in our future. But the station is nowhere near ready yet. There's an awful lot of work that still needs to be done."

A shuttle mission costs about $400 million, he said.

"To have (people) go up and float around and watch what happens . . . we've got a limited amount of space," in the shuttle, Buckingham said. "You've really got to have a reason to go up there."

Italian **astronaut** Umberto Guidoni, left, and space shuttle commander Kent Rominger talk Wednesday from the Rafaello module with Italian President Carlo Ciampi.

Tito ready for launch

Associated Press

BAIKONUR, Kazakhstan — U.S. businessman Dennis Tito said Wednesday that NASA would someday be glad that he was included on a Russian rocket to the international space station, saying his paid trip would be good publicity.

The investment firm founder, set to blast off Saturday with two cosmonauts, said he was baffled over why U.S. space officials had lobbied against his trip for so long. Tito reportedly paid the Russian space agency some $20 million for the ride. NASA grudgingly dropped its objections Tuesday.

"It's hard for me to understand" why, he said during preflight rituals that included the raising of Russian, Kazakh and U.S. flags at the cosmonaut hotel near the Baikonur launch facility Russia rents from Kazakhstan.

"I think this flight will be very good for NASA. I think NASA ulti-mately will be happy that I took the flight."

A Russian government commission Wednesday approved the Soyuz TM rocket for its Saturday launch, after engineers and space experts reported that all systems were functioning properly, said commission secretary Alexei Strelnikov.

"The safety level is 99 percent," said Vladimir Serdyuk, an engineer in charge of the assembly. "But even if something should go wrong, there is an emergency escape system that would allow the crew to descend safely."

Tito, a tidy, soft-spoken 60-year-old, said his flight would be good publicity for the international space station, and denied being simply a high-paying passenger.

NASA had said that Tito could get in the way of the crew's work because he doesn't have adequate training.

Article in "Florida Today" newspaper.

Rocket launch to carry student engineering project with NASA

UCF engineering technology students expect to capture high-altitude video of lightning from NASA rocket.

A high-resolution video camera in a payload assembled by UCF engineering technology students should yield the first close-up images of high-altitude lightning this summer. The 15-by-2 inch payload will ride a Super Loki rocket from Wallops Island in Virginia to an altitude of 25 miles some time between June 22 and July 9, if and when thunderstorms pass within 20 miles of the launch pad.

"NASA/Wallops has donated two free launches and the upper stages of the rocket," says engineering professor Nebil Misconi, who is leading the project. "Students, some of whom have graduated, have been working on the payload for six months."

The rocket will eject the camera at 25 miles and it will drift down on a parachute, transmitting images of the lightning first reported by shuttle astronauts a few years ago.

"They have taken pictures of the red and blue glow from space, but they are hundreds of miles away," says Misconi. "Two images were made a couple of years ago by accident during a different kind of experiment, but these will be the first images made this close to the storms."

The students are looking for relationships between the high-altitude lightning and the bolts closer to the ground.

The students have built two payloads, "and we plan to build one more, thanks to a grant from the UCF Student Government," says student Kris Muller.

"This has been a great experience learning to deal with the suppliers and NASA," he adds.

The packages will have to withstand preflight checks for shaking, shock and acceleration. At least one will be launched even if the weather does not cooperate during the launch window.

We will use one to demonstrate the design works," says Misconi, "and at least check out the camera and transmission systems even if we just get pictures of clouds."

— *Jerry Klein*

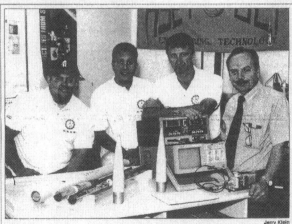

Jerry Klein

Left to right, UCF engineering technology undergraduates Kris Muller, Richard Coronado and Mike Singer make final preparations with Nebil Misconi, engineering technology professor, on the two payloads they built for two NASA launches in Virginia. A Student Government grant paid for the project.

The author in front of his office at UCF.

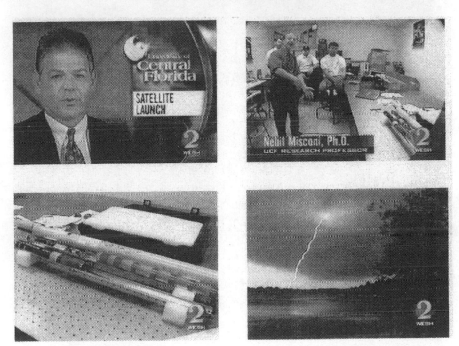

A lightning in the sky shown by NBC's TV channel 2 as an
example for what the experiment hopes to study.
Upper right photo: The students working on the payload in my laboratory.

Space Shuttle Payload Bay Redesign Project:

Carrying Tourists Into the 21st Century

By
Matthew Ducsay
Michelle Kiaaina
Michael Scalise
William Bailey

Senior Design Project
ETG 4950
Dr. N. Misconi

The front cover of the students report to the author.

Photos

7 June, 00

STRATOSPHERE LIGHTNING IMAGES SOUGHT

Jerry Klein, UCF News Bureau, (407) 823-2730

UCF Engineering Technology students assembled these rocket payloads to photograph lightning in the stratosphere.

A high-resolution video camera in a payload assembled by University of Central Florida engineering technology students should yield the first close-up images of high altitude lightning this summer. The 15-by-2 inch payload will ride a Super Loki rocket from Wallops Island to an altitude of 25 miles between June 22 and July 9, if and when thunderstorms pass within 20 miles of the launch pad.

"NASA/Wallops has donated two free launches and the upper stages of the rocket," says engineering professor Nebil Misconi, who is leading the project, "students, some of whom have graduated, have been working on the payload for six months."

The rocket will eject the camera at 25 miles and it will drift down on a parachute, transmitting images of the lightning first reported by shuttle astronauts a few years ago.

"They have taken pictures of the red and blue glow from space, but they are hundreds of miles away," says Misconi. "Two images were made a couple of years ago by accident during a different kind of experiment, but these will be the first images made this close to the storms."

They are looking for relationships between the high-altitude lightning and the bolts closer to the ground.

275

Editors:

The students work on the
payloads between 2 and 4
p.m. Fridays in the
Research Pavilion,
Research Park, room 469.
Nebil Misconi 321-255
3649 or 407 384 2152 on
Fridays.

Engineering technology students Mike Singer (L), Kris Muller
and Richard Coronado check the payload under the direction
of professor Nebil Misconi.

The students have built two payloads, "and we
plan to build one more, thanks to a grant from the
UCF student government," says student Kris
Muller.

"This has been a great experience learning to deal
with the suppliers and NASA."

The packages will have to withstand preflight
checks for shaking, shock and acceleration. At
least one will be launched even if the weather does
not cooperate during the launch window.

"We will use one to demonstrate the design
works," says Misconi, "and at least check out the
camera and transmission systems even if we just
get pictures of clouds."

-UCF-

More News   Back to UCF

Japanese space agency earns Goddard award

by Ernie Shannon

Representatives of the National Space Development Agency of Japan (NASDA) were presented with the Tropical Rainfall Measuring Mission (TRMM) outstanding performance award for their work on the Precipitation Radar and the launch vehicle to satellite interfaces. The NASDA team recently was at Goddard for a week-long set of meetings with the TRMM Project, Code 910.

The visit coincided with an "all hands" meeting for the project. The event included the presentation of a number of performance awards to recognize the contributions of civil service and contractor employees to the TRMM Program.

A highlight of the ceremony was the presentation of an 1/8 scale model of the TRMM Observatory to Hideo Takamatsu, NASDA TRMM project manager, by Vern Weyers, Code 400; Director of Flight Projects Directorate.

TRMM Project Manager Tom LaVigna, Code 490, said the visit and the awards ceremony was a significant event for the project. "The technical meeting was the 12th to be held between our teams. We are extremely pleased with the excellent working relationship we have with our Japanese partners. This visit, as with the others, was extremely productive in working various items and was especially significant for the formal signing of the Precipitation Radar to Observatory Interface Control Specification, a key project document."

Integration of the observatory flight subsystems to the TRMM structure has started and is progressing well. The Precipitation Radar will be delivered by NASDA to Goddard for integration to the observatory in November 1995.

Vern Weyers, Director of Flight Projects, left and Tom LaVigna, TRMM Project Manager are shown with Hideo Takamastsu, NASDA TRMM Project Manager when he was presented with a model of the TRMM spacecraft.

NASA launches first high school student payload

by Keith Koehler

A suborbital space payload, the first built and managed by junior and senior high school students, was successfully launched on a NASA sounding rocket at 5:00 p.m. EDT, Friday May 12, from the Wallops Flight Facility.

The launch culminated a year-long aerospace course that took 79 Florida students in the 1993-94 school year through an academic program that taught them "hands-on" rocketry, including payload development, data analysis, flight electronics, flight dynamics, data transmission and optics.

The students are from Cocoa, Melbourne and Palm Bay High Schools and Southwest Junior High in Palm Bay, Fla. Some students traveled to classes at Brevard Community College in Palm Bay.

The project is a cooperative venture between NASA, the State of Florida's Technological Research and Development Authority (TRDA) and the University of Central Florida (UCF). Harris Corp. and D.B.A. Systems, both of Melbourne, Fla., provided facilities for vibration testing.

The rocket, a ten-foot tall Super Loki-Dart, went past the stratosphere to 45 miles (73 kilometers) altitude to transmit data back to Earth. Its mission is to prove the value of small, inexpensive meteorological rockets as tools in remote optical sensing.

"Using the Super-Loki Dart rocket vehicle will provide an inexpensive way to study pollution in the Earth's atmosphere," said Dr. Nebil Misconi of UCF, the project scientist.

According to Frank Schmidlin, Code 972, the NASA principal investigator, there are two goals in this program. The first is the invaluable education experience the students are receiving. Still important, but secondary, is the data, which is to obtain a set of astronomical observations to deduce total content of atmospheric aerosols.

"This program enriches the participants' technical education and gives them practical knowledge of the importance of the space program in studying the environment. The students are gaining an up-close and personal experience with a space mission," said Frank Kinney, executive director of the TRDA.

The TRDA funded the educational program with a $50,000 grant in 1994. This was made possible through the Florida Department of Education and Challenger license plate sale funding, which support TRDA programs.

Wallops provided the rocket, final payload testing support, and launch range support, including data acquisition services.

277

Index

Printed in the United States
By Bookmasters